THE JEWISH PEOPLE

HISTORY · RELIGION · LITERATURE

THE JEWISH PEOPLE

HISTORY · RELIGION · LITERATURE

Advisory Editor
Jacob B. Agus

Editorial Board
Louis Jacob
Jacob Petuchowski
Seymour Siegel

THE JEW
and
THE UNIVERSE

BY

Solomon Goldman

ARNO PRESS
A New York Times Company
NEW YORK • 1973

181.3
G619j

Reprint Edition 1973 by Arno Press Inc.

Copyright, © 1936, by Harper & Brothers
Reprinted by arrangement with Harper & Row,
  Publishers, Inc. All rights reserved.

THE JEWISH PEOPLE: History, Religion, Literature
ISBN for complete set: 0-405-05250-2
See last pages of this volume for titles.

Manufactured in the United States of America

———◆———

Library of Congress Cataloging in Publication Data

Goldman, Solomon, 1893-1953.
  The Jew and the universe.

  (The Jewish people: history, religion, literature)
  Reprint of the ed. published by Harper, New York.
  1. Philosophy, Jewish. 2. Moses ben Maimon, 1135-
1204. I. Title. II. Series.
B755.G6 1973   181'.3   73-2200
ISBN 0-405-05265-0

142090

THE JEW
AND THE UNIVERSE

THE JEW
and
THE UNIVERSE

BY

Solomon Goldman

I 9 3 6

HARPER & BROTHERS PUBLISHERS

NEW YORK AND LONDON

TO ALICE

CONTENTS

PREFACE

THE RIDDLE OF THE UNIVERSE RE-
mains unsolved. Up to recent years scientists, or at least
inventors, confidently believed that they were already at the
Golden Gate of absolute Truth. For a long time metaphysicians spoke with the accents of finality. Theologians were
always wont to brandish the key to the arcanum. Logicians
still arrogate to their methods and canons the title of pure
Reason. Views of life bodied forth in the abundant language
of metaphor by the most sensitive and impassioned of artists,
or by the wisest and noblest of men, have been dismissed as
childish and irrelevant. Unfortunately, Aristotle, Kant, or
Hegel have brought us no nearer the truth than the wisdom
of Isaiah, St. Francis of Assisi, or Tagore. If we are im-
pelled by an incurable curiosity to discover the origin of the
Universe, Life and Intelligence, an endless search awaits us.

It is my conviction that in the prolonged search success
will crown only the labors of those who will recognize and
welcome Intuition as the legitimate helpmate of Reason, and
who will weigh the offspring of both in the scales of experimentation. The "purists" may perhaps achieve new
canons of logic and new ways of knowing, but hardly ultimate truth. The random intuitions of gifted and inspired men
may at times be more enlightening and revealing than volumes of syllogisms.

In Europe, however, pure Reason has been a zealous and
intolerant God. And Jews have not yet rid themselves of
the proclivity to worship at strange shrines. The glitter of
occidental logic and the obscurity of its metaphysics they
slavishly accepted as the Truth. They became abashed at
this splendor and, as a result, were embarrassed by the ab-

sence of rationalistic preciseness in their own literature. Hastily and contemptuously the Prophets, Sages and Rabbis were rejected as children everlastingly toying with fables and parables. Thinking and enlightenment were confused with, and limited to abstractedness. In Europe's gilded or dingy ghettos of half a century ago to be cultured or to belong to the *intellegentsia* meant to be "German" or "European." This became the fashion not merely in matters of dress and diet but more particularly in the sphere of thought and expression.

In 1912 my sainted and lamented teacher, Professor Israel Friedlaender, recommended to me the reading of Achad Haam's well-known essay on Maimonides, entitled The Supremacy of Reason. In those days Achad Haam was nothing less than a demi-god. His name was so frequently on the lips of the learned and intelligent, and pronounced with so much reverence that one somehow thought of him as the greatest Jewish thinker of all time. His opinions were considered incontrovertible and final. To my amazement and unhappiness I found it impossible to accept his interpretation of Maimonides. Professor Friedlaender, to whom I came with my doubts and notes, suggested with more enthusiasm than my immaturity warranted that I develop my reactions into a thesis. A busy rabbinic career has nipped in the bud many a scholarly and literary ambition. The musings of 1912 were soon forgotten and were not resurrected from the limbo of the past until 1935, when I was invited by the University of Illinois to deliver an address at the University on the occasion of Maimonides' octocentenary. The following pages are an expansion of last year's lecture and an elaboration of the reflections of 1912.

In these pages I have often stated the views of the ancients and medievalists in their own language and have frequently refrained from interrupting the continuity of their thought with the intrusion of my own opinions. I trust that the reader will not conclude that I have uncritically accepted all of their views. I remain perplexed even as any of Maimonides' contemporaries. Alas, the old Guides have not dissolved the mists of my confusion, neither have the most recent dispelled my doubts.

It remains my pleasant duty to express my thanks to Professor Louis Ginzberg, Professor A. Eustace Haydon, Professor Louis Finkelstein and to Mr. Maurice Samuel for their kindness in reading the manuscript. My special indebtedness to Professor Ginsberg I have further indicated in the notes. It is a joy to record that in the course of writing this book I derived considerable benefit from conversations with my friends A. H. Friedland, Leo I. Honor, Felix A. Levy and Joshua L. Liebman.

SOLOMON GOLDMAN

Sayner, Wisconsin.
July, 1936.

THE JEW

AND THE UNIVERSE

I. PERSONALITY AND THE UNIVERSE

MAN HAS SOUGHT TO COMPRE-
hend or solve the riddle of the Universe in one of two ways:
Either he examined reality logically and philosophically, and
viewed it as a concatenation of cause and effect, culminating
in a First Cause; or he related himself to the world organically, intuitively, and viewed it as the unfolding of God's
Creative Will. Among the Greeks the former is preëminent.
In the foreground of Greek culture stand its philosophers.
Distinguished and varied as were the achievements of the
Greeks, their foremost men are yet Socrates, Plato, and
Aristotle. One hardly seeks a world view in Phidias. When
we speak of the Hellenic approach to the Universe, we invariably think of the logical and metaphysical systems, of
one or another of its many brilliant, individual thinkers or
schools of thought.

Among Jews the intuitive approach prevails. In the great
writings of Israel designated Bible, Apocrypha, Talmud,
Midrash and Responsa, and containing the bulk of Jewish
literary productivity, it is difficult to discover a score of
logical syllogisms or metaphysical hypotheses. Throughout
this literature no attempts are made to state or define concepts. Indeed the whole apparatus of rationalism is absent.
"Reason" invariably yields the palm to intuition, speculation
to meditation, formulation to awareness. In many, many
thousands of pages of superb religious content we search in
vain for a definition of God, religion, soul, or idea. Concepts
and phenomena are not analyzed. They are seen whole and
in their immediate relation to man. The Universe is viewed
through and in terms of personality.

The literature, of course, only reflects life. The whole
structure of Jewish civilization is reared on intuition. Political

I

and economic concepts are no more defined than ethical or
philosophical. Life is taken organically, breathless as it were.
Its interests center in living man rather than in abstract
theorizing. No wonder the complaint is common among historians of the Jewish people that Jewish history is a history
of men and not of movements. It is indeed a history of
Patriarchs, Judges, Prophets, Rabbis, Messiahs, Zealots and
two or three Kings. Throughout, personalities predominate;
they dwarf and overshadow causes and events. "How small
appears Sinai when Moses stands on its summit. The mountain is only the footstool for this man whose head reaches
into heaven where he speaks with God."[1] Heine was probably unaware that he was indulging in rich "oriental" imagery for which there had long been noble precedent. Thus
the Midrash exalts: When Moses taught or sang, the whole
of nature stood still and reverentially listened to him.[2]

History, heaven and earth, God the Jew perceived mainly
through personality.[3] From time immemorial towering indi-
vidualities were both the symbols and focal expression of
all existence and pushed into the background all problems
of metaphysics and epistemology. Living man intrigued the
Jew's curiosity and challenged his reverence. The stage setting, the world and the fullness thereof were of secondary
importance; the human drama was the thing.

The first chapter of Genesis, with breathless rapidity,
albeit with precision, constructs the universe and its properties. With an impatient, impersonal *fiat*, let there be, the
Deity dissolves chaos, void, darkness, diffuses light, fashions
firmament, heaven, earth, stars, quickens vegetation, beast,
fowl and fish. *Y'hee*—let there be—*y'hee*—a word is sufficient. An indirect command will suffice for the whole of
matter and animation. But suddenly the Deity, as it were,
pauses and the Heavens resound: "We will make man in
our image, after our likeness."

Unlike Philo and the Gnostics, Rabbinic literature emphatically asserts that man was the direct creation of God

and not the work of the angels.[4] It could not have been otherwise. For to the very act of creation God was inspired by the souls of the unborn pious.[5] It was only upon their advice that the Creator resolved to fashion the world.[6] Not only its creation but its existence the world owes to the *zaddik*, i.e., the consummate personality, who is its foundation.[7] So indispensable is he to the order and stability of the Cosmos that he does not breathe his last until one equally worthy is born to take his place.[8] The soul of such a *zaddik* is sufficient to balance the world.[9] God would not have disdained creating the whole universe for just one such man.[10] His kind are not only its pillars[11] but also its true rulers.[12] Abraham was given the assurance that there will always be found thirty men his equals in piety and saintliness for without them the world could not exist.[13] This belief in the efficacy of the righteous to support the universe is current among Jews to this day.

The Talmud and Midrash abound with delightfully quaint parables and dicta, extolling and glorifying the elect, the superman. It is a subject worthy of thorough investigation. Here but a few random examples will have to suffice. So important in their eyes was personality, the precious individual, that it occurred to the Rabbis that the Bible allows more space to Eliezer's experiences than to some of the most important laws, only because the Damascene had the good fortune of being the servant of the First Patriarch.[14] At the creation of Isaac the whole of nature was transformed, the barren women became fertile, the blind began to see, the deaf to hear, the mute to speak; Heaven and Earth rejoiced.[15] To the glorification of Jacob there is no bounds.[16] It was because of him that the world was created.[17] In the moon, on the heavenly throne his face is engraved. He is the ideal man and his countenance represents the human race.[18] He is even called God.[19] His twelve sons, too, are mentioned as the cause of creation.[20]

Everywhere the Rabbis seize the opportunity to prize man above nature. He is to them the seal of the Cosmos.[21] They boldly identified "the spirit of God hovering over the waters" with the spirit of Adam.[22] The omission of the words "and God saw that it was good" from the account of the Second Day suggests to them the thought that the Omniscient Creator had foreseen that water would bring Moses to grief.[23] They did not even hesitate to declare that it was Moses who had taught God to be more compassionate with mankind than he had intended to be.[24] David, the Jews dared muse, wrote upon seven stones the names of the Patriarchs, Moses, Aaron, his own name and that of God.[25] In such a notion they sensed neither presumption nor blasphemy. For it was to men like Moses, David and the Messiah to come that the world owed its origin.[26] Abraham, Solomon and several others they unhesitatingly designated the "friends of God."[27]

This exaggeration of the grandeur of man was in no way due to a primitive view of nature. The conception of a physical world order, fixed and immovable was not foreign to the Jews.[28] No less a scientist than Alexander von Humboldt recognized this to be true. In the Cosmos he wrote: "It is a characteristic of the poetry of the Hebrews, that, as a reflex of Monotheism, it always embraces the universe in its unity. . . . Nature is to him (the Hebrew poet) a work of creation and order. . . . It might be said that one single psalm represents the image of the whole cosmos: The Lord, 'who coverest thyself with light as with a garment; who stretchest out the heavens like a curtain; who laid the foundations of the earth, that it should not be removed forever. He sendeth the springs into the valleys, which run among the hills: thou hast set a bound that they may not pass over; that they turn not again to cover the earth. They give drink to every beast of the field. By them shall the fowls of the air have their habitation, which sing among the branches. The trees of the Lord are full of sap; the cedars of Lebanon which he hath planted, where the birds make their nests;

as for the stork, the fir-trees are her house.' "[29] The God of Israel was not capricious and His universe was not subject to endless alterations and improvements. He had wrought well and for all time in order and perfection.[30] But that order the Jews had conceived as dependent upon the moral nature of man,[31] upon the dignity and distinctiveness of human personality. Only with personality goodness came into the world;[32] only personality gives the scheme of things importance.[33] Profound and revealing is the simile of Rabbi Jacob Tam.[34] "Even as the wise and skilled craftsman," said he, "will show off a beautiful piece of work, even so the Creator glorifies Himself with the pious. For they are the significant attestations of the importance of his work."[35]

In India the formless totality of the All—Sat, Atman or Brahma, was God. The personal creator, i.e., personality of the early Vedic age lost all significance in the development of Indian thought. The ultimate satisfaction of Hindu reason and emotion was found in the realization of this formless totality. The "highest effort of rationalistic thought in India has been to see God," in this totality.[36] "Buddhism," Professor Whitehead strikingly suggests, "is a metaphysics even as Christianity has always been looking for one."[37] In the words of Professor Sylvain Lévi, pure *idéation*, pure *idéification* constitute "still to this day, the most flourishing system in the Buddhist schools of Tibet, China and Japan."[38] Mohammedanism never quite abandons the impersonal, abstract *dhat*.[39]

In Ionia, the deep mystery of the universe *per se* overwhelmed men. There, along the Aegean, philosophers or scientists were groping for ultimate constitutive causes, for a neat formula that would contain them. What is the substratum of the cosmos? Thales, Anaximander and Anaximenes persistently speculated. Water,[40] the indeterminate, air they concluded. In Judah, on the other hand, they mused, what is water as a life-giving principle, beside an Abraham or a Moses.[41] If then the world has an origin, a common source, it emanates from personality. "It would seem," remarks Professor Schechter, "that the rabbis felt actual delight in heaping human qualities upon God whenever opportunity was offered."[42] If the world was created, then it was the achievement of a Moses. A Moses, it is true, a million times greater than the Moses they had known, but a Moses it was. The First Cause was not a prime mover but a moral being making for righteousness. It was not Styx, motion, change; the life-giving principle was personality, it was God.

The Greeks, with all their emphasis on physical beauty and prowess, on man as man, nowhere succeed in exalting personality to such heights.[43] It is true that the early cosmogonies were anthropomorphic, but the roots of that anthropomorphism are, as it were, not in man, but in mythical divinities, half-sensuous, half-spiritual. They do not possess the distinctive quality of human personality. Pan, Poseidon, or Demeter are natural phenomena, exercising, in some exaggerated manner, human functions. Worse still, these primal beings lack moral quality. They are not better but rather worse than man. Homer's canvas is crowded with heroes, but they too are so often mythical and so often weak. It is not quite clear what the hero of Troy was—a god or a human being. And what was the Trojan War about? Was it really the comely face of Helen that launched a thousand ships, or was it the sheer love of adventure that brought life to a halt in the Aegean, and sent its noblest sons to play at soldiering? But who is the hero of Sodom and Gomorrah? The angels? God? Or, any of the inhabitants of the wicked cities? The young child knows it was Abraham. And what was the issue involved? Again the *zaddik*, the righteous man—personality. "Wilt Thou indeed sweep away the righteous with the wicked? Peradventure there are fifty righteous within the city." To such towering peaks Hellenic heroes never ascend. Such prominence they never attain.

It was otherwise in Israel. Here, generations of Jews in all humility admitted that the benign grace of God was theirs

only because of the "merit of the Fathers."[44] Had they not
had in their favor the kindliness and the piety of the First of
the Patriarchs, the fugitives from Egypt might have perished
in the desert leaving no trace on its hot sands. It is to Abraham that they were obliged for the gifts Heaven showered
upon them during the forty years of wandering.[45] If it is not
one of the Patriarchs or Matriarchs then it is Moses, Aaron
and Miriam who loom large as the benefactors of the people
in the wilderness. The Manna, Jewish folklore details, came
down from heaven for the sake of Moses, the pillar of cloud
was Aaron's gift and the miraculous well the wanderers
owed to Miriam.[46]

Extraordinary men then have made the Jew seek and see
the universe through man. Ultimate being is not a *Ding an
sich*, it is not easily grasped; it is not sufficient to explain it
in thin metaphysical outline. It is rather Moses, Elijah, Isaiah,
Hillel. Absolute being is a lifeless assumption. Personality
is palpably living, effectively real. "There is a greatness in
the lives of those who build up religious systems; a greatness in action, in idea and self-subordination, embodied in
instance after instance through centuries of growth."[47] The
presence of Moses fills one to overflowing. All one's senses
are keenly stimulated by his nod, by his repose, his smile or
his frown.

Theologians have so often regretted the abundance of Biblical anthropomorphism. They marveled that this most spiritual of literatures should at the same time be so sensuous.
The defect, if it is one, we must admit is incurable. It pervades the Talmud and the Midrash as completely and as
deeply as it does Holy Writ. All the early attempts at puri-
fication by Philo, John and Onkelos proved ineffective. The
living stream of Christian religion, too, flows from the lux-
uriant anthropomorphism of the Synoptic Gospels. The most
that John could achieve with his, In the Beginning was the
Word and the Word was God—all that he achieved was to
father a theology. Gibbon may be unduly ironical in dealing

with matters religious, but it is hardly an exaggeration when he writes: "The most sagacious of the Christian theologians, the great Athanasius himself, has candidly confessed that, whenever he forced his understanding to meditate on the Divinity of the Logos, his toilsome and unavailing efforts recoiled on themselves; that the more he thought, the less he comprehended and the more he wrote, the less capable was he to express his thoughts."[48]

It was not the Gospel of John but the Synoptics that begat the Man-God. The Evangelists searched the literature of their people and their own memories for all that was living and perfect in Moses, Elijah, Jeremiah and depicted Jesus. They quite naturally persuaded themselves that the Man-God was greater than all his predecessors. They compared him to Moses and Elijah, to be sure, to the disadvantage of the latter. This approach of the writers of the Three Gospels was quite Jewish. The understanding and love of God, they well knew, had grown out of the nation's immortals, out of the people's historic experience. If Jesus was to be a God, he had to be fashioned a personality.

With the Jew the historico-experiential approach through personality was forever operative. Yehudah Halevi's presentation, at the very beginning of his poetico-philosophic work, still remains the classic Jewish mode. In his Kuzari, the Christian scholastic, begins the exposition of his religion with a credo: "I believe that all things are created whilst the Creator is eternal." The Moslem doctors begin: "We acknowledge the unity and eternity of God." The Rabbi says: "I believe in the God of Abraham, Isaac and Israel." This medieval philosopher, then, like the prophet, Rabbi or evangelist, points to the overwhelming influence of personality in all Jewish thinking.[49] Halevi, no mean philosopher, who knew something about the history of ideas, yet regarded the anthropomorphic speculations of the *Sheur Komah* of value.[50] Any wonder then that the Bible remained so wholesomely anthropomorphic.

This high value placed upon personality is the key to Judaism. Unlock the magic arcanum and it will reveal to you its hidden meaning, its veiled mysteries. Study man and you will find the Jew's world and the Jew's God.

Viewing the universe through man, Judaism never became merely a theory of the supermundane. Its dogmas and doctrines are not abstruse Socratic concepts, Platonic ideas, or Aristotelian forms; for the very good reason that life is not dialectics.[51] Its flow and ebb will tear down even the most solidly wrought syllogism of the mighty Stagirite. Judaism is intuition rooted in human experience. Human experience is varied, inconsistent, illogical and erring. Judaism displays all the glaring, egregious errors of experience.

The Rabbis and prophets never boasted of a particular taste for the rigor of logic. The spinning of subtle, formal distinctions without correspondence to human history and living environment was not exactly their *métier*. They knew neither of the Aristotelian-scholastic theory of Being nor of Kant's epistemological substitution. Objects of knowledge were not to them abstract shadows, but substances concrete and indefinable. They made no distinction between eternally valid truths and subjective, psychological determinations. To them these were organically interdependent. The Rabbis were not troubled because we cannot know things as they are in themselves and because what we know are only "phenomena" which the mind produces within itself. They did not lose touch with common sense reality, although they might have been hard pressed to define it.[52] They might have understood and even agreed with the idealist's allegations that "reality, considered by itself and apart from a mind that knows it, is full of insoluble puzzles and contradictions." They would, however, have been more than puzzled in their effort to grasp the meaning of the second half of the allegation: "These (puzzles and contradictions) disappear when reality is treated as not something by itself, but for mind."[53]

"Meditate upon His work," said Rabbi Meir (brilliant,

almost hair-splitting legalist of the second century), "and you will recognize Him Who spoke and with His speech brought the world into being."[54] Rabbi Meir was a keen logician, subtle enough to baffle the most acute minds of his day.[55] He was, according to some, intimate with Graeco-Roman thought.[56] He was, in addition, a skillful stylist, possessing a genius for reducing the most labyrinthic legal discussion to concise, lucid statement.[57] The famous Mishnaic style noted for its brevity, simplicity and clarity may have been his creation.[58] Was it beyond such a man to grasp Aristotelian abstruseness and clothe it in Hebraic garb? How far removed is his homily from the scholastic theorem: *Nihil est in intellectu quod prius non fuerit in sensu*.[59] Are not the opening words of Kant's Critique more or less a paraphrase of the words of the *Tanna*? "That all our knowledge begins with experience," writes Kant, "there can be no doubt. For how is it possible that the faculty of cognition should be awakened into exercises otherwise than by means of objects which affect our senses. . . ."[60] Is not metaphysics often divine poetry turned into prose? Rabbi Meir chooses to speak in metaphor, in language aglow with human experience. The scholastic and Kantian mode of expression he and his people would have found prosaic, cold, denuded of vitality, buoyancy.

Somehow the language of the metaphysician and the scientist loses the quality of things. Our dearest friends, our most cherished hopes, our deepest passions vanish into lean words and ethereal symbols. It was this, was it not, that made Ruskin speak of metaphysicians and philosophers as the greatest trouble makers the world has got to deal with? "When, glancing into the second volume of 'Hippolytus,' " Ruskin tells us, "we find the Chevalier Bunsen himself talking of a 'finite realization of the infinite' (a phrase considerably less rational than 'a black realization of white'), and of a triad composed of God, Man and Humanity (which is a parallel thing to talking of a triad composed of man, dog and canineness), knowing those expressions to be pure, definite and highly finished nonsense, we do not in general trouble ourselves to look any farther."[61] Rabbi Meir cannot be charged with such "nonsense." His words are not mere shadows; they are endowed with life, quality. The Jew having become accustomed to see the universe through dynamic men could not speak in any other way. He would not dispense with "attributes."

Should it be argued that Rabbi Meir was only a product of his surroundings and did what he did in blissful unawareness, we might well, then, turn again to the Kuzari. Yehudah Halevi, living in an environment and age given to abstract speculation, nevertheless, writes deliberately, consciously: "Do not believe him who considers himself wise in thinking that he is so far advanced that he is able to grasp all metaphysical problems with the abstract intellect alone, without the support of anything that can be conceived or seen, such as words, writing, or any visible or imaginary forms. 'Seest thou not that thou are not able even to collect the burden of thy prayer in thought alone, without reciting it? Neither canst thou reckon up to a hundred without speaking, still less, if this hundred be composed of different numbers.' Were it not for the sensible perception which encompasses the organization of the intellect by means of similar sayings, the organization could not be maintained. In this way, prophets' images picture God's greatness, power, loving kindness, omniscience, life, eternity, government and independence, the dependence of everything on Him, His unity and holiness, and, in one sudden flash, stands revealed this grand and majestic figure, with its splendor, its characteristics, the instruments which typify power, etc., the uplifted hand, the unsheathed sword, fire, wind, thunder and lightning, which obey his behest, the word which goes forth to warn, to announce what has happened and to predict."[62] May it not be then that Rabbi Meir chose the language of life as deliberately as did Yehudah Halevi.

Now, life, as it presents itself to man as he lives it, is contradictory, baffling, illogical. Therefore the Bible and Talmud, concerned with rich living values, are as full of contradictions as they are free from dogmas. "Those who would oppose grammar to usage," wise old Montaigne asserts, "are queer people."[63] Moses who dared the devastating, solitary heat of Sinai's flaming peak, and spent forty days in the company of God, studiously chiseling the divine word into the inert granite—is a mighty man indeed, a holy man, a perfect man—but mark him, consumed with anger, shatter the living word against Sinai's foot. Reduce him, if you can, to a formula, to a *Ding an sich* shadow. An enigma is this man Moses! He is personality! How much then more is his God, Who is the source of all Personality.

The Greeks whose eyes were riveted on natural phenomena pursued an entirely different course. To them the source of Reality was presumably thought. Therefore all knowledge was advertised as the product of logical demonstration. *À priori* truth was at least theoretically in ill-repute. It is true that in mathematics, in the theories of Ideas and Forms, in all the problems of metaphysics, the prejudice yielded, but, on the whole, in Greek speculation the myth of pure reason prevailed.[64] "Socrates, Plato, Aristotle, like their whole age, allowed themselves to be deceived by words."[65] Among Jews *à priori* assumptions were not concealed under a fog of verbiage. Intuition was placed frankly first, logic was a good deal behind.

Are then the Bible and the Talmud devoid of reason and intellectuality? Decidedly not. No more than the Greeks were deficient in the fruits of intuition. The differences among peoples are not so radical. Human beings are human beings everywhere, and the universe to which they react is, despite its multiformity, none-the-less the same. What differentiates one people from another is not kind or essence but presentation and emphasis. There were not wanting men in Greece who "felt" the universe as much as they reasoned about it. Plato himself never quite escaped the conflict between logic and intuition. Even so in the Bible and Talmud there is no want of reason and intellectuality. Perhaps in no other literature are education, learning, study, wisdom, knowledge or contemplation so paramount. To be intelligent was considered an inescapable obligation. There was a deep and profound thirst for knowledge. "The man who understands astronomy," said the Rabbis, "and does not pursue it, regards not the work of the Eternal and considers not the operation of His hands."[66] But they were painfully aware of the limitations of Reason. Indeed Reason is its own greatest limitation. The pagans, on the other hand, were not always moved solely by intellectual curiosity to delve into the mysteries of nature. There was at least one important school of thought which found its impetus to philosophize elsewhere than in Reason. Many pagans pursued knowledge only to save themselves from the terrors of their religion. For Epicurus the study of celestial phenomena, for one thing, "had no other end in view than peace of mind and firm conviction."[67] Religion had been so degraded that it had become only a burden of fear. It produced criminality and impiety,[68] and persuaded men to evil deeds.[69] Lucretius' philosophic and didactic poem had for its purpose the setting "free the mind from the close knots of superstition."[70]

Like Socrates, who was often Hebraic in spirit, the Prophets and the Rabbis fought shy of origins. Such matters, thought the Athenian—"*aut maiora, quam hominum ratio consequi posset, aut nihil omnino ad vitam hominum adtinere* —were either too difficult for the human understanding to fathom, or else were of no importance whatever to human life."[71] Socrates, however, was a logician and enjoyed the sport of gliding on the thin ice of precise definitions.[72] Whether the Prophets and Rabbis anticipated Erasmus and believed that every definition was a misfortune, we do not know,[73] but they certainly seem to have acted on this assumption, and therefore never became philosophers or theologians.

Being neither the one nor the other, their world view is an unsystematic expression of intuitive knowledge. Monotheism with them was never stated as an Aristotelian theorem, but was conceived in terms of personality and expressed as an historic process. "The Torah," said Luzzatto, "saw no reason for teaching belief, for the Jews had already believed from the days of Abraham, and if they had not been believers, a commandment to the effect would have been useless."[74]

II. The Rabbis and Their Problems

THE ABSENCE OF SYLLOGISMS IN biblical and talmudic writings is not, we hope, to be confused with a want of reflection. Indeed all the problems—epistemology excepted—which puzzled Aristotle, Maimonides and Aquinas had, long before them, vexed the Prophets and the Rabbis. All questions concerning ultimates, such as are subsumed in ontology and cosmology, recur again and again. There is scarcely a fundamental proposition in medieval philosophy, or, for that matter, in Plato and Aristotle, which the Rabbis did not conceive and state a thousand times —in their own way, of course—a way aptly described by Dr. Kadushin as organic.[1] They unquestionably assumed that our thinking reaches out beyond the material into the spiritual and unknown—into *ta meta ta physica*, even though they did not conceal their ignorance of the unknown with empty phrases. That there is a "permanent substratum" or *hypokeimenon* at the bottom of all changing phenomena they devoutly believed. That there is an essential difference between matter and spirit, between man and beast, that the world has meaning, they never questioned. That the moral order of the universe is fixed was the very soul of their Torah concept; that God is the Being of being, eternal, infinite, uncaused, the very essence of thought; they had to learn from no one.

Have the Rabbis achieved final results, have they found permanent solutions to the problems of God, evil, etc.? Of course not! Have Aristotle, Spinoza, or Husserl achieved anything more conclusive? "He who thinks he knows the greatness of God, lessens it; he who would not lessen it, knows it not."[2] Be it said for the Rabbis that their speculations were never converted into rigid dogma. Their religion never lost its ductility. If what Dr. Kadushin claims is true, namely, that they did have a theology, then Professor Schechter's stricture is equally true, namely, that the Rabbis were never aware of it.[3]

It is, however, ludicrous to assume that there can be any conception of unity in the Godhead without some attempt at reflection.[4] To profess monotheism implies the assumption of the rationality and intelligibility of the world.[5] So much reflection cannot be denied the Rabbis. They certainly wanted to know God, see His essence face to face, understand His nature and His ways. They had even said, as in the case of Abraham, Job, Hezekiah and the Messiah to come, that the existence of God could be discovered by reason alone.[6] The Rabbis unquestionably would have urged that the *imitatio dei* was impossible without the *recognitio dei*, but, of course, *recognitio* they would have argued was not solely intellectual, but rather intuitive awareness.

This awareness was, of course, always the accompaniment of a particular experience. Not given to abstract reasoning, unconscious emphasis equated such an experience with the totality of life. In this they differed little from the scientist. The scientist, Professor Planck assures us, begins by taking a leap into the transcendental. But once he has taken that leap he neither discusses it nor worries about it. "If he did, science could not advance so rapidly. And anyhow—which is fundamentally a consideration of no less importance—this line of conduct cannot be refuted as inconsistent on any logical grounds."[7] Even so, the Rabbis. Their thinking was immediate, practical, social. Plato and Aristotle were prone to speculate, as it were, in a vacuum. Even in the later schools of the Stoics, Epicureans and Sceptics, "ethics were almost entirely divorced from the wider social interest."[8]

It is true that the Rabbis yielded more to imagination and intuition than to inquiry and reason, yet doubt and questioning were forever cropping up. In the Books of Job and Koheleth, the Rabbis had an inexhaustive source of skepticism. Many of Job's dicta were conceded to be blasphemous.

"His mouth," some had said, "should have been stuffed up with dust rather than be responsible for many of his utterings."[9] For similar reasons some wanted to exclude the Book of Ecclesiastes from the Biblical Canon,[10] an attempt which made the "mild" Spinoza rage against the "audacity of the Rabbis."[11]

The Rabbis discussed the origin of the world, and the stuff and substance it was made of. They speculated about the physiology of the human body and, interestingly, had noted that at first the hand was of one piece, and that only after Noah's time was it divided into fingers.[12] They wondered whether *Tohu* and *Bohu*—chaos and void—were primordial matter.[13] They did then speculate on the eternity of the universe, even though they never abandoned the principle of *creatio ex nihilo*.[14] They were aware of the concepts of space and time, and spoke of God as the *Makom*, or *extensio* of the universe.[15] "We do not," said one of the Rabbis, "know whether God is the place of the world, or, the world is His place."[16] Rabbi Eliezer ben Jacob interpreted the name "*Shaddai*" to mean that the "whole universe and the fullness thereof was not worthy (kedai) of the Godhead."[17] God's power was unlimited and beyond man's comprehension. "All that thou seest," said Rabbi Huna, "is merely an infinitesimally small part of God's ways. Man cannot conceive the meaning of thunder, hurricane, storm, the order of the universe, his own nature; how can he boast of being able to understand the ways of the King of all kings?"[18]

They puzzled over God's immateriality and perceived Him as pure spirit, known to man only by his deeds. "When I judge the creatures, I am '*Elohim*'; when I make war on the wicked, I am '*Zebaot*'; when I suspend (judgment) for a man's sins, I am '*Shaddai*'; and when I am compassionate, I am '*Jehovah*.'[19] The famous Rabbi Jose ben Halafta was sufficiently spiritual, or radical, to declare: "Never did the '*Shechinah*' descend to earth, and never did Moses or Elijah ascend to Heaven."[20] Rabbi Meir was enough of a metaphysician to parry skillfully a carping interlocutor. When asked by a Samaritan to explain Jeremiah, chapter 23, verse 24: "Behold I fill heaven and earth." "How then could God," said the Samaritan, "speak to Moses between the two divisions of the ark?" Whereupon Rabbi Meir replied: "If the figure of a man changes according to the size of the looking glass, how much more likely is such an achievement for God."[21]

We see, however, the mind of the ancients best in the consideration of such problems as more intimately affect human conduct. They were much more concerned with the questions of evil, freedom of the will, and man *per se* than they were with primordial matter. There was more directness in their view of man than in the pronouncements of materialist philosophers. Both in the Bible and in Rabbinic writings there is unquestionably an awareness that man is of the earth, an integral part of the world's scheme, subject, like all of creation, to the will of God or the laws of nature. Man, however, was considered a special case. This, the ancients conceded, without indulging in the kind of apologetic circumlocution so characteristic of modern writers, idealists and materialists alike. Always thinking in terms of personality made the Rabbis zealous for the manhood of man, and inspired them to crave for him a large share in the hegemony of the world.

The story is told that Rabbis Ishmael and Akiba, walking through the streets of Jerusalem in the company of a stranger, were accosted by a sick man in search of a cure. The Rabbis gladly offered a remedy. "Who," remonstrated the stranger, "inflicted that man with his disease?" "The Holy One Blessed Be He," the Rabbis replied. "And you," said he, "dare inject yourself into an affair that is not yours. He inflicted the pain and you presume to cure it?" Said the Sages to him: "What is your trade?" "A farmer," he said pointing to the sickle in his hand. "But who created the soil, who the vineyard?" questioned the Rabbis. "The Holy One Blessed Be He," re-

plied the stranger. "And you bring yourself into a matter
that is not of your making? He created it and you eat its
fruit?" "Oh," said he, "don't you see the sickle in my hand?
If I don't plow, manure, weed, nothing will grow." To
which the Rabbis impatiently rejoined: "Fool, have you not
heard that it is written 'Man is likened to grass'? The tree,
if it is not manured and weeded, produces nothing. Even so
for the body, medicine is the manure and a human being is
the doctor."[22]

This human being was to the Prophets and Rabbis all-
important. Man is, as it were, God's collaborator. It is then
not surprising to find, in both Bible and Talmud, emphasis
placed on the freedom of the human will. The difficulties
inherent in the doctrine did not escape the ancients, but they
were too proud to declare man an automaton. In matters of
conduct his freedom was regarded as axiomatic. "The theory
of man's perfectly free will," records Maimonides, "is one
of the fundamental principles of the Law of our Teacher
Moses, and of those who follow the Law. . . . Against this
principle we hear, thank God, no opposition on the part of
our nation."[23] That this axiom did not fit snugly all conditions did perturb, but not seriously upset the Jewish mind.
The prophetico-rabbinic view is here, as elsewhere, intuitive
and immediate. It is nowhere presented in the form of an
iron-clad syllogism. There are some generalizations on the
subject, but it is as characteristic of Judaism as it is, or, was
of science, to concern itself more with the concrete. The fine
spun Aristotelian differentiations between Choice, Desire,
Passion, Wish, Opinion or Deliberation, and the division of
acts into voluntary and involuntary are not precisely stated,
but are certainly implied in Rabbinic literature.

The Jew's firm conviction that God is just is the source of
the unshakable belief in man's freedom. "If," says Maimonides, "man has free will, it is . . . intelligible that the
Law contains commands and prohibitions, with announce-
ments of rewards and punishments."[24] Aristotle has no more

solid foundation for his freedom of choice. "It is manifest,"
he says, "that man is the author of his own acts," since the
lawgivers "punish and exact redress from those who do evil
. . . and honor those who do noble deeds, in order to encourage the one and repress the other."[25]

Aristotle's reference to lawgivers is rather weak, vague and
indefinite. It lacks fire. The Jewish appeal was different. The
whole of biblical literature, the noblest utterances of the
Prophets become meaningless gibberish if man is not his own
master. If he acts under constraint then the burning, horta-
tory and indignant utterances of the Jeremiahs and Amoses
are "mocking the poor."[26] Everywhere in the Bible and Talmud man is urged to choose between good and evil, life
and death. Man was warned not to eat from the Tree of
Knowledge, but he did eat. His knowledge imposes upon him
the responsibility of his freedom. Therefore, "see, I have set
before thee this day life and good, and death and evil."[27]
Remember, "for this commandment which I command thee
this day, it is not too hard for thee, neither is it far off. It
is not in heaven that thou shouldest say: 'Who shall go over
the sea for us, and bring it unto us, and make us to hear it,
that we may do it?' "[28] It is in your power to act. Therefore
"thus saith the Lord of Hosts, the God of Israel: 'Amend
your ways and your doings.' "[29] It is in your power. On this
there is universal agreement.

> "Stand ye in the ways and see,
>   And ask for the old paths,
>   Where is the good way, and walk therein,
>   And ye shall find rest for your soul."[30]

In the Talmud emphasis, equally emphatic and categorical, is given to man's status as a free moral agent. The famous
Rabbi Akiba put it in two words *ha-Reshut Netunah*, freedom
is granted.[31] The greatest personality of the long Talmudic
period here laid bare the "solid rock on which the whole
structure of Rabbinic Judaism was founded."[32] A later Tal-

mudic authority expanded, but did not alter, the principle. Rabbi Hanina bar Papa suggested that before conception an angel brings the drop of semen before God and says: "Master of the universe what is thy will concerning it? (Shall the man be) strong or weak, wise or foolish, rich or poor? But (the angel does not ask shall he be) wicked or righteous? For it is the opinion of Rabbi Hanina that "Everything is foreordained except conduct."[33]

Categorical as these classic formulations sound, there is nevertheless a deep awareness in Bible and Talmud that man's conduct is not always voluntary.[34] The story of the Egyptian Pharaoh whose will God Himself had chained did not fail to disturb some minds. The utter helplessness of man found eloquent expression.

> "O Lord, I know that man's way is not his own;
> It is not in man to direct his steps as he walketh."[35]

> "Man is like unto a breath;
> His days are as a shadow that passeth away."[36]

There was difference of opinion as to whether the sins of the fathers were visited on the children.[37] The same prophet who placed the responsibility for conduct on the individual keenly sensed the need for the creation of a new type of individual. "And I will sprinkle clean water upon you, and ye shall be clean; from all your uncleannesses, and from all your idols, will I cleanse you. A new heart also will I give you, and a new spirit will I put within you; and I will take away the stony heart out of your flesh, and I will give you a heart of flesh."[38]

In the Talmud the same thing is apparent. The weakness of man was deeply appreciated, the overwhelming odds against him were not minimized. A human being is today here and tomorrow in the grave.[39] What is he but ashes, blood, bile.[40] Many expressions escape the Rabbis implying that even conduct is foreordained. Thus some Rabbis believe that he who is born under the planet Zedek (Jupiter) would

be righteous. He who is born on a Thursday would be particularly charitable and kind.[41] Heaven too was always ready
to give extra aid in the exercise of one's will. So much depended on the initial step.[42]

Yet the deep sense of justice, which made God the em-
bodiment of justice, necessarily made of man a free moral
agent. There never did, there never could develop in Judaism
such controversy about the freedom of the will as frequently
prevailed in the Christian Church. Predestination, God's foreknowledge or grace could never come to interfere, from the
point of view of the Synagogue, with man's moral obliga-
tions. The Law was there to be observed. The Pelagians
who declared that the grace of God is bestowed according
to our merits were denounced as heretics. Saint Augustine,
writing to the monks of the monastery of Hadrumentum,
urged them not to overstress the defense of the freedom of
the will, to be careful to make it dependent on the grace of
God. For without the grace of God, man's will would be
helpless. "That is why the Lord, speaking about the fruits
of righteousness, says to His disciples, 'Without Me ye can
do nothing.' "[43] A Jewish teacher, in marked contrast, declared in behalf of God: "When they forsake Me I will be
indulgent, perhaps they will observe the Law. For even if
they forsake Me but keep the Torah, its light would lead
them back to Me."[44]

The conviction that man is a free moral agent was
prompted not only by the belief in divine justice, it buoyed up
out of the inner consciousness of strong men. Men such as
Elijah, Amos, Ezra, Hillel or Akiba unquestionably experienced extraordinary strength, an inner mastery over external
and internal temptation and pressure. It is reported of Hillel
that the most persistent irritation could not bring him to
"lose his temper."[45] Rabbi Akiba had married late in life.
He loved his Rachel with all the tenderness and depth of his
mighty spirit.[46] From this marriage, the first offspring was
a youth of extraordinary talent, whom the father dearly

loved.[47] The news of the son's imminent death reached the
father while he was lecturing at the academy. The man of
iron did not interrupt himself. Calmly, he held his class the
whole day.[48] Who is a hero? The academies proclaimed:
He who masters his passion.[49] He is greater than the con-
queror of cities. The Akibas and the Hillels were not isolated
instances of supreme self-control. It was true of many generations of Pharisees. It should be remembered, that unlike
their Christian prototypes, they were not recluses but social
beings, a part of the scramble of daily affairs. They were
cobblers, bakers, tailors, peddlers, merchants, and their temp-
tations were numerous.[50] Now and then one of them may
have faltered, yet are we exceedingly doubtful whether the
most prying gossip would have found among them anything
lewd or salacious. Even the daring Boccaccio would have hesitated to turn their painful moral defeats into the occasions
for laughter.

Men who lived for centuries as the *Tannaim* and *Amoraim*,
inured to the most rigid discipline, were quite naturally conditioned to regard their wills as free. The Rabbis, however,
were acute students of human nature. Their insight into the
human psyche is amazing. Psychologists would do well to pay
more attention to the rich storehouse of "case" material in
Rabbinic literature. The Rabbis were deeply cognizant of
the weakness of the flesh, and often expressed judgments
about human nature that are decidedly deterministic. "When
a man plans a sin," they complained, "Satan dances at his
door until he has done it."[51] Ah, this Satan, he dogs a man's
footsteps unabatingly daily but *Yom Kippur*.[52] There is no
escape from his power, unless one turn angel,[53] beast,[54] or
retire to a cemetery.[55] Worse still. He spitefully fans the
desire for that which is forbidden.[56] Alas, one can't be over-
confident even unto the day of death.[57]

This utter helplessness of man against his impulses would
frequently move the greatest of Palestinian *Amoraim* to
tears.[58] The struggle is unrelenting. More than one saint had

reason to lament *oi li miyizri*.[59] He attacks and besieges the
body like a king.[60] He comes in, apparently, very shy and
timid, like a guest, but once in, he establishes himself as perfect master.[61] Even an Abaye would not trust himself in his
hands.[62] How then dare any man challenge temptation?[63] A
Rabbi Hiyah bar Ashi would pray daily: "O Merciful One,
save me from the evil tempter."[64] For he gets such an early
start on the *Yezer Tov*. Already in the embryo the evil
tempter is securely established.[65] Once there, it acts like a
foreign substance in the body, seeking the destruction of all
that is good and noble.[66] When in the yonder, God shows
this evil tempter to the righteous, he looms in their eyes as
huge as an enormous mountain. They weep out of sheer
fright at the great height they scaled.[67] Even the greatest
named him with seven evil names. He is evil, uncircumcised,
impure, an enemy, a stumbling block, a rock, a lurker.[68] Even
his Creator calls him evil,[69] and regrets having created him.[70]
It should be noted, since we have singled out above Rabbi
Akiba as absolute self-master, that it was he who had said
that the evil tempter first appears as the thread of a spider's
web but soon becomes like the cable of a ship.[71]

We shall see later that millennia of controversy among
logicians, metaphysicians, theologians and, in recent years,
among scientists, have given us no deeper awareness of the
problem of human responsibility, and no solution more adequate.

The problem of evil was also an ancient obsession in Jewish literature. Neither the Prophets nor the Rabbis were so
imprudent as to say a final word about it. In the Bible the
pain, sorrow, injustice, futility, *ennui* to which human beings
are heir find vigorous and vehement expression.

"Right wouldst Thou be, O Lord," protests Jeremiah,
"Were I to contend with Thee;
Yet will I reason with Thee:
Wherefore doth the way of the wicked prosper?
Wherefore are all they secure that deal very treacherously?

Thou hast planted them, yea, they have taken root;
They grow, yea, they bring forth fruit."[72]

Such painful protests are not limited to the sensitive Jeremiah. The anguished cry at the misery of society recurs again and again in Holy Writ. It was to be expected that among Jews it would take the form of embittered plaint against social injustice.

"Thou that art of eyes too pure to behold evil,
And that canst not look on mischief,
Wherefore lookest Thou, when they deal treacherously
And holdest Thy peace, when the wicked swalloweth up
The man that is more righteous than he;
And makest men as the fishes of the sea,
As the creeping things, that have no ruler over them."[73]

"Why standest Thou afar off, O Lord?
Why hidest Thou Thyself in times of trouble?
Through the pride of the wicked the poor is hotly pursued."[74]

"Lord, how long shall the wicked,
How long shall the wicked exult?"[75]

"Wherefore do the wicked live,
Become old, yea, wax mighty in power?"[76]

"Let me be weighed in a just balance,
That God may know mine integrity."[77]

Such biblical verses are too numerous and too well-known to require further citation, but it was not only social injustice that grieved prophet and psalmist. The precariousness of human existence *per se* troubled them. They were deeply aware that

"As for man, his days are as grass;
As a flower of the field, so he flourisheth.
For the wind passeth over it, and it is gone;
And the place thereof knoweth it no more."[78]

That man was born to weariness and vanity the authors of Koheleth and Job had stated with unmatched eloquence, emphasis and pathos. Indeed the problem of human suffering in all its nuances did not escape them. They were overwhelmed by the inexorable cruelty of natural phenomena, the waste and ruin wrought by storm, drought, lightning, locust, flood, earthquake, disease; by the wickedness of man to man; by the depth, baseness and fury of human passions.

The Rabbis were not behind the prophets in their deep awareness of the world's ills. Even though they tried to reassure themselves that the good outweighed the evil,[79] they were yet too kindly and sympathetic not to see life's miseries. When a Gamaliel heard a mother weep for her dead child his heart quaked at her sorrow.[80] Even the pain of the dumb brute pierced the Rabbis to the quick.[81] They loved life too much to regard evil a blessing. They could not, like so many other orientals, take denial or pessimism as their religion. On the other hand, reared in a divine tradition so different from that of an Epicurus, they could not charge God either with impotence or malevolence.[82] So much of pagan skepticism and fatalism, as we have already noticed, was due to the bad repute of the gods. They were so frequently envisaged as malicious demons, spiteful, envious, seeking the destruction of mankind as a mere whim or sport. The poets "represented the gods as inflamed by anger and maddened by lust." They displayed to "gaze their wars and battles, their fights and wounds, their passions, their adulteries . . . their unions with human beings. . . . With the errors of the poets may be classed the monstrous doctrines of the magi and the insane mythology of Egypt."[83] These gods and their superstitions ever hung over men's heads like the sword of Damocles and poisoned and destroyed their peace of mind.[84] "Man's life lay . . . foully groveling upon the ground, crushed beneath the incubus of pagan superstition."[85] To inspire human beings with hope one first had to cast down religion and trample it under foot.[86]

The God of the Universe, however, was not an Olympian *roué*.[87] The Rabbis could not abandon the firm conviction

that justice was the foundation of His throne.[88] They despised evil so profoundly and believed in justice so desper-
ately that even though they regarded God the Creator of
the whole world and all there is therein, they could not at
times resign themselves to regard Him as the direct source
of evil. Nothing evil descends from on high.[89] Only the
angels of peace and mercy, they opined, stand close to the
Divine Presence, the angels of wrath are at a great distance.[90]
So anxious were they to widen this distance between God
and evil that they eagerly grasped at every straw. In Genesis
they pointed out it is written: "And God called the light
day; but when speaking of the 'darkness,' it reads: 'He
called,'[91] for 'the Holy One, Blessed Be He, does not cause
His Name to rest on evil.'[92] He cannot even bear to look
at the wicked or wickedness."[93]

The Rabbis labored hard to account for what seemed to
be much flagrant injustice in the world. The problem gnawed
them to such an extent that they made God admit that by
creating the tempter He was in a measure responsible for
man's sins.[94] It was a conundrum, they opined, that gave
Moses no rest. He too wanted to know the "ways of God."
"Master of the universe," he pleaded, "let me know Thy
ways. Why is there the righteous who suffers and the wicked
who prospers?"[95] So convinced were the Sages that the problem of evil vexed Moses that they ascribed to him the author-
ship of the Book of Job.[96] The prophet Habakkuk they
credited with even greater persistency. He marked out a circle
about himself and threatened to remain upon his watch until
he would obtain an answer:

> "How long, O Lord, shall I cry,
> And thou wilt not hear!
> I cry out unto thee of violence
> And thou wilt not save!
> Why dost thou shew me iniquity,
> And beholdest mischief?
> And why are spoiling and violence before me?
> So that there is strife, and contention ariseth."[97]

The notion that punishment and suffering were the visitation of God's love gradually evolved as the most plausible, popular and comforting explanation of much of the world's evil. Rabbi Akiba propagated this view with quenchless zeal and unbending courage.[98] Even like unto a potter, the Creator tests only His very best specimen.[99] So many of life's most genuine values, many thought then as even now, can be acquired only through pain, trouble and poverty.[100] Israel emerges from the vale of tears armed with a new resilience.[101] He who is sufficiently strong to face his trials with gladness bringeth salvation unto society.[102] Certainly sorrow refines character. Man is tender and pain hard to bear. When Abraham first tasted its sting, he cried: "If the generation of the Deluge, O God, had known pain they never would have rebelled against Thee."[103] Desire, too, is a source of sorrow; yet but for it the family, society, civilization are inconceivable.[104]

Suffering, the ancients philosophized, was inescapable.[105] It was inherent in the very woof and web of life.[106] All that God did was unquestionably for the good,[107] even death was good.[108] Man ought then to pronounce a benediction over the evil as well as over the good.[109] But even as with the prophets so with the Rabbis the cry of anguish or even protest was never silenced. *Lo hen velo secharan,* neither suffering nor its reward pleaded the grief-stricken Rabbi Johanan.[110] Heaven and earth Thou bearest but my trespass Thou wilt not bear![111] How can you, Oh Eternal Sovereign, expect both absolute justice and human society to exist side by side?[112] The Eternal Sovereign was not too expectant. He created the world with His blessings yet even then wondered whether it could resist evil.[113] Courageous were Jeremiah and Daniel, the Rabbis applauded. The excessive evil of their times caused them to limit the praise of God. He was a God of truth and they would not lie unto Him.[114] Alas, life was hard and the logic of events inscrutable. There was death due to no sin and suffering caused by no iniquity.[115] How could they forget

the brutal, dreadful death of Rabbi Akiba? Even Moses in
Heaven could not restrain himself but cried before the Most
High: *zo Torah vezo secharah*. Is this the Law and its reward? Silence, Heaven thundered, it is part of the original
plan of creation.[116]

It is true that in the end the Rabbis found comfort in a
verse.[117] An intuitive experience, the memory of a personality sufficed to silence all doubt. "Philosophers," says a
comparatively recent Jewish thinker in all earnestness, "made
of God a First Cause, then bound Him to the thing caused,
or effect. The truth is just the opposite. It is written: 'Thou
God art alone'."[118] The verse is undoubtedly no solution,
but neither is the concept, nor the idea, nor the form, nor
water, nor motion, nor the principle of concretion, nor even
the Supreme Mathematician.[119] On the other hand, to give
their verse vigor, the Rabbis assumed little beyond an intelligent and beneficent power in the world—an assumption
that metaphysicians and logicians neither prove nor abandon,
that even the skeptic Hume, a goodly few centuries after the
Rabbis, still regarded as universal.[120]

III. AWARENESS VERSUS FORMULATIONS

THE JEWISH VIEW OF THE UNI-
verse then though neither metaphysical nor logical was decidedly not unreflective. It contained the elements of the most
elaborate philosophic systems. Why these were never constructed in Judea is not difficult to conjecture. Speculation so
speedily approaches an impasse. To engage in investigation
of the essence of God, the purpose of evil, the nature of the
will is to embark on a never-ending voyage. The Hillelites
and Shammaites had battled over some of these conun-
drums for years, but only to a draw.[1] There were other
labors awaiting their energies and talents, and life cannot
wait on dialectics. To live means to act, and to act men have
to take some things for granted. Jewish thinkers did take
something for granted. They fell back on tradition and discouraged metaphysics.

> "Search not the things that are too wonderful for thee;
> And seek not that which is hid from thee.
> What thou art permitted, think thereupon;
> But thou hast no business with the secret things."[2]

In matters affecting human relations or conduct, generations of scholars displayed breath-taking ingenuity. When
necessary they could indicate distinctions finer than the finest
silken thread. The acts of men may prove a blessing or curse
to themselves or to their fellowmen. Here definite rules are
imperative. Here the Rabbis experience no difficulty in showing what master logicians they really were. They elaborated
the Law with meticulous care, even as the prophets had
provided the *élan vital*. Driven, however, by the very ex-
igencies of life to create and mold a society, Jewish thought
gradually learned to take the universe for granted and to
concentrate on the moral life. What God was the prophets

did not know, but they were certain to the marrow of their bones that He loved righteousness and hated wickedness. "Jewish monotheism was reached neither by postulating the unity of nature nor by speculation on the unity of Being— the physical or the metaphysical approach of science and philosophy—but by way of the unity of the moral order in the history of the world, identified with the will and purpose of God."[3]

The world view of Jewish thinkers was not reared on pure thought; it was an outgrowth of life, sprung from the paradox inherent in the burden of existence and the joy of living. The prophets and Rabbis were much more concerned to endow life with some value, to wrest for man some modicum of happiness, than to reduce the universe to a symbol or a formula. Even the quantitative and measurable aspects of things with which the scientist is concerned are excellent only for the laboratory. These the physicists find amenable to their methods. But man cannot forever live in a laboratory. A world of motion, number and weight is hardly satisfying. These measurements do not even give "direct information about external reality. They are only a register or representation of reactions to physical phenomena."[4]

The ultimate criterion of the Rabbis' thinking was not scientific measuring, or intellectual certitude, but the good life. The comprehension of the riddle of the universe was secondary, but its goodness came first. Philosophic content might be vague, but conduct must be fixed. They would have applauded wholeheartedly Antisthenes' maxim that "virtue is an affair of deeds and does not need a store of words or learning."[5]

We doubt whether there is anything to regret in this want of the speculative propensity which characterized Judea. The blessings that dialectics brought the Greeks were not tangible. "The discourse of the philosopher would vibrate without effect on the ear of the peasant." The Greeks were influenced but little in their practice by their philosophy.

The metaphysical systems, it will not be denied, purified to some extent religious belief, but it was no match against heathen practice. Even the philosophers remained impervious. "Socrates sacrificed in the usual way to the gods, although he held advanced ideas with regard to prayers and oaths. No doubt Plato and Aristotle passed for pious so far as their religious practices were concerned, in spite of the fact that they put new content into ancient forms. The former frequently made the speakers in his dialogues refer to the gods in quite the traditional way, and in his Timaeus he set forth a kind of systematic theology; in his Laws, written in his old age as a supplement to his Republic, he planned for his ideal state a religious organization, involving a plurality of gods, not dissimilar to that of the actual Athenian state; he represented his chief spokesman as proving the existence of the gods, giving warrant for the familiar practices of religion and justifying the ways of gods to men; moreover he proposed to have statutes against impiety and the introduction of religious rites not recognized by law. Aristotle clearly had slight respect for the common notions as to the gods, but for all that he regarded the worship of many gods as natural, and he thought that worship was indispensable for the existence of a state; therefore in his Politics he made a place for a polytheistic religion, defined the duties of priests and other sacred officials, and provided that all the expenses of public worship should be borne by the state."[6]

It was not only heathen worship that retained its hold on the Greeks. When the Hellenic world tottered and the death knell had sounded for its Pantheon, the deities went down to their graves wasted with licentiousness and debauchery. The punctilious inquisitions into the precise nature and origin of ethical concepts failed to purify the common notions of the gods. Moral skepticism levied a heavy toll on pagan society. Even in the most refined of homes brilliant discussions ended in riotous banqueting. Not even the exquisite art of Plato could check the impatience of Patrician youths.[7] In the eighteenth century Hume charged that Philosophers and Theologians were busy establishing the natural attributes of Deity, leaving the moral doubtful and uncertain. The Greeks might have been charged that with them, both the natural and moral attributes were little more than an endless logomachy.[8] The Rabbis despite the fact that they did not quest for precise formulae of cognition, being, substance, essence or accidents were not unaware of the intellectual difficulties. But they urged, with every fiber of their being, on the basis of experience, that the moral attributes of God were most certain. Even though they did not reduce it to a logical distinction, they nevertheless were fully convinced that between the actual and ideal there was an active relation, and that the source and end of that relation, as well as of all phenomena, was a moral Deity. Shall we then accuse the Rabbis of naïveté and mental indolence, or, on the contrary, discover in their thinking an approach that was most suited to their purpose.

The distinguished modern philosopher, Samuel Alexander, apologetically suggests that his account of the universe is based on common-sense experience, and, therefore, cannot be compared with the "clean-cut descriptions of the philosophical mathematicians."[9] The hypothesis of his own system is "that Space-Time is the stuff of which matter and all things are specifications." Consequently, Space and Time have no existence apart from each other and the reality is Space-Time.[10] Of what kind of common sense does Professor Alexander speak? How far does he succeed in vesting the universe with quality, which is ever the first prerogative of common sense? Exasperated, Professor Russell for himself is compelled to confess that his metaphysics is short and simple, that the external world may be an illusion, that order, unity and continuity may be nothing more than inventions on a level with catalogs and encyclopedias.[11]

If after these millennia European wisdom is so confused, was it then some good angel that led the Rabbis to prefer, as it were, verses to syllogisms? Was it sound intuition that caused them to eschew metaphysical systems and the claims of pure reason? Did they perhaps sense the impossibility of relating the "real" world of the philosopher to the world of daily experience?

The Rabbis and prophets were wise in passing on to us an awareness, a gleam, a divination which have proved richly suggestive. Their systems, had they constructed them, we suspect would not have fared quite so well.[12] According to Professor Lange modern times "had no task more important than to burst asunder the fetters" of the Aristotelian-scholastic system.[13] The Rabbis at least saved us the pother. That they set a limit to their questionings neither reflects on their intellectual acumen nor honesty. After all, they differ but little from the profoundest of philosophers, who were compelled to accept unknown first principles, upon which depended the whole web of their intermediate propositions and conclusions.[14]

Well, the Rabbis dispensed with the web of propositions. They did not define the Deity. They assumed that as to the existence of God there was no question whatever. As a result of primitive mythology, an omnipotent mind governing the universe had long been an accepted fact.[15] They regarded it however either as impossible or impudent to attempt to form an exact notion of the Supreme Being.[16] To define God as *sphaera intelligiblis, cuius centrum ubique, circonferentia nusquam*—an intelligible sphere whose center is everywhere and circumference nowhere, they would have thought both barbarous and blasphemous. To engage in the endless discussion of immanence and transcendence might have tested their patience. Dialectic niceties about the moment of contact between the Creator and created concerned them little. Yet, it would have been no exaggeration for them to have stated: "We know Him simply and naturally as we know our fellowmen."[17] If we are meticulous we argue that it is impossible to know God as simply and as naturally as we know our fellowmen without really comprehending His nature, but do we really comprehend the nature of our fellowmen? To what extent do we know them?[18]

Now, Professor Alexander is much more precise in his reasoning than the ancient Rabbis. He does not hesitate to plumb the meaning of reality in order to define the God-head. But what can we make of this statement? Says Professor Alexander: "If you ask me what God is, I can only answer He is a being whose body is the whole world of nature, but that world conceived as actually possessing deity, and therefore He is not actual as an existent but an ideal, and only existent insofar as the tendency towards His distinctive character is existent in the actual world."[19] Shades of Ruskin, here we have a sentence that vies favorably with Prussian metaphysics. Professor Alexander defines God in terms of Deity and the Deity as God. If this is lucid and conclusive, then no plaint can be lodged against the Rabbis. "An adequate scientific knowledge," to quote Professor Lange again, "of the absolutely transcendental is impossible, and modern systems which call up the phantom of an intellectual knowledge of transcendental things, are in truth no whit higher in this respect than the Platonic."[20]

IV. The Occidental Myth

It is difficult for the occidental nourished on the syllogism to allow that there are either elements of reason, or appreciable intelligence in any other scheme of thought than his own. Any view of the universe which cannot be stated in major and minor premises, he regards as irrational, uncivilized, oriental. There is always the supposition that European philosophers, with their airtight systems, have actually gone far in their comprehension of the universe. There is the arrogant innuendo that the Kants and the Hegels were in the possession of truths unknown to Chinese, Hindoo, or Jewish teachers. As a matter of fact, there is nothing more in this assumption than local superciliousness.

The best of the philosophers have achieved little beyond the improvising of a special argot for their trade, and beyond making occasionally a leap in the dark. These paltry efforts or achievements, it has flattered Europeans to acclaim, "pure reason," the supremely intellectual. If a Tagore betrays his ignorance of the mystery of the universe in some beautiful, poetic phrasing, he is dismissed as a benighted Hindoo mystic, with more beard than wisdom. When a Hegel, however, majors, minors and middles, analyzes and synthesizes, and leaves behind a trail of hair-splitting speculations and disputations, we, for no good reason, believe that we are nearer the truth. Strange how easily we are dazzled by the ingenuity of expression and deluded by the sheer variety and novelty of statement, to overlook the miserable poverty in definite results from which philosophy has suffered through the ages.[1]

The general impression that European philosophy reposes solidly on reason is a deception evidently maintained by some sort of philosopher's agreement. With hardly a thread

of truth in the fabric, it is puzzling how the fiction found
such ready acceptance. Philosophy no less than religion, reason no less than intuition, takes for granted just that for
which the heart craves proof. There was never a dogma more
false or arrogant than Hegel's belief that he could solve all
the problems of reality with logic alone. "He who devises
some bungling explanation of nature, including the rational
actions of mankind, starting from mere conjectural *à priori*
notions which it is impossible for the mind to picture intelli-
gently to itself, destroys the whole basis of science, no matter whether he be called Aristotle or Hegel."[2] Aristotle at
least was of a different mind. Writing in an age when philosophers did not as yet claim omniscience, he frankly admitted that not everything can be demonstrated.[3] At any
rate, he conceded the starting point of a demonstration was
not a matter of demonstration.[4] Certainly for the "what is
it" there is no proof.[5] Like any good believer Aristotle declared that "the question of what Being is and what is the
substance of things baffles us."[6] Man can simply not advance
beyond an unavoidable stopping point—*anágkē dè stēnai*.[7]
We might as well confess that metaphysical knowledge was
beyond our human powers.[8] Indeed, Aristotle was so uneasy
about the shortcomings of logic that a remark, of unusual
interest to Freudians, escapes him. "There is," says he, "something about exactness which seems to some people to be
mean, no less in argument than in a business transaction."[9]

But carp the illuminati, the Rabbis' most serious deficiency
was the failure to provide the scaffolding between the verse
and their God idea. Well, have the philosophers fared better? Aristotle, after pronouncing all those strictures about
logic, proceeded not with verses and metaphors, but with
categories and syllogisms, first to declare God the *Primum
Movens Immobile* and the final end of the universe, and
then had grave difficulty to connect Him with the finite at
all, and only achieved a verbal relation "by a metaphysical
tour de force."[10] Even then, he left us stranded in the dual-

ism of a transcendental God and the world He governs. Indeed, both Plato and Aristotle thought with presuppositions, which they were unable either to explain or to explain away; Plato with a presupposition of a given multiplicity, which he seeks to reduce to unity: Aristotle with a presupposition of a confused unity or continuity, which he is never able distinctly to resolve into its elements, or, to show to be individually determined in all its parts.[11] There has simply not yet been discovered in Philosophy a tenable connection between a materially conceived nature and an idealistic metaphysics.[12] Always the logician has to produce something *ex machina* to get anywhere.[13]

Myths, however, die slowly and dialectics is fascinating. In many parts of Europe it has proved irresistible. Let us not forget, though, that already the ancients, who knew something about philosophic schools, noted that "some schools took their names . . . from their teachers, as Socratics, Epicureans, or the like; some take the name of Physicists from their investigation of nature, others that of Moralists because they discuss morals; while those occupied with verbal jugglery are styled Dialecticians."[14] Plato complained that the Sophists spent their time in the study of unreality.[15] Forsooth he hated the Sophists with the vehemence of a sectarian.[16] Sophistry, echoes Aristotle, seems to be philosophy but is not.[17] Epicurus rejected dialectics as superfluous.[18] In more recent times John Ruskin admonished us: "I have often been told that any one who will read Kant, Strauss and the rest of the German metaphysicians and divines, resolutely through, and give his whole strength to the study of them, will, after ten or twelve years' labor, discover that there is very little harm in them: and this I can well believe; but I believe also that the ten or twelve years may be better spent."[19]

In a less generous moment, Ruskin ridiculed: "All that has been subjected to us on this subject seems object to this great objection; that the subjection of all things (subject to no exceptions) to senses which are, in us, both subject and abject, and objects of perpetual contempt, cannot but make it our ultimate object to subject ourselves to the senses, and to remove whatever objections existed to such subjection. . . . There is some meaning in the above sentence," concludes the impassioned Scotchman after a burst of devastating irony, "if the reader cares to make it out; but in a pure German sentence of the highest style there is often none whatever."[20] Professor Buechner, who cannot be accused of an anti-German bias, was sufficiently repelled by the involved sentences of his metaphysical contemporaries to warn them that disquisitions not intelligible to an educated man were not worth the printer's ink that was spent on them.[21]

Readers of Yehudah Halevi will recall how he belabors philosophers for their vagueness and their artificial theories.[22] When Spinoza subjected scholastic metaphysics to analysis, he discarded their God conception as *"asylum ignorantiae."* The modern metaphysician does not even resort to a supermundane asylum. "Those for whom," says Bradley, "philosophy has to explain everything . . . need not trouble themselves with my views."[23] More recently Professor Whitehead accuses metaphysicians, Spinoza not excepted, of invoking God to save their elaborate systems from collapse.[24] Charles S. Peirce, the father of Pragmatism, is even more merciless. "Metaphysics," he says, "is either meaningless gibberish—one word being defined by other words, and they by still others, without any real conception ever being reached, or else is downright absurd; so that when all that rubbish being swept away, what will remain of philosophy will be a series of problems . . . the truth about which can be reached without those interminable misunderstandings and disputes which have made the highest of the positive sciences a mere amusement for idle intellects, a sort of chess. . . ."[25] When the scientist turns metaphysician he is no more intelligible. Bertrand Russell, himself no mean scientist or philosopher, or both, is puzzled by many of his contemporaries. He cannot, for example, make up his mind whether he should accept the existence of God because according to Eddington atoms do not obey the laws of mathematics, or, because they do, according to Jeans.[26] With Bergson, Russell has little more patience. He dismisses the Parisian philosopher's metaphysics as being pleasant like cocktails, "but it has no better claim than cocktails have, to be included in the technique for the pursuit of knowledge."[27]

It was not our intention with the foregoing citations to heap ridicule on dialectics and metaphysics, or to deny that their pursuit has been responsible for some noteworthy contributions to the sum total of human knowledge. It was our purpose only to suggest that the time-honored Greek logic and metaphysics as applied, or misapplied, by untold generations of Europeans are not the only approach to the universe; their methodology is not the only evidence of thought or seal of truth. Surely the recent collision, or is it rapprochement, between science and metaphysics somewhat dims the luster of "systems."[28] Current scientific thought has come dangerously near the intuitive or "irrational."

In many quarters it is today conceded that the demarcation between the intuitive faculty and reason has been too wide and too bold. It is now asserted with equal boldness that the former was a trustworthy source of direct knowledge.[29] Scientists, such as Einstein, Schroedinger, Planck and others speak enthusiastically of religious insight as the guide of the scientific insight, the validity of which cannot be questioned.[30]

That scientists should come to take such a position was to be expected. Unlike the dialecticians, they have exercised themselves with facts and not with mere logical speculations, a practice Polemo so long ago earnestly urged upon all, but which was willfully disobeyed by many.[31] Confronted with facts, the scientists were driven closer and closer to grips with reality. To their amazement they discovered that of its essence nothing was known, that philosophers and metaphysicians had, in the main, been spinning subtle cobwebs.

The philosopher's contempt for matter and, consequently, for facts as it is well known, was his legacy from the Greeks.[32] It is true that Diogenes had mocked Plato saying: "Table and cup I see; but your tablehood and cuphood, Plato, I can no wise see," but then who was so queer as Diogenes. It was a simple matter for the magnificent Plato to dismiss him with a "better than thou" gesture—with a *noli me tangere*—which the most sanctimonious ecclesiastic might well have envied. Said Plato: "That's readily accounted for. For you have the eyes to see, the visible table and cup, but not the understanding by which ideal tablehood and cuphood are discerned."[33]

The modern scientist will not be so easily brushed aside. He is a little more certain of his "understanding." He might even remind Plato, with all due courtesy, that he, Plato, the philosopher, was pitifully ignorant of cup and table; that he, the scientist, was caught and confused in a vortex of non-existent particles, making any Athenian cup and table more ideal and phantasmagoric than all of Plato's cuphoods and tablehoods. No, he, the scientist, was not yet ready to speak of cuphoods and tablehoods. It would commit him too soon to a theory of the universe, to an acquaintance with its inner structure. His knowledge is to date so vague and fragmentary that he must balk at cosmic correlation.[34] Preoccupation with facts has made our scientist a trifle more modest. He theorizes a little more cautiously. "As a scientist," says John Burroughs, "one cannot admit anything mystical or transcendental in nature; while, on the other hand, the final explanation of the least fact is beyond us. We know certain things about chemical affinity, for instance; but what makes chemical affinity?"[35]

We no longer look down, from some lofty celestial height, upon the sublunar realm as something too simple to woo our intellectual powers. We have discovered that it is just a little difficult to define, let alone to understand, even transient, vulgar matter. Indeed, we must admit that we can no longer find salvation even with a materialistic philosophy of the universe. Not because of any religious scruple—religion is not the serious barrier. We are, alas, intellectually abashed. Sir Jeans and others have, unceremoniously, declared the universe to be a concept of "pure thought."[36]

"Mind," says Professor Eddington, "is the first and most direct thing in our experience; all else is remote inference."[37] Professor Planck is even a more pronounced heretic. "I regard," he declares, "consciousness as fundamental. I regard matter as derivative from consciousness."[38] We cannot get behind consciousness. Everything we talk about, everything we regard as existing, postulates consciousness. Matter is a "rhythmic whirl of events," if you will. It is the most unreal thing. If it *is* a thing under the sun, it has but a bare shadow, symbolic existence. It is, *mirabile dictu*, an emanation from mind. Tangibility and visibility are the poorest witnesses to Reality. In a word, again, the ideal is the real.[39]

In such a universe Diogenes' pots and pans are a reckless *à priori* assumption. It requires no less license to assume the existence, or, at least, the understanding, of atoms than it does of gods.[40] These pestilent little particles, *illa atomorum . . . turbulenta concursio,* have been discovered to be complicated solar systems, and the problems of their inner essence and their outer structure multiply daily *ad infinitum*. The laws governing atoms or pots and pans have ceased to be simple and uniform. Indeed the doctrine of simplicity and uniformity is a "marked case of wishful thinking."[41] The declaration of some physicists is strongly reminiscent of Protagoras' famous dictum: "As to the gods, I have no means of knowing whether they exist. For many are the obstacles that impede knowledge, both the obscurity of the question and the shortness of human life."[42] Replace gods by atoms and the quotation might be attributed, let us say, to Professor Compton. Indeed, times have altered strangely. The Chicago professor is much more certain of the gods than the Greek was of the atoms.

V. The Impotence of Science

THE REMARKABLE ADVANCE OF the exact sciences has not made confusion less confounded. The best that we can say for our age is that there is perhaps a general sense of new beginnings. Whether that sense is inspired by the break-up of the closed circle of nineteenth-century materialism and mechanism, or, by the budding of something new under the sun, remains to be seen.

O gluecklich, wer noch hoffen kann
Aus diesem Meer des Irrthums aufzutauchen!

As the remarkable century was drawing to an end, Professor Jevons cautioned that "before a rigorous, logical scrutiny, the Reign of Law will prove to be an unverified hypothesis, the Uniformity of Nature an ambiguous expression, the certainty of our scientific inferences to a great extent a delusion."[1] The physicist was rapidly abandoning mechanism as well as materialism. New vistas seemed to open up for *homo sapiens.* Just then the behaviorist came along and shut out all hope. Man, he said, was nothing more than a machine, a highly refined and complicated mechanism, it is true, but a piece of mechanism nevertheless. We gasped for breath. The psychologist was making of man a machine, on the basis of analogy of the physical world, just when the physicist began to doubt the mechanistic constitution of nature. The behaviorists would not be put down. Mind, they persisted, was matter at the present apex of its evolution. After eons of permutations and combinations, movements and vortices, matter had become rarefied and refined—something like Aristotle's celestial spheres. Our mental states, therefore, are only epiphenomenal, i.e., they are the reflection or glow of material processes but not cognitive. Physicist and

43

biologist probing the depth of matter report the universe to be idealist; psychologists penetrating the complicated nodosity of consciousness report it to be materialist. The physicist and biologist are becoming "spiritual"—allowing for mind, purpose and design; the psychologist has turned behaviorist or determinist ruling out both will and reason, and giving us a world bereft of mind and ruled by "chance."

We are sorely troubled. In the nineteenth century the zenith of civilization and salvation was in sight. Science was in a mad rush to unlock the last few doors to absolute truth and bliss. Solutions to the riddle of the universe were being patented. Synthetic systems were offered with every conviction and assurance of finality. In the last two or three decades our position has altered incredibly. We have plunged down to somewhere near the nadir. The unlocked doors have infinitely multiplied; the keys in our possession do not fit. We have lost our feeling of maturity and security. We rather feel like silly schoolboys again. We do not know where to begin our lesson and there is no teacher to help us. At any rate, all teachers are more or less discredited. Theology and Philosophy were deposed by Science, and, of late, Science has been so wayward and à couvert that we can but guess its intentions. With the contradiction in the heart of science, we have just noted, all traditional questions of metaphysics are reopened. Scientists are turning philosophers and in some instances even theologians, and a new search for finality is on the way.

Toward the end of the eighteenth century Baron von Holbach asked impatiently and contemptuously: "What shall we say of Berkeley, who tries hard to convince us that everything in the world is but a chimerical illusion, and that the whole universe exists only in ourselves and in our imagination, and who makes the existence of everything doubtful by the help of sophistries that are insoluble . . ."[2] In our own day the same Berkeley and his "sophistries" is referred to, and so largely quoted by Jeans, Eddington and Whitehead because they are "anxious to find philosophical justification for their own attitude towards the latest theories in atomic physics."[3]

Most modern philosophers, even such as are optimistic about the future, admit that at this time any attempt at metaphysical construction is premature. Already toward the close of the last century, it was conceded that "the very undertaking to construct a philosophic theory of things exclusively upon the physical sciences must, in these days, be described as a philosophical one-sidedness of the worst kind."[4] The explanations offered by science of numerous particulars are unquestionably final. But these very explanations of details have made the problem of "ultimates" ever more embarrassing.[5] Science, it is charged, is repeating with impunity the perennial error of philosophy. In its construction of a world picture, metaphysics so frequently limited itself to a consideration of the universe in terms of astronomy, physics and mathematics. Even when the philosopher did deal with esthetics, he either reduced it to mathematical formulae, or employed art as *analogia*. Even so, science has attempted a world view limited only to a few selected abstractions of Reality, in the sum total of things, perhaps, not of the utmost importance. It is not at all the real world, although it may be of primary significance for the understanding of the whole.

The quantitative account offered by science is undoubtedly fundamental and of interest. But a quantitative description of the universe may be no more enlightening as to its essence than a quantitative description of Shakespeare or Michelangelo would be of their specific genius. Science so often makes the impression of a huge burly giant tied hand and foot. There is a presence of tremendous, threatening power, but for the moment so pitifully helpless. Grand and significant as science has been in the exposition and manipulation of quantity, so helpless is it in the face of quality. Let all the scientists of the earth gather and they cannot as much as create one mosquito and give it the quickness of life.[6] Even a good joke, a hearty laugh, a beautiful face, an etching, a fugue, a sigh, a contour, a bolero do not come within its ken.[7] So much the worse for science and the sadder for man. To tell us that an idea, a wish, a hope, color, taste, texture, or even substance do not exist in the outer world but are the whimsicalities of our non-existent mind is neither enlightening nor comforting. To build up a Chinese Wall between inner experience and outer occurrences, and to place heavily armed guards to allow no communications and relations, will not make either for greater happiness or larger knowledge. That is where science just now stands. It has created an impasse between motion and emotions, particles and sensation, actions and thought. It denies the possibility of saying anything about their functional interrelations.[8]

The physicist's world has no characteristics beyond motion, shape or number. Even for the imaginary ether and assumed electron he only offers symbols and mathematical equations. And if asked by a bewildered humanity what the symbols stand for, "The mysterious reply is given that physics is indifferent to that; it has no means of probing beneath the symbolism."[9] It will not budge a fraction of an inch. The least recognition of the minutest speck, say of color, scientists fear will seriously upset their neat and exact measurements, applicable just because of its stubborn exclusiveness, universally. Only motion and energy will they measure; because they can measure them here and measure them on Mars. All other data of experience they must exclude, because they cannot describe them with punctilious exactitude.[10] In the meantime we are left in a barren, dry world sine life, sine beauty—a world of universality and generalization. "But," said Ruskin, "it is the distinctiveness, not the universality of the truth, which renders it important."[11] "To see in all mountains nothing but similar heaps of earth; in all rocks, nothing but similar concretions of solid matter; in all trees, nothing but similar accumulations of leaves, is no sign of high feeling or extended thought."[12] At any rate, it is not a universe for the five senses which, while responsible for many an illusion, are not themselves an illusion. "Vain is all that array of words which have been prepared and marshaled against the senses."[13] "Strip mankind of sensation and nothing remains."[14] Sensation, appetite are too vividly realistic to be abstracted into nothingness. Shall we say that pain does not exist in the world because science has no mathematical formula for it? If pain does not exist, how do we know that there is *anything* in the universe corresponding to the few aspects selected and abstracted by the physicist's mind?

"I shall consider human actions and appetites," says Spinoza, "as if I were dealing with lines, planes, or bodies."[15] It is certainly a stupendous achievement, and has gained for Spinoza a reputation among the foremost intellects of all time. May we not, however, say of him what he has himself said of Descartes under similar circumstances? "It is my opinion that he has shown nothing beyond great intellectual acumen."[16] The question is do lines and planes exhaustively describe a toothache.[17] Can any concise *propositio*, *demonstratio* or the longest *scholium* even of a Spinoza convey the exquisite torture that is the sufferer's, or, what it does for the moment to his view of life, God, his neighbors, etc.? Has not all this a better chance to find adequate expression in the quivering, abundant, language of Shakespeare? Could we turn from Spinoza's lines, planes and bodies to the society of men, women and children with their foibles, caprices, pranks, superstitions, likes and dislikes? Could Spinoza himself have felt any warmth in his lines if he had not first been man and then the geometrician philosopher?[18]

Does not the whole system of Spinoza presuppose firmly embedded convictions, mercurial sensation, gnawing appetites that will not be denied? Is it from Geometry *per se* that he has drawn the sweet, passionate love that pervades the *Ethics*? Does he really travel unaided through the arid desert

of lines and points, from the first to the fifth part of the
book? Has he not, before he left on the trying journey,
loaded his skins, and does he not from time to time scent
the presence of an alluring oasis? Was really his love for
God born out of the proposition, "It pertains to the nature
of substance to exist."[19] What made Spinoza capitalize God?
What made him insist that "Besides God, no substance can
be nor can be conceived?[20] Is it too much to detect here an
echo of the early *heder* instruction, "Thou shalt have no
other gods before Me"?[21]

Whence comes that reverence that constrains him to pro-
pose that God acts from the laws of His own nature only,
and is compelled by no one?[22] What makes him, gentle soul,
speak out against "adversaries" that "seem to deny the omnipotence"? Was the heretic humming, as he was writing this
proposition, the familiar phrases from the services on the
Day of Atonement? *"Kol yachol* and *mi yomar lecho mah
tipha'al."* What was there back of his mind when he rose in
this very *scholium* to the crescendo, "There could be no
other resemblance than that between the Dog, the celestial
constellation and the barking animal"?[23] Did he hear a
reverberation of the eloquent words of the prophet, *"el mi.
tedammiyun el umah demut ta'archu lo"*—To whom then
will ye liken God? Or what likeness will ye compare unto
Him?[24] May we not suspect that the propositions, "we delight in whatever we understand by the third kind of knowledge, and our delight is accompanied with the idea of God
as its cause,"[25] or "the intellectual love of God which arise
from the third kind of knowledge is eternal,"[26]—may we no
suspect that such propositions came naturally to a man who
for fifteen or twenty years recited twice daily meditativel
and passionately, "And thou shalt love the Lord, thy God
with all thy heart, and with all thy soul, and with all th
might"? May not Spinoza have been deceived, or, at an
rate, unduly sanguine when he hoped that his lines and point

might kindle that *amor Dei* and keep it burning *ad aeterni-tatem?*[27]

Has he, or, has anybody as yet, brought into inner harmony with one another lines and affections, abstractions and sensations? Does not this yet remain the unanswered question?

The common man asks the mathematician to write down an equation for two apples and two nails. The Professor goes to the blackboard and writes that which every second grade pupil knows $2 + 2 = 4$.

"Ah, my dear Professor," pleads the common man, "four what? Four apples or four nails?"

"Neither," says the Professor, "but four things, all of which possess the property of number and it is this element common to all of them that I have added."

"Thank you for your trouble. I don't know that you satisfy me at all. You see my apples are an exquisite red, abundant like a full moon. From previous experience with similar apples I know that its taste is delightful. An apple, Professor, is really a thing of beauty. There is something soul-satisfying about it. I am not much of a student of history or literature. But I do remember that a comely, lovesick maiden so far away and so long ago passionately chanted:

'As an apple-tree among the trees of the wood,
So is my beloved among the sons.
Under its shadow I delighted to sit,
And its fruit was sweet to my taste. . . .
Stay ye me with dainties, refresh me with apples;
For I am love-sick.'[28]

Some such apple chased a pair of lovers, nude and embarrassed from the delights of Eden into the miseries of life. Another such apple caused such a commotion among three pretty goddesses that whole literatures have been written about it and the tale not yet ended. Well, I do not want to be crude or show my ignorance, but I do protest in behalf of my apples. You lump them together with two nails and tell me I have four things. It won't do, sir, it won't. You are really saying nothing about my apples at all. You are giving me an equation expressing, what I believe you Professors call quantity. But quantity describes only extrinsic relation; it says nothing about the thing itself intrinsically. You have fixed your gaze on properties "external and superinduced." The qualitative, organic whole you have tacitly dismissed from your mind. But you can't let me down this way. Long ago one of your greatest philosophers maintained that "to the knowing of any substantial being, an accurate collection of sundry ideas is necessary." Of course, I know that even professors may choose the line of least resistance. "It is easy enough to know the simple ideas that make up any relation," but who will show us the heart of things?[29] What you have done is ignore completely the differences between the apples and the nails, and stressed only their likeness. It won't do, sir, it won't. You will have to search for a new equation."

The scientist goes asearching, but even more than the philosopher he wonders whether a qualitative world view is conceivable either on the basis of Philosophy or Science. Is he not compelled, even like the metaphysician, to bridge the gap between the absolute and the concrete with an "as if"?

How to pass from mind to the material world with mathematics and logic as lifebelts remains an insoluble mystery. "Verily," says Professor Eddington, "it is easier for a camel to pass through the eye of a needle than for a scientific man to pass through a door." The obstacles the scientist encounters at every threshold are not to be scoffed at. Professor Eddington's account of the perplexities is a veritable jeremiad. "I am standing on the threshold about to enter a room. It is a complicated business. In the first place I must shove against an atmosphere pressing with a force of fourteen pounds on every square inch of my body. I must make sure of landing on a plank traveling at twenty miles a second round the sun—a fraction of a second too early or too late the plank would be miles away. I must do this whilst hang ing from a round planet head outward into space, and with a wind of ether blowing at no one knows how many miles a second through every interstice of my body. The plank has no solidity of substance. To step on it is like stepping on a swarm of flies. Shall I not slip through? No, if I make the venture one of the flies hits me and gives a boost up again; I fall again and am knocked upwards by another fly; and so on. I may hope that the net result will be that I remain about steady; but if unfortunately I should slip through the floor or be boosted too violently up to the ceiling, the occurrence would be, not a violation of the laws of Nature, but a rare coincidence. These are of the minor difficulties. I ought really to look at the problem four-dimensionally as concerning the intersection of my world-line with that of the plank. Then again it is necessary to determine in which direction the entropy of the world is increasing in order to make sure that my passage over the threshold is an entrance, not an exit."[30] Be it said for Professor Eddington that modern physics has not invented the difficulty. It has only replaced a river by a door. When old Heraclitus suggested that he could not enter the same river twice, Cratylus spurned the suggestion, proving with all the vigor of logic at his command that it cannot be done even once.[31]

If then the scientist finds it impossible to pass through a door and the philosopher to enter a river, one would imagine it rather difficult to construct, with the tools at their command, God, man and society. Is it *laesa majestas* to hint that western thought has revealed no ultimate truths unknown elsewhere? May one make bold to suggest that its reputation has been seriously inflated, and to welcome the process of deflation which has of late been in operation? It may lead to a more tolerant attitude toward views of the universe rooted in intuition rather than in logic, expressed in metaphor rather than in dialectics.[32] Perhaps we shall prostrate ourselves a little less frequently before the *Ding an sich*, or *meta ta physica* systems. It might even happen that syllogist-

ically minded Jews could discover some intelligent Biblical
or Talmudic observations anent God, man and the world. It
might yet be conceded that the Jewish mind was not totally
bereft of thought.[33] It will hardly seem necessary to label
every Jew who does some thinking, Aristotelian. There might
even come an end to the lament, current among Jews from
the days of Bahya ibn Pakuda, over the shortage of books
presenting Judaism as an elaborate theological system.[34]
That lament may prove a *bechiyah ledorot*, an eternal lament.

For it seems that looking at the universe organically, syn-
thetically, qualitatively, or briefly, in terms of personality, is
deeply imbedded in the Jew's consciousness. He cannot get
himself to divest the universe of life, or, empty life of value.
Even when he philosophizes, he invariably remains a social
thinker, a Jewish teacher, though paying his respects to the
wisdom of Jawan—to "pure" Reason.

To this day Jews laboring in the vineyard of metaphysics,
sooner or later, abdicate in favor of social values or personality. Thus, Professor Alexander, after a profound and
weighty discussion of origins running for two bulky volumes,
concludes that we cannot "prove the existence of a being
called God, whether worshipful or not, except on the basis
of experience. *No one is now convinced by the traditional
arguments for God's existence.*[35] The reason is that at some
time or other they introduce conceptions which are *à priori*
in the bad sense of that phrase, in which it means not something experienced which is pervasive of all things, but something supplied by the mind."[36] The only argument for which
Professor Alexander still allows any validity is the argument
from design. "Because," he adds, "such adaptation implies in
human products the operation of a designing mind, the conception is extended from this particular case, by an illegitimate use of analogy, to experience as a whole."[37] In other
words, with the Prophets and Rabbis, he sees God through
personality, except that the ancients were little concerned by
the illegitimacy of the analogy.

Professor Bergson, another Jew, questions: "How could you ever manufacture reality by manipulating symbols?" and concludes: "Symbols and points of view . . . place me without him (man); they give me only what he has in common with others, and not what belongs to him and to him alone, but that which is properly himself, that which constitutes his essence, cannot be perceived from without, being internal by definition, nor be expressed by symbols, being incommensurable with everything else. Description, history and analysis leave me here in the relative. Coincidence with the person himself would alone give me the absolute."[38] Professor Bergson's attack seems to be directed at the thesis that life cannot be grasped and understood merely on the basis of physico-mechanical causes. It is true that he does not remain consistent, and citations could be produced to prove the contrary, but no student of philosophy will deny that Professor Bergson leans heavily on the extra faculty—"intuition."[39] Bergson's universe is not the "closed circle of physics the circumference of which is constituted by symbols of the physicist's own manufacture."[40] He is evidently too much of a Jew for that. His philosophy "seeks to explain all the richness and variety of the world, the movements of the tides no less than the desires of the lover, the formation of the rocks as well as the thought of the philosopher."[41] But that richness and variety is easier to live than reason about, and Bergson like Rabbi Meir prefers life to dialectics.[42]

VI. The Purpose of Maimonides

The Bergsons and the Alexanders are Jews by birth only. They have of Judaism, only, what the blood stream can carry of such matters. Otherwise, their Jewishness has been suppressed into the subconscious. Like most ordinary mortals, the philosophers have been too much with the world. They have been too servile to escape it, even for an occasional contact with the four-thousand-year-old culture of their own people. Or isn't it their people? It is undoubtedly out of the way to credit their intuitionism to their blood stream. We shall have to look elsewhere for genuine Jewishness. But wherever we will find it we will discover the personality, organic, intuitive view of the universe predominating.

Elsewhere in this work we pointed out that in the basic literature of the Jewish people, in its Bible, Apocrypha, Talmud, Midrash and Responsa, there is hardly a trace of logical formulation or metaphysical hypothesis. Such a lacuna in a literature the composition of which stretches over twenty-five centuries is more than accidental. Contrast this long period with the two or three centuries of energetic mental activity in Greece. The difference will be apparent to the most superficial observer. In the one, reality is explored by means of reason. In the other, it is sought in intuition. These two approaches to the universe, which are, in the final analysis, no more than two aspects of the human mind, nevertheless differentiate one of these peoples from the other. It is of course natural, since these approaches are only two aspects of the mind, that we should find the rationalist among the Jews and the intuitivist among the Greeks. The pure rationalist however, who stakes all on reason is among Jews a *rara avis* indeed. Even in the halcyon days of Greek influence over Jewish thought, it could not boast of a complete victory. Quite the contrary is true. It is just in those men who drank deep from the fountains of Greek philosophy that we discover how difficult it is for a Jew to turn Hellenist. The names of Aristobulus, Philo, Halevi, ibn Gabirol instantly leap into the memory. But we shall perhaps best learn how deeply rooted the personality or organic view of the universe is in the Jewish mind from an examination of the life work of the greatest Jewish philosopher of the Middle Ages.

Maimonides whose octocentenary the civilized world celebrates this year was equally at home both with Shem and Japheth.[1] He is perhaps the most classic illustration of the Jewish rationalist. "Never," says he, "should man throw his reason behind him, for his eyes are not in back but in front."[2] Although it is known that Saadia Gaon had made a similar pronouncement,[3] he may, nevertheless, be considered more theologian than philosopher.[4] Maimonides is the rationalist *par excellence.* In him Reason predominated.[5] He, it is claimed, put Aristotle on a level with Moses and subjected tradition to rigorous, logical analysis. Unlike most of his medieval contemporaries, he was not seeking to achieve harmony between theology and philosophy;[6] he abandoned philosophy. He criticized such Jewish thinkers as Saadia and Bahyah for their dependence, in important matters, on the *mutakallemim.* He made philosophy and religion synonymous. Faith with him was not the "correlative of reason, but rather the consummation of the reasoning process."[7] In this he went beyond any Jewish thinker that preceded him.[8] He was only partly approached by the Christian, Thomas Aquinas. It was not until centuries later that Locke became the first Christian to make faith a species of reason, and therefore religion a department of philosophy.

Maimonides assumed that the theories of the philosophers could in no way be opposed to the teachings of the prophets and sages. "Had not the Most High," he queries, "declared through Moses: 'Surely that great nation is a wise and under-standing people,'[9] our present ignorance (of philosophy) is solely due to the fact that wicked barbarians have deprived us of our possessions, put an end to our science and literature and killed off our wise men. All this was long ago predicted by the prophets: 'The wisdom of their wise men shall perish and the understanding of their prudent men shall be hid'?"[10] After a lapse of centuries, "having been brought up among persons untrained in philosophy, we are inclined to consider philosophical opinions as foreign to our religion, just as un-educated persons find them foreign to their own notions, but in fact it is not so."[11] There were, therefore, for Maimonides no two truths labeled divine and human.[12] There was only one truth, and Reason its only source.

It is pointed out with considerable enthusiasm that a goodly part of the *Guide* is devoted to an attack on the theo-logical harmonizers of his day. Maimonides was impatient with an intellectual dichotomy. He vigorously decries the at-tempt to create a special science and metaphysics to meet the demands of faith. To him all such efforts result from sheer ignorance. Between science and religion there is no such gulf. Quite the contrary. Religion that is unscientific, or unphiloso-phical, is no religion.[13] In his keen analysis of Arab dialectics (*Kalam*), Maimonides is supremely brilliant. Centuries later the great Leibnitz himself was captivated by its incisiveness of argument and pithiness of phrase.[14]

In the desire of the *mutakallemim*, says Maimonides, to establish the existence of God they denied order to the uni-verse. The Cosmos according to them was chaotic, a barrel without hoops, threatened each moment with complete col-lapse. Such a chaotic universe, always falling apart, they had maintained, makes the existence of God an absolute neces-sity. There can no longer be any discussion on this point, but to clinch the argument for ever and anon, the *mutakallemim*, or dialecticians, conceived the theory of the "creation of acci-dents." To show how completely and immediately dependent the universe is on God, they maintained that substance is not continuous, that it has no character of its own. Its continuity was lodged with the ever-new accidents that were coming into being. But these accidents themselves were short-lived, because time itself is only a collection of time atoms that appear and vanish like the stars in the night. What then can be responsible for the stability of the universe about us if not an ever-ready, creative, active God? Thus, every moment all of the most insignificant occurrences about us depend instantly for their existence upon God. Without His intercedence, collapse is inevitable. "They say," points out Maimonides, "that God generally acts in such a way, e.g., the black color is not created unless the cloth is brought into contact with indigo, but this blackness which God creates in the instant when the cloth touches the black pigment is of no duration, and another creation of blackness then takes place; they further say that after the blackness is gone, He does not create a red or green color but again a black color."[15]

Maimonides' criticism of the timid theologians was piercing and merciless. He is giving Reason rein and it gallops freely on the highway of rationalism. In Maimonides then we should find the living First Cause, the qualitative ineffable, the law-giving Space-Time continuum. Alas, we will discover only a supremely brilliant effort in that direction. We will find a great Jew, steeped in the lore of his people, troubled by life's perplexities, by the illogic of experience, making an heroic attempt to force the turbulent, ever-flowing current of Judaism into Aristotelian phraseology. But equally often we will behold the current smash the vessel, and Maimonides, in the end, save himself by viewing life in the rich colors of personality.

Why Maimonides was led to employ Aristotelian phraseology, and abandon the methods of the Rabbis, does not immediately concern us. Logic and intuition, it will be remembered, have nothing to do with race. Each is only a function of the human mind. It may be that Maimonides was born a logician, pure and simple. It may also be that he was moved by the rivalry between Judaism and the philosophico-scientific thinking of his day. The Rabbis had little reason to be concerned over the conflict between Judaism and Greek thought. To them paganism embraced little more than the stupidities of the pagan masses. Its incurable idol worship, its admixture of mysticism and licentiousness could inspire the Rabbis only with contempt for the pagan world. Their acquaintance with the "wise men of Athens" was on the whole rather superficial. These foreign sages were reputed shrewd but hardly profound.[16] As long as the ethics and the metaphysics of the Greeks remained unknown, Revelation remained unchallenged. Between the echoes of a perverted mythology that reached Palestine and the ethics of Judaism there was no point of contact. Of course, the vices of other nations, even as are our own virtues, are easily exaggerated. It was not until the early Middle Ages that the Jews discovered that there was more to the classic legacy than the escapades of Zeus and the adventures of Apollo. Certainly, by the time of Maimonides the learning and wisdom of the Greeks enjoyed incomparable respect. That Maimonides was cognizant of the conflicts in people's minds is self-evident; that it determined his life's work is open to question.

.   .   .   .   .

From the eighth century on, Jews enjoyed comparative peace in the Pyrenean Peninsula. Under friendly Mohammedan rulers, Jewish life in Spain flourished economically, politically, culturally. Noted Jewish merchants, bankers, philosophers, physicians, astronomers and statesmen were legion. Hasdai ibn Shaprut guided the destiny of Cordova; Samuel ha-Nagid was at the helm of Granada; Saragossa basked in the dazzling brilliance of ibn Gabirol; Seville learned astronomy from ibn Albalia. Rich though Cordova was in men of genius, the Maimon family was yet noted for scholarship and piety. Tradition traced its genealogy through the Hillelites to King David.[17] For generations the Maimons had enjoyed position, prestige, peace. They were equally at home in the heritage of their people and in the culture of their environment. They wrote Hebrew with ease and spoke Arabic with elegance. They were proud and loyal citizens and good, learned, pious Jews.

In this free and cultured environment, the precocious[18] lad, Moses, the son of Maimon, was diligently studying Bible and Talmud, and voraciously perusing Arabic books. Suddenly, in the year 1148, the Cordova Jewish community, its dignity, its affluence and its eminence, cracked into bits like a useless earthen pot. The frenzied dictator Abd al-Mu'min, intolerant of differences, drove the Jews from a city where they had lived for centuries. The thirteen-year-old Maimonides had his first draught from the cup of Jewish sorrows. For seventeen years the Maimon family reenacted the eternal tragedy of the wandering Jew; their weary heads and bleeding feet seeking a resting place. It was not until 1165 that they found a home in Fostat, old Cairo.

Those seventeen years were naturally the formative years in the life of Maimonides. Fortunately, the son of Maimon, driven from his native city by the cruelty of fanaticism and barbarism, did not for a single moment question: *Warum sind wir Juden?* Rather, there matured in him, during those years, the resolution to dedicate his master mind to his people and its heritage. In the midst of wandering and persecution, he labored zealously to broaden his knowledge and deepen his insight. At the end of his Commentary on the *Mishnah*, Maimonides writes: "While my mind was ever troubled amid the God-decreed expatriations from one end of heaven to the other, I wrote notes on many an *halacha*, on journeys by land, or while tossed on the stormy waves at sea."[19] Every page of his writings bears witness how richly he benefited both from his trials and studies. He became the greatest scholar of his generation, and his love for the heritage of his people has been rarely equaled.[20] Any-

one, who has read the philosophic and rabbinic works of
Maimonides and particularly his Responsa and Letters, will
readily guess the *leitmotif* of the man. He was consumed
with a passion to explain Judaism to the Jews, to persuade
them of its pristine value, to convince them that it was a
faith and a culture worthy of every sacrifice, of every trial,
even of the trial of martyrdom.

The eastern lands he had come to had suffered much at
the hands of the Crusaders, even as the lands he had left
had been victimized by the Almohades. The glorious sun of
Israel's golden age was, at any rate, in that part of the world,
rapidly sinking into an abyss of ignorance, confusion and
superstition.[21] Persecution, alas, does not merely inflict physical suffering. What is far worse, it engenders fear, despair,
listlessness and pusillanimity. Maimonides rose as the beacon
tower to dispel the darkness, to encourage the weak, and
to lead the troubled.[22] They, who think that the man's mission was to teach metaphysics or even to harmonize Judaism
with Aristotelianism, miss the very motive of his being.

At best his philosophy was only a byproduct of his main
purpose. In a remarkable passage, allegorically clothed,
Maimonides writes: "Before I was fashioned in the womb,
the Torah knew me, and before I came forth it had dedi-
cated me to its study, and guided me to disperse its springs
abroad. It was my lovely hind, the wife of my youth with
whose love I was ravished from my earliest days. Even
though many foreign women, Moabites, Amonites, Edomites,
Sidonites became her rivals, the Lord knows that they were
at first acquired to serve only as her perfumers, cooks and
bakers, to show the peoples and the princes her beauty, for
she is exceedingly beautiful. Nevertheless I robbed her of the
attention due her, for my heart was torn to many pieces with
all kinds of studies."[23]

His chief purpose can hardly have been philosophizing.
It is evident that it was rather to comfort the suffering, to
salvage Jewry, and expound Judaism. When Jerusalem was

smoldering in flames, Rabbi Johanan ben Zakkai built Yab-neh. When Jewry in the middle ages was sinking, Maimon-ides resolved to save it with his mighty intellect. "It was not my intention, when writing this treatise, to expound natural science or discuss metaphysical systems; it was not my object to prove truths which have already been demonstrated, or describe the number and the properties of the spheres: for the books written on these subjects serve their purpose, and if in some points they are not satisfactory, I do not think that what I could say would be better than what has already been explained by others."[24] A profound student of Maimon-ides, Professor Israel Friedlaender, states: "The enormous scientific activity of Maimonides is consciously directed to-wards this one goal; the perpetuation of Judaism by mak-ing the people understand and, in understanding, love Judaism, thus enabling them to fight for it and suffer for it."[25]

He was a searching spirit, his mind keenly logical, his outstanding intellectual quality was systematization, syn-thesis, orderliness.[26] He believed with the Rabbis that the systematizer takes precedence over the casuist.[27] He gloried in pithy sentences and concise paragraphs that merge into a mosaic of thought. He had studied the *Halachah* long and hard. He had at his fingertips all its labyrinthic intricacies and winding paths.[28] He was impatient of loose ends. He was in search of an arrangement into which all things might fit. It was his practice to state his argument briefly, clearly, point by point. He delighted in such numerical divisions, as twenty-five proofs, five reasons, eight categories, six classes, etc., etc.[29]

Maimonides knew the Jewish and Arabic philosophers and had studied exhaustively astronomy, mathematics and medi-cine. He was acquainted with all that his generation had of Plato, neo-Platonism and Aristotle. He was eminently equipped to philosophize, to expound, to teach, to guide. But was Maimonides, like Averroes the Mohammedan, or

Aquinas the Christian, ever tempted to write a commentary on Aristotle? Not at all. During the years of his homelessness, as we have already seen, his mind was completely occupied with the Talmud. His first great published work was a commentary on the Mishnah. Already in this work, which Maimonides began at the early age of twenty-three, the intellectualist is much in evidence.[30] He evidently had learned much from the philosophers. He did know his logic. He acknowledges his indebtedness to many authors of many lands. But in this work, as in his later works, Maimonides is primarily concerned with conduct, with the patterns of associative living.

It is significant that his largest literary efforts revolve about the.Law. We shall see later that this interest Maimonides acquired from his Jewish *milieu*. But his absorption in the Law he differs notably from the distinguished Mohammedan and Christian thinkers of the Middle Ages. A glance at the titles of their books will show that they were almost exclusively absorbed in the problems of logic and metaphysics. Thus Al-Kindi translated Aristotle's metaphysics, *Analytica Posteriora,* etc., Ptolemy's Geography, and spent his life annotating and commenting on the Greeks.[31] Avicenna, when he turned from medicine, was primarily the philosopher. His *Najāt* contained much logic. His other important work, the *Ishārāt,* is a treatise on theorems and propositions.[32] Al-Fārābi wrote mainly commentaries on the Greek philosophers, an Introduction to Logic and a work on Intelligence and the Intelligible.[33] Averroes was the author of treatises on the sky, the soul, metaphysics, commentaries on Aristotle, Plato, Nicolaus and notes on Al-Fārābi's logic and Avicenna's theorems. He also devoted a special book to polemics with the theologians, entitled "Vanity of Vanities."[34] Aquinas, the greatest of the Christian scholastics, began his literary career with such treatises as *de Principiis Naturae* and *de Ente et Essentia.* Already as a child he pressed on his teachers the question, "What is God?"

Throughout his life the question remained his preoccupation.[35] His other *Magna Opera* are the well-known *Summa Theologica*, the *Summa Contra-Gentiles* and the *Quaestiones Disputatae*.[36]

The central theme of early scholastic philosophy, the question of universals raised by Roscellin and never quite abandoned, Maimonides dismissed in a score of lines.[37] It is true that Maimonides' literary work also began with a treatise on logic, but it was a work of the smallest compass, written at the early age of sixteen,[38] for a friend who was anxious to acquire the logician's terminology. In sheer magnitude, all of this work in medicine, astronomy and philosophy will not equal one-third of his Code. Perhaps we should except the *Moreh Nebuchim*, the Guide of the Perplexed. But when we compare the close to 1900 references in the Guide to Biblical and Rabbinical literature, in addition to numerous citations from Maimonides' own legal writings, with a bare 70 references to all of Greek and Arabic Jewish philosophy, excepting only his discussion of the *Kalām*, we will understand where the man's interest lay.[39] Indeed, he declared that the primary object of his philosophic treatise was only "to explain certain words occurring in the prophetic books" and to "enlighten a religious man who has been trained to believe in the truth of our holy Law," to offer "an exposition of the esoteric ideas contained in the prophetic books . . . to explain certain obscure figures which occur in the Prophets."[40]

In the spirit of the Torah, like a true heir to a ben Zakkai, he imparted his philosophy only in private communication to the most distinguished and worthy of his disciples, Joseph ibn Aknin.[41] He writes to this disciple: "God knows that I hesitated very much before writing on the subjects contained in this work, since they are profound mysteries; they are topics which, since the time of our captivity, have not been treated by any of our schools as far as we possess their writings; how then shall I now make a beginning and discuss them? But I rely on two precedents: First, to similar cases our sages applied the verse 'It is time to do something in honor of the Lord: For they have made void Thy Law,'[42] secondly, they have said: 'Let all Thy acts be guided by pure intentions.'[43] On these two principles I relied while composing some parts of this work."[44]

Maimonides, of course, could have referred also to the noble tradition that he was following. He was, after all, not the pathbreaker in Jewish philosophy. The work of Saadia, ibn Gabirol, Halevi, ibn Daud, ibn Pakuda had been going on for two centuries. Even though Maimonides does not mention them by name, there is hardly a chapter in the Guide which does not betray traces of their influence. It is true that Maimonides is considerably at variance with them and frequently refutes their theories. As we have already noticed, he criticizes with unusual vehemence their dependence on *Kalām*. He rejects impatiently their proof of the existence of God based upon Creation. He rejects the division of the laws into reasonable and traditional.[45] However, he did find in these great predecessors authority for philosophizing. They had already searched Scripture and had found proof for the absolute existence of God.[46]

With all this precedence and caution, Maimonides nevertheless assures us that he is writing the book for one man in ten thousand, but, even with this one, he pleads: "I adjure any reader of my book, in the name of the Most High, not to add any portion of it except such passages as have been fully treated of by previous theological authorities; *he must not teach others anything that he has learned from my work alone, and that has not been hitherto discussed by any of our authorities.*"[47] He advisedly makes his treatise more difficult than it need be, in order that he might withhold "from the multitude the truths required for the knowledge of God." That, Maimonides regards as the Divine Will "from which it is wrong to deviate: 'the secret of the Lord is with them that fear Him.' "[48] Lest we find this *Apologia* insufficient, Maimonides reminds us that the "ancient philosophers and scholars of other nations were likewise wont to treat of the *principia rerum* obscurely, and to use figurative language in discussing such subjects. Thus Plato and his predecessors called Substance the female, and Form the male."[49]

Maimonides' system of thought, then, should be examined not as an appendage to Aristotle, as the child of Reason, but as a continuation of Judaism, as the offspring of intuition.[50] His work was not a dialectic effort evoked by the challenge of Reason, but, was rather stimulated by an earnest desire to expound Judaism as he understood it. Maimonides did not set out to resolve his own conflicts, or, to offer philosophic bait to those who had turned their backs on the Law. Of his own position he was confident; for the renegades he had no time. He was absolutely certain of the truth of his interpretations, views and doctrines.[51] In a spirit of the gentlest humility, he nevertheless speaks with utmost finality.[52] Unlike the other Jewish philosophers of the Middle Ages,[53] Maimonides nowhere betrays the least suspicion of his fallibility. He nowhere invites the reader to question, doubt, or correct his views. Like every true genius he believed that the truth was his.[54] While he does not claim that he could resolve every doubt of the seekers of the truth, he was nevertheless confident that he could settle "the greater part of their difficulties."[55] Maimonides concludes his Introduction with a statement, which to the modern ear might even sound very much like boasting: "This book will then be a key admitting to places, the gates of which would otherwise be closed. When the gates are opened and men enter, their souls will enjoy repose, their eyes will be gratified, and even their bodies, after all toil and labor, will be refreshed."

It is interesting to note the difference in approach between Maimonides and Aquinas. The latter, in his Preface to the *Summa Theologica* declares that he is writing the book "to teach those things which have to do with the Christian religion *in the way which best accords with the instruction of beginners*,"[56] and that he will attempt "to treat briefly and clearly all that appertains to sacred doctrine, so far as the subject matter will allow." To students of Maimonides, this citation from Aquinas will be strongly reminiscent of the former's introduction to the *Mishneh Torah*. There Maimonides makes the supremest effort, exerts every fiber of his great mind to be as simple and as explicit as he possibly can. That book he writes for "beginners." So interested is he to make his Code approachable by all, that he even revived a Hebrew style and vocabulary which had long been in disuse. He regretfully abandons the language of the Bible because he dare not presume that he is master of it; the language of the Talmud because it would be understood only by the few. He chooses rather to employ the diction of the Tannaim, because it will prove easier for the greater majority. But even in the Code where the bases of faith are reduced to the simplest of terms, he offers on matters metaphysical only "a drop from the ocean."[57] Aquinas the Christian is anxious to impart to all the knowledge of essential dogmas, whereas Maimonides, the Jew, is eager to teach the multitude the way of conduct, reserving philosophy for the few.

In his Guide, then, Maimonides sets out to teach those adequately prepared the profounder implications of Judaism. The problems he raised were not unknown in Israel; the conclusions he reached were within the spirit of the Bible and Talmud. He was fastidious about his method—a method not widely known in Israel. The new vessel has prevented many from recognizing the old wine. It is true that opening an old bottle and pouring its contents into a new one will somewhat affect the taste of the wine. Even so reconstructing a prophetic image, or a rabbinic parable into logical formulation and concise definition, will create at first a feeling of strangeness, but close study will reveal the vigorous spirit of Bible and Talmud. Maimonides then though logician and philosopher is persistently expressing the Jewish view of the Universe.

VII. Joshua, Soldier or Metaphysician

At the very beginning of a consideration of Maimonides' philosophy, it should be made clear, as already hinted,[1] that Maimonides did not set out to harmonize the truths of philosophy and religion. He recognized no such dichotomy. To him religion was philosophy. In this he not only anticipated but went considerably beyond Aquinas. The latter too had rejected the theory of "double truth" so much in vogue among Christian Averroists. Christian dogmatism, however, made it impossible for Aquinas to remain as consistent as Maimonides was. Some phases of pagan mythology had become in the New Testament fundamentals of the Christian creed. These constituted too much of a load even for the elastic conception of Reason characteristic of the Middle Ages.[2] Aquinas dogmatized as follows: "There are certain things to which even natural reason can attain, for instance, that God is, that God is one, and others like these, which even the philosophers proved demonstratively of God, being guided by the light of natural reason." He was, however, compelled to insist that certain other things "that are true about God wholly surpass the capability of human reason, for instance, that God is three in one."[3] The attempt to prove the Trinity by natural reason he dismissed as an offense against the dignity of faith.[4]

Maimonides found no such obstacles. The survivals of early mythology in the Old Testament had not hardened into dogmas of the faith. The Bible was to Maimonides easily the source of both reason and religion. It was, one might say, religion or philosophy popularized. "The Torah speaks the language of man,"[5] "for," says Maimonides, "its object is to serve as a guide for the instruction of the young, of women and of the common people." That being its object,

it veils the metaphysical contents to those, who come un-
prepared. To begin with metaphysics would lead only to
confusion. "I compare such a person (who would begin with
metaphysics) to an infant fed with wheaten bread, meat
and wine; it will undoubtedly die, not because such food is
naturally unfit for the human body, but because of the weakness of the child, who is unable to digest the food and cannot derive benefit from it."[6] The Torah, therefore, in addition to all its other merits, possesses this one, too, that it
makes it possible for one of lower, or moderate intelligence
to learn great philosophic truths about God. It would be
ludicrous to convert the generosity of revelation into ignorance and superstition.

Spinoza, of whose vehement attack on Maimonides we
shall speak anon, does not hesitate to appropriate this argument and make it his own. "For as we cannot," says he,
"perceive by the natural light of reason that simple obedience
is the path of salvation, and are taught by revelation only,
that it is so by the special grace of God, which our reason
cannot attain, it follows that the Bible has brought a very
great consolation to mankind. All are able to obey, whereas
there are but very few, compared with the aggregate of humanity, who can acquire the habit of virtue under the unaided
guidance of reason. Thus, if we had not the testimony of
Scripture, we should doubt of the salvation of nearly all
men."[7]

On the other hand, Spinoza categorically and conten-
tiously denies that there is either the least hint in Holy
Writ of metaphysical concepts or the least intention to convey them to any one, be he ignorant or learned. How he
struggled in his *Tractatus Theologico-Politicus* to delimit the
Bible to ethics and to deny it any claim to philosophy! "He
supposes," says Spinoza of Maimonides, "that the prophets
were in entire agreement one with another, and that they
were consummate philosophers and theologians.[8] . . . Scripture does not aim at imparting scientific knowledge . . . it

demands from men nothing but obedience, and censures obstinacy but not ignorance."[9] How irate the angelic thinker can become when he attacks Maimonides on this score! "The sole object" (of Maimonides and others), he storms at the beginning of his treatise, "seems to be to extort from Scripture confirmations of Aristotelian quibbles and their own inventions, a proceeding which I regard as the acme of absurdity."[10]

It is true, argues Spinoza, that "faith consists in a knowledge of God, without which obedience to Him would be impossible, and which the mere fact of obedience to Him implies."[11] But Moses, Jeremiah and John have summed up that knowledge in a short compass, namely, it consists in knowing that God is supreme, just and supremely merciful— "the one perfect pattern of the true life."[12] Otherwise Scripture gives no express definition of God or His attributes. Faith therefore looks for nothing but obedience and piety, whereas philosophy has no end in view but truth.[13] Maimonides, Spinoza protests, who was the first to make Scripture agree with reason, "ascribed to the prophets many ideas which they never even dreamed of."[14] Elsewhere he adds: "I am consequently lost in wonder at the ingenuity of those whom I have already mentioned, who detect in the Bible mysteries so profound that they cannot be explained in human language, and who have introduced so many philosophic speculations into religion that the Church seems like an academy, and religion like a science, or rather a dispute. It is not to be wondered at that men, who boast of possessing supernatural intelligence, should be unwilling to yield the palm of knowledge to philosophers who have only their ordinary faculties; still I should be surprised if I found them teaching any new speculative doctrine, which was not a commonplace to those Gentile philosophers whom, in spite of all, they stigmatize as blind; for, if one inquires what these mysteries lurking in Scripture may be, one is confronted with nothing but the reflections of Plato or Aristotle, or the like, which it would often be easier for an ignorant man to dream than for the most accomplished scholar to wrest out of the Bible."[15] At the conclusion of his examination of Biblical interpretation, he states: "We dismiss Maimonides' theory as harmful, useless and absurd."[16]

It is in the nature of things that absurdities should occur in the theories even of the greatest thinkers. Nor does it argue superiority in subsequent generations to whom these absurdities are patent. Spinoza's views of the Bible were no more logical or no less absurd than those of the medievalists whom he criticized so vehemently. Many of these views were forced on him, perhaps unconsciously, because in his day and age a man could not speak his mind freely in matters religious. Readers of the philosopher's Letters and Tractatus are not unaware of the apologetic note running through these writings. In the midst of his discussion of the Bible, he pleads: "I am certified of thus much: I have said nothing unworthy of Scripture or God's Word, and I have made no assertions which I could not prove by most plain argument to be true. I can therefore rest assured that I have advanced nothing which is impious or even savors of impiety."[17] Spinoza failed evidently to realize that he was simply indulging in a practice not unknown to the Middle Ages.[18] He was after all in a certain sense reestablishing the dichotomy already known to Averroes and to many Alexandrian Averroists who posited the eternity of matter and denied the immortality of the soul, and who, to escape the orthodox authorities of Islam, laid down the doctrine of a "double truth." Spinoza does not weary of repeating, "it is indisputable that theology is not bound to serve reason nor reason theology, but that each has her own domain. The sphere of reason is . . . truth and wisdom; the sphere of theology is piety and obedience . . . to sum up we may draw the absolute conclusion that the Bible must not be accommodated to reason, nor reason to the Bible."[19]

From our modern vantage ground Maimonides seems to

have the edge of the argument. He certainly penetrates the spirit of the Bible and Talmud deeper and interprets it much more accurately than did Spinoza. In speaking of Joshua and the stopping of the moon, Spinoza makes the following comment: "Many, who will not admit any movement in the heavenly bodies, explain away the passage until it seems to mean something quite different; others, who have learned to philosophize more correctly and understand that the earth moves while the sun is still, or at least does not revolve around the earth, try with all their might to wrest this meaning from Scripture, though plainly nothing of the sort is intended. Such quibblers excite my wonder! Are we bound to believe that Joshua, the soldier, was a learned astronomer?"[20] No one, of course, compels either Spinoza or anybody else to believe that Joshua was an astronomer.[21] That isn't at all the point. The question is, was Joshua a common soldier to the author of the book bearing his name? Does he not report of him: "And there was no day like that before it or after it, that the Lord hearkened unto the voice of a man."[22] Wasn't Joshua the successor to Moses upon whom the lawgiver had put his honor?[23] Was not Joshua, the son of Nun, full of the spirit of wisdom?[24]

Here is where Spinoza refused or failed completely to understand the spirit of the tradition and its literature. Maimonides, in the spirit of that tradition, makes the prophet, the man of intuition, the highest type of man, the supremest of human beings, and not the philosopher. It is the prophet who may enter into the "presence of the King." Moses is not only the lawgiver and the prophet, in the narrow sense of the word given to it by Spinoza, but he is unquestionably the great metaphysician as well. In other words, from the point of view of the tradition, there was nothing that a human being could possibly know, of which Moses had remained in ignorance. The prophet does not only have the imaginative faculty, as Spinoza contends, but the intellectual as well.

A cursory glance at rabbinic literature suffices to convince

us that Maimonides had more faithfully and logically interpreted its meaning than did Spinoza. The Rabbis tell us
that the sinful generations preceding Noah enjoyed a peaceful longevity without trials and woes, in order to be able to
devote themselves to astronomic studies.[25] The division of
time into weeks, months and years, or the calendar, mankind owes to Seth.[26] Enoch was the father of astronomy.[27]
The patriarchs and, even the matriarchs,[28] as well as all the
sons of Jacob, enjoyed the gift of prophecy.[29] The members
of the tribe of Issachar were excellent mathematicians.[30]
To Moses, of course, the Rabbis declared God had revealed
all the mysteries, both cosmic and historic.[31] A total of
twenty-four thousand celestial gates of wisdom, understanding, ingenuity, knowledge and all other treasures, were
opened to him.[32] "There was nothing kept back in heaven."

In Talmudic literature Joshua, the son of Nun, is decidedly
not Spinoza's common "soldier." On the contrary, he was
one of four to whose honor and memory posterity coined
special medals.[33] He is esteemed as the ideal scholar.[34] So
profound and original was Joshua that he was able to deduce
from reason many of the laws revealed to Moses on Sinai.[35]
"Joshua," we are told, "put on the garments of Moses' wisdom and girded his loins with the lawgiver's knowledge."[36]
Tradition likewise ascribed to him the knowledge of astrology and magic.[37] As late as the middle ages Joshua was still
spoken of as the ideal man, one of the few who went through
life sinless.[38] A similar view was taken of all the worthies
mentioned in the Bible. Othniel, the son of Kenaz, a person
of much less importance than Joshua, is praised for his extraordinary erudition and acumen.[39] Josephus, who had read
much of the Greeks and lived for a long time in Rome,
nevertheless counted Samson among the prophets.[40] The
praise of Solomon, as scientist and philosopher, exceeds all
bounds. Both in rabbinic and apocryphal literature he is
made the father of wisdom—an unsurpassed student of "beginnings." In the middle ages he was still regarded the

supreme thinker whose books of wisdom were Aristotle's primary source.[41] Even the idolator Jeroboam, son of Nebot, prior to his apostasy, enjoyed the privilege of expounding the Story of the Chariot in the company of the prophet Ahijah the Shilonite.[42]

This was the *Anschauung* of tradition. Generations of scholars and thinkers had been considered as particularly worthy of sharing the divine mysteries. It was in this spirit that the Psalmist who entreated:

> "Show me Thy ways, O Lord;
> Teach me Thy paths,"

concluded that the council or secret of the Eternal is "with them who fear Him."[43]

What a quibble then it is and misrepresentation to boot, to maintain that the men whom God vouchsafed, according to Spinoza himself, revelation on matters ethical, were denied every hint of philosophy and science. Or, to use Spinoza's own language, "the prophets," he says, "were endowed with unusually vivid imagination, and not with unusually perfect minds."[44] Maimonides makes the more logical assumption: If the Bible is the Word of God, and Spinoza does not seem to have doubted it, then it is the vehicle of the whole truth, and not of any particular phase of it. That, at any rate, was the view of Jewish tradition, the tradition which both Maimonides and Spinoza were elucidating. Spinoza's assumption that the prophetic mind was not unusually perfect is as arbitrary as any of which Maimonides was ever guilty. No less specious is Spinoza's argument that "prophetic knowledge is inferior to natural," because the latter "needs no sign and in itself implies certitude."[45] Spinoza seemed to have forgotten that, as against the scientist, the prophet was reaching out into the unknowable, about which neither science nor philosophy is any too certain. Neither Maimonides, nor Descartes, nor Kant nor Spinoza himself, was ever able to

persuade any empiricist that the metaphysical rests on certitude.

It is inconceivable, says Spinoza, that Moses should have
taught the Israelites, the erstwhile slaves of Egypt, infested
with its superstitions, "sound notions about Deity."[46] How,
indeed, could he have taught slaves anything about the art
of right living, "the master art, so difficult and correspond-
ingly so fruitful?"[47] Is proper conduct such a simple matter
for slaves to understand, or, is it so completely independent
of ·intelligence and knowledge? Spinoza failed to remember
that tradition had already anticipated and met his difficulty.
It assumed that the generation which was worthy of standing
at the foot of Sinai and hear the divine Voice was not only
not an ignorant generation, but on the contrary, one extraordinarily endowed.[48]

Spinoza's refusal or inability to examine tradition in its
own light involved him in an almost childish absurdity.
Either his early training, or the age he lived in, made impossible an outright rejection of the Bible. He therefore explains the selection of Israel, as follows: "The Hebrew nation
was not chosen by God in respect to its wisdom nor its tran-
quillity of mind, but in respect to its social organization and
the good fortune with which it obtained supremacy and kept
it so many years. This is abundantly clear from Scripture.
Even a cursory perusal will show us that the only respects
in which the Hebrews surpassed other nations are in their
successful conduct of matters relating to government, and
in their surmounting great perils solely by God's external
aid; in other ways they were on a par with their fellows, and
God was equally gracious to all. For in respect to intellect
(as we have shown in the last chapter) they held very ordinary ideas about God and nature, so that they cannot have
been God's chosen in this respect."[49]

What drove Spinoza into this absurdity was his desire to
prove, as against Maimonides and the other medievalists,
that Biblical literature contains no philosophy. He was, there-

fore, compelled to show why it was that God's elect were not in possession of this precious boon. But why God should have given philosophy to the Greeks and the special knack of conducting "matters relating to government" to the Jews, Spinoza does not undertake to explain. Why God's "external aid" should have been granted to a people which, according to Spinoza, is intellectually inferior, the sage of Amsterdam does not reveal. Spinoza had forgotten the simple, obvious truth that every religion sets out to satisfy all the needs of man, including "his thirst for knowledge." In the early centuries Christianity made converts among the pagans, because —writes Tatian—they found in this "barbarian philosophy" a cosmogony more satisfactory than any supplied by their own thinkers.[50]

Spinoza himself occasionally falters. His subconscious respect for the heroes of his childhood gets the better of him. "I was imbued," Spinoza writes, "from my boyhood up with the ordinary opinions about the Scriptures."[51] Indeed, his early training is sufficient to make Spinoza forget himself, to such an extent, so as to name Moses a metaphysician who comprehends the absolute essence of God.[52] The prophets too, though primarily interested to lead society to ethical conduct, sought to understand the Divine mysteries. The prediction of future events, he agreed, the great prophets regarded as a matter of no importance.[53] Even, like Maimonides, Spinoza quotes Solomon with commendation and concludes that, "Scripture literally approves of natural reason."[54]

Maimonides then was on sure Jewish ground when he saw no dichotomy between religion and philosophy, or revelation and reason. He was simply viewing the Universe, as Jews always had, organically. When he assumed that in the Bible there was a storehouse of metaphysics or of divine mysteries he was doing no violence to tradition. That these mysteries were carefully concealed no one doubted. To get at them all one had to do was to manipulate or interpret the text.[54]

VIII. THE METHODS OF MAIMONIDES

THE PRACTICE OF SEARCHING THE Bible for concealed truths was, already, in the days of Maimonides, hoary with age.[1] The vogue of allegorizing was widespread. It was as common in literary circles as in religious. Homer, to take but the most conspicuous example, was considered divinely inspired, and the text of the Odyssey was thoroughly searched for its hidden mysteries. Books proving the *Apotheosis vel consecratio Homeri* were not rare.[2] Cherished texts everywhere tempted the reverend and ingenious mind, but most of all was that true of the Jews' sacred writings. "These," says Philo, "are no mythical fictions, such as poets and sophists delight in, but modes of making ideas visible, bidding us resort to allegorical interpretation guided in our rendering by what lies beneath the surface."[3]

This practice Philo himself pursued to the limit. Every verse, incident, name was bent to suit his fancy. Adam became mind; Eve, sense, perception; Hagar, learning of the scholars; the three Patriarchs, the three natures of the Deity; Instruction, Holiness and the practice of Justice;[4] Rachel, superficiality; Leah, exacting virtue. The Manna became the Word of God, the soul's food; the wilderness where it fell, "the wilderness of passions and wickedness."[5] The verse in Exodus: "Now Moses went out to take the tent and to pitch it outside the camp, far off from the camp; and he called it 'the tent of meeting,' "[6] Philo interprets as follows: "The soul that loves God, having disrobed itself of the body and the objects dear to the body and fled abroad far away from these, gains a fixed and assured settlement in the perfect ordinances of virtue. Wherefore witness is also borne to it

76

by God that it loves things that are noble, and it was called 'the tent of witness.' "[7]

So general was the practice of allegory that it led many an author, outside of the field of religion, to hide the truth under a veil of verbiage. How far this went we can learn from the fact that Italy's great poets, Dante and Petrarch, as well as Boccaccio, regarded it as the duty of the poet *veritatem rerum pulchris velaminibus adornare.* Maimonides was most probably not acquainted with Philo's sermonic allegories. He may not have heard that Homer and Virgil had given birth to an extensive literature of hermeneutics, but Maimonides certainly did hear of Nahum ish Gamzu, Rabbi Akiba and of scores of other great Talmudic allegorizers. Maimonides was certainly acquainted with the remarkable utterance reported in the name of Rabbi Jonathan. This scholar had said that when Moses came to write the verse, "Let us make man in our image, after our likeness," he pleaded with God. "Master of the Universe, why do you provide heretics with an opening (to doubt or mock)?" Write, said the Eternal and let him who would err, err.[8] He knew what liberties the Rabbis had taken with the Biblical text. They made the most of the smallest peculiarities of expression, of the most trivial grammatical whimsicalities. Revering the Torah as the source of all wisdom, the Rabbis elaborated a comprehensive system of hermeneutics to wrest its meaning. They quite naturally assumed that any noble thought which occurred to them had already been revealed to Moses on Sinai.[9]

The Rabbis were in their own ways "rationalists," and frequently took the very heart out of a Biblical verse or miracle.[10] They explained the sweetening of the waters at Marah as altogether due to natural causes. Some completely allegorized the incident and interpreted the tree Moses threw into the spring, to mean the tree of life, namely, the Torah.[11] God's playing with Leviathan suggested to them His contempt for the heathen powers.[12] The wells Isaac dug symbolized for the Rabbis the ensigns in the desert, or, the Five Books of Moses.[13] "I am that I am" was taken to teach the immutability of God in His attributes of goodness, faithfulness and sublimity.[14] There was not wanting a Rabbi Jose who boldly declared: "It is written 'the heavens are the heavens of the Lord but the earth had been given to the children of men.'[15] From this we conclude that the Shechinah never descended below, and that Moses and Elijah never ascended above. It was only the Divine Voice that created the illusion of a real presence on Sinai."[16] The Menorah was interpreted as a symbol of study, and its branches symbolized the seven planets.[17] The eloquence of Balaam's ass was explained away even in ancient times, despite Josephus' effort to support the literalness of the Biblical account.[18]

The method then was not new with Maimonides. In his day, conditions had not yet altered. Old texts were still the fountainhead of all wisdom. Authority once established is not easily shaken.[19] Even a century later, Dante, for example, was ready to concede that nature had revealed all her secrets to Aristotle. "It was enough," said he, "for all people that I address, to know *per la sua grande autorita* that the earth is fixed and immovable."[20] To produce argument, where Aristotle was quoted as the authority, he thought would be absurd.

Be it said for Maimonides that he employed the method with exquisite skill and scientific exactitude. One of his noted commentators even speaks of the *Moreh* as a comprehensive commentary on the whole Torah, "all in accordance with the truth."[21] Professor Israel Friedlaender, himself a gifted linguist and stylist, who carefully searched the language of Maimonides,[22] states: "He knew the subject of his interpretation in its minutest details and was constantly guided and controlled by the Biblical text. . . . With the Alexandrians allegorical interpretation was a play of imagination; with Maimonides it was the work of science."[23] He developed his system of homonymology to perfection. Allowing his approach, his discussions of terms are philological classics. He penetrated the very soul of Hebrew words. Even the uninitiate will marvel at the master's touch in his exposition at the beginning of the "Guide" of the Hebrew words for shape, figure, form, likeness, *zelem, toar, demut, tabnit* and *temunah*.

In the very first chapter, in which Maimonides discusses the meaning of these terms, he practically conveys the quintessence of the whole of his philosophy. In a brief sentence he tells us that he will prove in the Guide: "The incorporeality of the Divine Being, and His unity, in the true sense of the word." Parenthetically he adds: "There is no real unity without incorporeality." Students of Maimonides know how central this thought is in his system. *"Zelem,"* Maimonides skillfully expounds, "signifies the specific form, viz., that which constitutes the essence of a thing, whereby the thing is what it is; the reality of a thing in so far as it is that particular being. In man the 'form' is that constituent which gives him human perception; and on account of this intellectual perception the term *zelem* is employed in the sentence 'in the *zelem* of God he created him.' "[24] In Philo, of course, Maimonides was anticipated except that the terminology of the Alexandrian Jew was Platonic, and not as in Maimonides, Aristotelian.[25] The neo-Platonist writes: "Right well does he (Moses) say this (man was created as the image of God), for nothing earth-born is more like God than man. Let no one represent the likeness as one to a bodily form; for neither is God in human form nor is the human body God-like. No, it is in respect of the Mind, the sovereign element of the Soul, that the word 'image' is used. . . ."[26]

IX. Maimonides' Central Thesis

We have said enough, we hope, to show the state of mind and method Maimonides would bring to the exposition of Biblical literature. Assuming as he did that there was only one truth, an old Jewish assumption indeed, and finding an old Jewish method, Maimonides' task was determined for him. What was that task? Briefly, to prove that the popular phraseology of the Bible only veiled the profoundest metaphysical truths. What was the essential truth upon which all else is based? It was the doctrine of the Incorporeality of God.

The Jew Maimonides would quite naturally have a horror of either images or plurality. That, at once, inspires the essence of his philosophy. Begin with an aversion to all images of the Deity and any form of plurality, feed this aversion on logic and metaphysics, and every trace of corporeality and all its essential and accidental attributes will be consumed in wrath. The Rabbis though their metaphysical diet was meager equally despised plurality, *shetei reshuyot*, and images.[1] The notion of absolute oneness and incorporeality immediately leads to the denial of the eternity of matter and the affirmation of *creatio ex nihilo*. In a world of one God, too, if we are to credit Him with any intelligence and power, there would be order and purpose. But order and purpose imply justice. Or is justice primary and the matrix of all these concepts. Many indeed see monotheism as an emanation from the Jew's sense of absolute justice. Philo states his objection to polytheism in a remarkably striking utterance: "Its propounders," he says, "do not blush to transfer from earth to heaven mob-rule, that worst of evil polities."[2]

With so much in his tradition to begin with, Maimonides

MAIMONIDES' CENTRAL THESIS 81

proceeded to elaborate the niceties of faith even as the Rabbis had the niceties of practice. Just as the latter were eager to search out the very soul of the Law, so was Maimonides meticulous in stating the very essence of belief. "When reading my present treatise (The Guide)," he tells the reader: "bear in mind that by 'Faith' we do not understand merely that which is uttered with the lips, but also that which is apprehended by the soul; the conviction that the object (of belief) is exactly as it is apprehended."[3] For such meticulousness Maimonides, metaphysically bent, might even find support in the Bible. Everywhere in Holy Writ the demand is made upon the whole human being, upon the heart, for impassioned concentration.[4] To honor God with mouth and lips and not to grasp him with the heart was to practice only the religion of rote. It was a simple matter for a metaphysician to give such verses in the Bible an intellectual as well as an ethical meaning.[5]

Now what was the gravest danger to the ideal religion, the religion of monotheism? It was, quite naturally, the tempting, contagious belief in corporeality. At its touch, Maimonides saw the flower and fruit of Jewish faith transformed into a poisonous growth. It was not merely as a dogma, in and of itself, that the belief in incorporeality was of the highest importance, but primarily because it was the cornerstone of all rational religion. We must see this clearly if we are to make allowance for the vehemence with which Maimonides belabors corporeality. Let us turn the pages of the Guide for some illustrations. "The primary object of every intelligent person must be to deny the corporeality of God and to believe that all those perceptions (of Him spoken of in the Bible) were of a spiritual, not of a material character. Note this well."[6] "All people must be informed and even children must be trained . . . by simple authority that God is incorporeal; that there is no similarity in any way whatever between Him and His creatures."[7] "That God is incorporeal, that He cannot be compared with His crea-

tures, that He is not subject to external influences, these are
things which must be explained to everyone according to his
capacity, and they must be taught by way of tradition to children and women, to the stupid and ignorant, as they are
taught that God is one, that He is eternal and that He alone
is to be worshiped. Without incorporeality, there is no
unity. . . ."[8] *"Bear in mind that by the belief in the corporeality, or in anything connected with corporeality you
would provoke God to jealousy and wrath, kindle His fire
and anger, become His foe, His enemy and His adversary in
a higher degree than by the worship of idols. If you think
that there is an excuse for those who believe in the corporeality of God on the ground of their training and ignorance, or their defective comprehension, we must make the
same concession to the worshipers of idols;*[9] their worship is
due to ignorance and to early training; 'they continue in the
custom of their fathers . . .*[10] there is no excuse for those,
who being unable to think for themselves, do not accept
(the doctrine of the incorporeality of God) from the true
philosophers. I do not consider those men, who are unable
to prove the incorporeality of God, as infidels, but I hold
those to be so who do not believe it."[11] Maimonides, we can
see, was as grimly determined to destroy every notion of
corporeality, even as centuries later, Spinoza was bent on
making God material.

Was the theory of incorporeality anything new among
Jews? Of course not. It may be that the untutored Jew, with
limited understanding and imagination, never completely
abandoned the belief in a corporeal Deity.[12] The multitude
do not easily conceive existence unless in connection with
a body, and that which is not a body nor connected with a
body has for them no existence.[13] Perhaps to this day the
declaration of the average Jew that God has no body nor
the likeness of a body is largely verbal. Why should we
assume that it is easier for the plain man to conceive an immaterial and formless spirit or being than for him to visual-

ize the atom as a hump in Space-Time, or as a wave of probability? Indeed, modern science is constrained to admit that
"the picture of the atom, as a concrete something conceived
as a miniature solar system, is, indeed, only a concession to
the incurably pictorial character of our imagination."[14] Bertrand Russell suggests that "the idea that there is a hard lump
there, which is the electron or proton, is an illegitimate intrusion of common-sense notions derived from touch. For aught
we know, the atom may consist entirely of the radiations
which come out of it. It is useless to argue that radiations
cannot come out of nothing. We know that they come, and
they do not become more really intelligible by being supposed to come out of a little lump."[15] "Weak humanity needs
imagery in which to clothe its vision."[16]

The hold of polytheism on the popular mind through
many Christian centuries is sufficient proof that the "unlearned and simple men could not understand what was not
presented in color and pictorial form."[17] So general and
evident was this compromise with the old cults, that St.
Augustine up to the time of his acquaintance with Ambrosius
believed that the God of the Catholic Church had human
shape.[18] We might then concede that many Jews did or do
imagine God in some likeness, but that in no way makes
Maimonides the father of the belief in incorporeality.[19] That
God was spirit was a very old Jewish conception. The Rabbis, who excommunicated Spinoza, were not Aristotelian, but,
imbued with Jewish tradition, they regarded his opinion that
God is corporeal as the rankest heresy.

The Bible abounds with passages expressive of the horror of a concrete material Godhead, and of the strongest
propensity to see Him only as spirit.[20] Maimonides certainly
does not begin with a *tabula rasa*. The biblical attacks upon
idols, the vengeance wreaked upon them when the opportunity presented itself, the irony of a deutero-Isaiah or a
Jeremiah heaped upon them were well known to Jews.[21]
There was frequent opportunity in the Synagogue to rehearse

the old injunctions and sarcasms. There was always the austere, unflinching Second Commandment. "Thou shalt not make unto thee a graven image, nor any manner of likeness, of anything that is in heaven above, or that is in the earth beneath, or that is in the water under the earth."[22] How entreatingly the Deuteronomic writer pleads: "Take ye therefore good heed unto yourselves—for ye saw no manner of form on the day that the Lord spoke unto you in Horeb out of the midst of the fire . . ."[23] ye heard the voice of words, but ye saw no form, only a voice."[24] How well Jews remembered the famous Haphtarah, *Nahamu, Nahamu Ami.* Had they not heard long before philosophy became the vogue in Israel:

> "To whom then will ye liken God?
> Or what likeness will ye compare with Him?"[25]

Biblical critics have noticed that in the Book of Leviticus, a particular effort was evidently made to divest the Deity of all tangibility. Throughout that book God is transcendent. He does not swear or repent, He does not speak to men in dreams; there is no mention of angels or of visions. The biblical tradition anent incorporeality is deep and definite. Did it require extraordinary sensitiveness to find an immaterial God in the account of the Deity's first appearance to Moses. " 'Behold, when I come unto the children of Israel, and shall say unto them: The God of your fathers hath sent me unto you; and they shall say to me: What is His name? what shall I say unto them?' And God said unto Moses: 'I AM THAT I AM'; and He said: 'Thus shalt thou say unto the children of Israel: I AM hath sent me unto you.' "[26] Similarly the experience of Elijah, that "the Lord was not in the wind neither in the earthquake, nor in the fire, but in a still small voice" tended to convey an immaterial conception of Deity.[27]

Very early we find attempts to explain away the anthropomorphisms of the Bible. They will be found in the *Tik-*

kune Soferim, the Septuagint, Onkelos, as well as in rabbinic literature.[28] When circumstances, and the limitations of language, compelled the Rabbis to speak of God in human terms, they prefixed such statements with a specially devised term *kevayahol* (as though it were possible to say so).[29] It was natural for men who had a horror of image-making, and who nevertheless could not be satisfied with a lifeless ethereal First Cause, to waver between sensuous and figurative expressions of God. This is not the place to produce evidence how skillful the Rabbis were in ironing out anthropomorphisms. Jewish scholarship in the past century has dealt adequately with the subject.[30] The voice mentioned in the Sinaitic theophany was allegorized.[31] This Voice, the famous Rabbi Simon ben Lakish, Palestinian scholar of the first part of the third century, declared had no echo, i.e., it was immaterial.[32] Creation, the teachers insisted, was by "word" only.[33] When the Rabbis did speak of creation with one hand, both hands, the right hand or the left hand, they only meant to emphasize the relative importance of the things created.[34] In Genesis, chapter VIII, verse 21, we read: "And the Lord smelled the sweet savor." The sensuousness of the verse was widely and vehemently attacked in some Christian circles. The Rabbis, on the other hand, resorted to interpretation and explained the smelling to mean God's knowledge. The savor symbolized Abraham, Hananiah, Misha'el and Azariah, and the many other martyrs, who were ever ready to die for the Sanctification of the Name. The verse then, according to the Rabbis, meant that God gladly accepted the sacrifice of Noah for the sake of his descendants.[35]

In consonance with the spirit of tradition, Maimonides' immediate rationalist predecessors accepted the incorporeality of God as an old-established creed. It is true that Yehudah Halevi, by far more poet than metaphysician, was reluctant completely to spiritualize the Deity. His poetic fancy embraced speculation even on God's measurements.[36] Lacking the rigor of the logician he was tolerant of loose ends—an indulgence which Maimonides found impossible. The inconsistencies which strike us in the Bible and Talmud have their natural counterpart in Halevi.[37] Maimonides, however, codified opinions as well as practices. It was therefore left to him to eradicate incorporeality root, branch and all.[38]

Being a logician and systematizer, he seizes on every hint in the Prophets, Psalms, Proverbs, Job or the Rabbis to formulate the rigid dogma of incorporeality.[39] For this purpose he needed no stimulus either from Aristotle, or from Arab commentators. It was in the best tradition of a people that was instinctively hostile to images of the Deity. Maimonides was only providing formulation for that which the Prophets and Rabbis had believed intuitively.

X. No Means Yes

ONCE INCORPOREALITY IS ESTAB-
lished, the Deity needs must be completely dehypostatized.
"When a being is without corporeality," says Maimonides,
"it cannot occupy space, and all idea of approach, contact,
distance, conjunction, separation, touch, or proximity is inapplicable to such a being."[1] If God has no body, then, of
course, he has no ears, no throat, no eyes; then, of course,
he hasn't any of the five senses. If he has not the senses,
their functions cannot be ascribed to Him. Neither can locomotion be attributed to God, since "everything that moves is
corporeal and divisible." Therefore we cannot ascribe rest
to God, "for rest can only be applied to that which also
moves."[2] The Biblical passages, then, which nevertheless
speak of God's seeing, smelling, etc., must, of necessity, be
taken in a spiritual sense. "God requires no instrument
wherewith to operate in order to perform anything."[3]

But what is this thing designated as spiritual? Ah, that
is the crux of the problem. Maimonides does not know, nor
does Aristotle, nor anybody else. It is, if you will, a figment
of the imagination, an act of faith, an immediate agreement.
Suppose we press Maimonides, or any other philosopher, and
plead now, describe exactly what you mean. Give us an
explanation that will satisfy to some degree, an explanation
that is not merely verbal, or logical. Just how can one
comprehend a voiceless voice, a sightless sight, or a touch-
less touch? Will not the mind, in the end, proceed to form
some kind of an image? Will not the plain man, the non-
metaphysician or for that matter even the metaphysician after
all continue to sin in his heart? How then shall we impress
this idea of incorporeality upon the mind, and forever shut
out the remotest possibility of ascribing materiality to God?

Maimonides, the logician, who followed an argument to its logical conclusion, like all his fellow philosophers, naturally saw the intimate relation between a thing and its qualities. The only way to know a thing is through its qualities, and it is through qualities that relations with the world can be established. To the mind one is inconceivable without the other. Once you think of a substance, you will instantly think of its dimensions, its position and a thousand other relations. On the other hand, "qualities" being determinants, or accidents they must converge into something. "The accidental always implies a predication about some subject."[4] You cannot, therefore, think, for too long, of qualities without attaching them to something or somebody. Someone says "tall" and you see before your eyes Uncle Ichabod, with his long legs. If you dwell on quality, it will lead you to substance. It will be no different with regard to God. You will not escape relating God and the attributes. Should you ascribe to God even only the attributes of wisdom, justice and mercy, you will proceed to imagine some sort of a corporeal being, and you will end by creating the Deity in human shape or form. You will under any circumstances assume relation between God and the attributes, or make of God some kind of "substratum of accidents,"[5] but no relation can exist between God or any being or attribute.

To imply any such relation would bring us back where we were, namely, we would again be confronted with the danger of ascribing materiality to God, or at least, predicating of God that which was identical with His existence. Hence Maimonides launches out with all the vigor of his logic against attributes. "If you have a desire to rise to a higher state, viz., that of reflection . . . you must understand that God has no essential attribute in any form or in any sense whatever, and that *the rejection of corporeality implies the rejection of essential attributes.*[6] Those who believe that God is One, and that He has many attributes, declare the unity with their lips, and assume plurality in their thoughts."[7]

A large portion of the "Guide" is devoted to proving that attributes cannot be affirmed of God.[8] Here, of course, Maimonides employs the logician's tool. His proofs and even his very language, as we shall see in a moment, are to this day the legacy of the metaphysician. Maimonides points out that every affirmative description of an object can be made in one of five ways; by defining its essence or some phase of its essence, or by describing its quality, relations, or actions. That makes affirmative assertions of God impossible. His essence is beyond definition. To speak of a portion of His essence would destroy its simplicity and make of it a compound. All quality is an accident and therefore ruled out by the simplicity of God's essence. All relations too are accidents, even such as time, space or existence, and therefore inappropriate in reference to God. All actions emanate from His essence and are therefore indefinable.[9]

In almost similar language, Professor Alexander describes, or denies the possibility of describing his Space-Time concept. "Space-Time is . . . the source of the categories, the non-empirical characters of existent things, which those things possess because of certain fundamental features of any piece of Space-Time. *These fundamental features cannot be defined. For to define is to explain the nature of something in terms of other and in general simpler things, themselves existents. But there is nothing simpler than Space-Time, and nothing beside it to which it might be compared by way of agreement or contrast.* They cannot even be described completely. *For description, like definition, is effected by reference to existent entities.*[10] Not only all our language but all our conceptions are derived from existents, including in existents those of mathematics, particular figures or numbers. The utmost that we can do is therefore to describe in terms of what is itself the creation of Space-Time with its various features, and however little our description borrows from metaphor, it cannot but be a circuitous way of describing, what is prior to the terms we use in our description, and can therefore in the end only be indicated and known by acquaintance. Space-Time itself and all its features are revealed to us direct as red or sweet are. We attempt to describe what is only to be accepted as something given, which we may feel or apprehend; to describe, as has been said in the foregoing, the indescribable."[11]

But to return to Maimonides. "No attribute," he argues, "coming under the head of quality in its widest sense can be predicated of God."[12] Therefore, "those who believe in the presence of essential attributes in God, viz., Existence, Life, Power, Wisdom and Will, should know that these attributes, when applied to God, have not the same meaning as when applied to us, and that the difference does not only consist in magnitude, or in the degree of perfection, stability and durability. It cannot be said, as they practically believe, that His existence is only more stable, His life more permanent, His power greater, His wisdom more perfect, and His will more general than ours, and that the same definition applies to both. This is in no way admissible, for the expression 'more than' is used in comparing two things as regards a certain attribute predicated of both of them in exactly the same sense, and consequently implies similarity (between God and His creatures). When they ascribe to God essential attributes, these so-called essential attributes should not have any similarity to the attributes of other things, and should according to their own opinion not be included in one of the same definition, just as there is no similarity between the essence of God and that of other beings."[13] God, the universal essence must be apprehended as *incorporeal*, i.e., *apart from all attributes*.[14]

Maimonides, let us remember, also attacked the belief in attributes not only because he was reared in the belief of the incorporeality of God, but equally because, as a Jew, he had since his childhood accepted God's unity.[15] Unity and cor-

poreality were to Maimonides a contradiction. "Without incorporeality there is no unity, for a corporeal thing is in the
first case not simple, but composed of matter and form
which are two separate things by definition, and secondly,
as it has extension it is also divisible."[16] To assume corporeality and at the same time to profess unity, Maimonides
maintained "is like the doctrine of the Christians, who say
that He is one and He is three, and that the three are one."[17]

It will be conceded that for the concept of unity, even as
for the concept of incorporeality, Maimonides did not have
to depend on Aristotle, for here, too, he was completely in
the spirit of Jewish tradition. "Unto thee it was shown, that
thou mightest know that the Lord, He is God; there is none
else beside Him," was said to his ancestors and not to those
of Aristotle.[18] "Hear, O Israel, our God the Eternal is One"
had been on the lips of Jews for millennia. The Book of
Isaiah which Maimonides undoubtedly knew from childhood expresses God's oneness in winged words.

> "Ye are My witnesses, saith the Lord,
> And My servant whom I have chosen;
> That ye may know and believe Me, and understand
> That I am He;
> Before Me there was no God formed,
> Neither shall any be after Me."[19]

"I am the First and I am the Last and besides Me there is
no God,"[20] was a verse deeply imbedded in the Jewish consciousness.

In rabbinic literature the Unity of the Godhead received
time and again vigorous endorsement. "One," said the Rabbi,
"is the very name of God."[21] On the verse "I am the Lord
thy God" they offer an arresting homily. God in His first
utterance to the people of Israel made sure to impress upon
them His Unity. He warned them against all error. "(Do not
mistake ME for many) because I appear in many forms—at
the Red Sea like a warrior, at Mount Sinai like a scribe and
teacher, to Solomon as a youth and to Daniel as an ancient.

I am He at the Red Sea, at Sinai, etc."[22] Before his death
Moses, according to the Rabbis, prayed to God to open all
the gates of Heaven and the abyss, so that all might see that
there was no one beside God.[23]

Being neither logicians nor metaphysicians, the Rabbis did
not inquire into the nature or essence of God's oneness, or
of unity in general. They were unquestionably certain that
the Oneness of God admits of no plurality, and that His
unity suffers no diversity, but the "theology" of the Prophets
and the Rabbis is "based not upon cold speculation but upon
warm feeling." Dry, barren reasoning was not their hobby.
"The most characteristic feature of the rabbinical system of
theology," writes Professor Ginzberg, "is its lack of system.
With God as a reality, revelation as a fact, the Torah as a
rule of life, and the hope of redemption as a most vivid
expectation, one was free to draw his own conclusions from
these postulates in regard to what he believed."[24] Never indulging in mere philosophizing, they sensed no contradiction
in ascribing Oneness to other entities, such as the letter *aleph*,
the Torah and Moses.[25] The assertion that God was one
without possessing the attributes of unity, might have brought
wonderment to their eyes. All the attributes that they
ascribed to God were to a Being with a personal character
and not a First Cause. They spoke freely of the justice and
the mercy of God, without ever sensing the need of reconcil-
ing the apparent contradictions theologians have found between these qualities.[26]

Maimonides, on the other hand, obsessed with the idea of
absolute simplicity, needs must rule out the remotest possibility of inner pluralities. True unity, he would ascribe only
to a substance simple without composition or multiplicity,
one in all respects and aspects. That meant not only the
elimination of accidental qualities, but also the distinction
between genus and species, as well as, the distinction between existence and essence. Weaving his syllogistic threads
relentlessly, he concludes that the Oneness of God is neither

quantitative nor qualitative. He is himself rather apologetic about this vagueness: "The investigation of this subject, which is almost too subtle for our understanding, must not be based on current expressions employed in describing it, for these are the great source of error. It would be extremely difficult for us to find, in any language whatsoever, words adequate to this subject, and we can only employ inadequate language. In our endeavor to show that God does not include a plurality, we can only say 'He is one,' although 'one' and 'many' are both terms which serve to distinguish quantity. We, therefore, make the subject clearer, and show to the understanding the way by saying 'He is one but does not possess the attribute of unity.' "[27]

The Rabbis probably would have thought that things, for which adequate words could not be found in any language, were a little beyond them. They preferred to speak of the unity of God, and to assume that they themselves and others knew what they had in mind. But Maimonides had studied metaphysics, logic and science; he had learned to distinguish between essence and accident. Attribute, he had come to see, was something "not inherent in the object to which it is ascribed," but rather that it was an accident, i.e., "superadded to its essence."[28] Number itself is also such an accident, superadded to a thing's essence, but to add anything to God, would mean "the existence of many eternal beings." Therefore, Maimonides is compelled to write "God is one without possessing the attribute of unity," [29] and to warn us that "there cannot be any belief in the unity of God except by admitting that He is one simple substance, without any composition or plurality of elements; one from whatever side you view it, and by whatever test you examine it; not divisible into two parts in any way and by any cause, nor capable of any form of plurality either objectively or subjectively."[30]

Maimonides realized that he had here stepped into the endless, futile debate among scholastics, anent the question of universals.[31] There were the nominalists, to whom all abstract and universal concepts were only names, or words; the conceptualists, who recognized the presence of universal representations in the mind, but denied them real existence in reality. In addition to these two views, there were the moderate and the exaggerated realists. Maimonides himself evidently belongs with the moderate realists. "It is an established fact," he writes, "that species have no existence except in our own minds. Species and other classes are merely ideas formed in our minds, whilst everything in our minds, everything in real existence, is an individual object, or an aggregate of individual objects."[32]

He is somewhat vehement in his denunciation of the extremist. "Some thinkers," he says, "have gone so far as to say that the attributes of God are neither His essence nor anything extraneous to His essence. This is like the assertion of some theorists, that the ideals, i.e., the *universalia*, are neither existing nor non-existent, and like the views of others, that the atom does not fill a definite place, but keeps an atom of space occupied; that man has no freedom of action at all, but has acquirement. Such things are only said; they exist only in words, not in thought, much less in reality. But as you know, and as all know who do not delude themselves, these theories are preserved by a multitude of words, by misleading similes sustained by declamation and invective, and by numerous methods borrowed both from dialectics and sophistry. If after uttering them and supporting them by such words, a man were to examine for himself his own belief on this subject, he would see nothing but confusion and stupidity in an endeavor to prove the existence of things which do not exist, or to find a mean between two opposites that have no mean. Or is there a mean between existence and non-existence, or between the identity and non-identity of two things?"[33]

Maimonides might have been a bit more charitable with his fellow philosophers, for six chapters later he himself employs language not one wit less vague. Eliminating all attributes, he was compelled to eliminate existence. "It is known that existence is an accident appertaining to all things, and therefore an element superadded to their essence. This must evidently be the case as regards everything the existence of which is due to some cause; its existence is an element superadded to its essence. But as regards a being whose existence is not due to any cause—God alone is that being, for His existence, as we have said, is absolute—existence and essence are perfectly identical; He is not a substance to which existence is joined as an accident, as an additional element. His existence is always absolute, and has never been a new element or an accident in Him. Consequently God exists without possessing the attribute of existence. Similarly He lives, without possessing the attribute of life; knows, without possessing the attribute of knowledge; is omnipotent without possessing the attributes of wisdom; all this reduces itself to one and the same entity; there is no plurality in Him."[34]

The reader of the Guide cannot help but note that here Maimonides had plunged into deep waters. Assuming the incorporeality and unity of God and further assuming that attributes were accidents, superadded to essence, he was compelled to maintain that we cannot even speak of the existence of God, because existence is itself an accident, superadded to the essence of a thing. He was making the old Aristotelian differentiation between "some things that can exist in separation and others that cannot."[35] Like all the Arab and Jewish philosophers, he accepted the division of being into *ens per se* and *ens per accidens*. He was then compelled to conclude, rigid logician and systematizer that he was, that existence is always an accident superadded to the essence of the thing. Had Aristotle, the Scholastics or Maimonides been more unflinchingly logical they would have been compelled to admit, that to penetrate the essence of things means to dissolve the distinction between substance and accident altogether. Saadia and most other Jewish philosophers were only a little less consistent. On the brink of the precipice they took a deep breath and ascribed positive attributes to God, particularly that God was living, omnipotent and omniscient. Arbitrarily they maintained on the basis of Scripture with the help of Reason, most pliable that the attributes added nothing to God's essence.[36]

Maimonides though constrained by the discipline of inexorable logic to deny existence and other attributes to God, nevertheless, remains a devout Jew praying every day to a personal God, the God of the Bible and Talmud, whose existence Reason made absolutely necessary, since the whole course of Jewish history proved it. His fine-spun logic really makes no difference. His God, the Jewish God, never merely became a "verbal abbreviation,"[37] or, as with the Buddhists "pure ideation."[38] God with Maimonides remained sovereign and transcendent, and not only a function of man's thought. The Guide concludes with a most pious utterance, prophetic and rabbinic in language and spirit. "God is near to all who call Him, if they call Him in truth, and turn to Him. He is found by every one who seeks Him, if he always goes towards Him, and never goes astray. Amen."[39] This God, Maimonides was convinced, had suffered with Israel in its sorrows and rejoiced with it in its joys.[40] It is a God whom one loves suitably only, "when one loves Him with a mighty, boundless love till one's soul is bound up in the love of God, so that it occupies him steadily like one lovesick whose mind can not forget the woman he loves even for a moment, and he meditates upon her when sitting, standing, eating or drinking. The love of God must yet excel this."[41] Even the arch heretic Spinoza, who, we saw, had imbibed in his childhood and youth the spirit of the Bible and Talmud, could not help but write: "We know Him better than we know ourselves, because without Him we could not know ourselves at all."[42]

But how does Maimonides square experience with logic?

Your genuine metaphysician is no coward. Once he has started, we wager, he will square you a circle. This is said in no disrespect of Maimonides, but we do suggest that the reputation of logic is somewhat inflated. It has certainly not kept logicians from proposing logical absurdities. Maimonides was propelled by the preciseness of his definitions to make his subject even more perplexing. Yehudah Halevi, the poet, under such circumstances retreats to a more robust and sensuous conception of the Deity. When the King in the *Kuzari* asks: "How can I individualize a being, if I am not able to point to it, and can only prove its existence by its action?" the Rabbi replies: "It can be designated by prophetic or visionary means. Demonstration can lead astray. Demonstration was the mother of heresy and destructive ideas. What was it, if not the wish to demonstrate, that led the dualists to assume two eternal causes? And what led materialists to teach that the sphere was not only eternal, but its own primary cause, as well as that of other matter? Worshipers of fire and sun are but the result of the desire to demonstrate. There are differences in the ways of demonstration, of which some are more extended than others. Those who go to the utmost length are the philosophers, and the ways of their arguments led them to teach of a Supreme Being which neither benefits nor injures, and knows nothing of our prayers, offerings, obedience, or disobedience, and that the world is as eternal as He Himself. None of them applies a distinct proper name to God, except he who hears His address, command, or prohibition, approval for obedience. He bestows on Him some name as a designation for Him who spoke to him, and he is convinced that He is the Creator of the world from nought. . . ."[43]

Maimonides, more daring, strains the strings of argument. Since, from the point of view of the logician, to say affirmatively what God is may involve us in logical difficulties with materiality and plurality, we would do better to say only what God is not.[44] This is simpler and less precarious.

"Know that the negative attributes of God are the true attributes; they do not include any incorrect notions or any deficiency whatever in reference to God, while positive attributes imply polytheism."[45] Once the logician in him has started on this track, he goes to its end: "I do not merely declare," he writes, "that he who affirms attributes of God has not sufficient knowledge concerning the Creator, admits some association with God, or conceives Him to be different from what He is; but I say that he unconsciously loses his belief in God. . . ."[46] By affirming anything of God, you are removed from Him in two respects; first, whatever you affirm, is only a perfection in relation to us; secondly, He does not possess anything superadded to His essence. . . ."[47] With every additional positive assertion you follow your imagination and recede from the true knowledge of God." On the contrary, "every time you establish by proof the negation of a thing in reference to God, you become more perfect (in your knowledge of God)."[48]

In God existence being no accident but identified with His essence, the more we eliminate attributes or accidents, the more our mind can dwell on God's essence or His absolute existence, which is the same thing. "The smaller the number of things is, which a person can negative in relation to God, the less he knows of Him . . . ; but the man who affirms an attribute of God, knows nothing but the same; for the object to which, in his imagination, he applies that name is to a non-existing being, for there is in reality no such object."[49] Should it occur to us to ask Maimonides: "But aren't there in the Bible numerous qualitative descriptions of God?" His ready answer is that they describe His works, and only through His work can we obtain knowledge of God.[50] "Whenever any one of His actions is perceived by us, we ascribe to God that emotion which is the source of the act when performed by ourselves, and call Him by an epithet which is formed from the verb expressing that emotion."[51] The attributes have no objective existence with respect to God—they are simply man's subjective judgments about himself. The "negative" theologians generally resolved this difficulty in this way. Why they did not see in acts attributes is nowhere satisfactorily discussed.[52] Should we insist that descriptions may be found in the Bible which are nothing but attributes, and are not easily classed as "works," Maimonides will assure us that the Bible by affirming negates the opposite. Thus, when we are told of God's existence, the true meaning is that He does not, not exist.

One cannot deny that Maimonides' theory of negative attributes is decidedly un-Jewish in mood, even though it was entertained, in a less extreme form, by other Jewish thinkers. It is true that it was not impossible for the speculating, allegorizing Maimonides as well as for his fellow philosophers to find hints for a system of "negative theology" both in the Bible and Talmud. When God is made transcendent, removed, nameless, it becomes difficult either to conceive Him or to describe Him in any way. It is not beyond a metaphysician to convert the verse, "thou shalt see my back; but my face shall not be seen,"[53] into a system of negative theology. Isaac's blindness was attributed in rabbinic literature to the momentary glimpse he had had of the *Shechinah* on Mount Moriah.[54] David, the Rabbis had said, praised God with all the limbs of his body, but his efforts proved unsatisfactory.[55] In other words, his attempt to define or to describe the Deity proved futile. The prohibition to pronounce God's Name, to some extent may have been due to the absolute awe in the presence of the Nameless One.[56] However, the theory, in its cold logical precision and metaphysical confusion found no place either in the Bible or Talmud. While it is true that the Rabbis preferred to dwell only on such attributes as related God to His "active direction of men and the world,"[57] it is neither their temperament nor method to strike off their emotional reactions in such neat phrases, as "God is pure action, having no potentiality."[58]

The emphasis in the Septuagint on the Namelessness of

God is undoubtedly of Jewish origin. The meticulousness, however, with which Philo makes God beyond conception or expression is not Jewish, but a product of Hellenistic influence.[59] In Asiatic religion and in Christian theology, where dogmas were always precisely defined, the "negative" theory was much more in vogue. In Buddhism, where both existence and consciousness were considered evils, a negative metaphysics certainly found fertile soil.[60] The Vedantic philosophers posited that no concept or figure, be it Atman or Brahma, could express the essence of God. The Deity was "without end, without age, without shore; it has neither without nor within." It can best be indicated negatively; *neti, neti*—it is neither "that" nor "this." The Brahma is *Nirgunna*, i.e., without attributes. Silence, they maintained, was the correct answer to what it is.[61] We shall soon, interestingly enough, see Maimonides interpret silence in the same way. Into Christian theology the theory, in its most crystallized form, came from Dionysius the Areopagite who had divided theology into positive and negative. Negative theology, he declared, denied that God's essence was anything that had existence, which we could either conceive or name. God was defined as a Not-Being, or a Nothing.[62] In Judaism such pronouncements intrigued only the extreme mystics.

Philosophers were led into this impasse simply because all thinking, or every human effort for that matter, needs a conclusion—*anangkē de stenai*. Abstractions may be spun too thin. So much of the effort results in devising new vocabularies, adding little to the clarity or comprehensibiliy of the subject. "Every attempt to define *things* breaks down."[63] What difference there is in the comprehension of ultimates between speaking with the Rabbis of God and the world, or with Plato of ideas and things, or with Spinoza and Lotze of substance and modes has not yet been made clear.[64] In all instances, we, after all, confront the same difficulty, namely, that of establishing any kind of relation between the elements contrasted. If a "thing" is *extra omne genus*, then, silence about its nature is perhaps the best of philosophies. But philosophers and theologians have never been known to suffer from a shortage of words.[65]

It may be that their inventiveness and ingenuity proceed not from choice, but from the very nature of their subject. Vide, the modern scientist has developed the same capacity for abstruseness. He, too, driven by the urge to pronounce the last word, has only added to our vocabularies and perplexities. He has denied attributes not only to God, the world too he has robbed of all quality. "The world as seen by science is not the world as it really is."[66] Some time ago color, temperature, sound, texture and taste disappeared from the whole of nature, and found a rather questionable habitation in the hallucinations of the perceiver's mind. For a time so-called primary qualities were treated with some courtesy, but then the physicists mislaid matter in "an island of universes," and could only indicate structure and relation, in the feeble lines invariably employed by the spiritualist's medium. Mass, momentum, stress became only expressions containing potentials and their derivatives. Even ether and ether waves became abstractions. These abstraction waves somehow make up an electron, for the sole purpose, evidently, of exemplifying this quality of abstractness in a more acute form.[67] For these language was out of the question. Since "a piece of matter is nothing more than a series of events obeying certain laws,"[68] mathematical formulae had to suffice. How else could one describe the particle which is itself only a charge of negative electricity, which is, nevertheless, a charge in nothing.

We have then in the twentieth century a negative science even as the medievalists had a negative theology. Both of them are the result of pushing thought to the limit, and of attempting in words or symbols that to which there no longer is anything corresponding in our imagination. We refuse to halt with the limitation of experience. Having no experience of divine attributes or operations, i.e., of the divine nature, our speculations turn into verbal conjectures. Maimonides was driven by the same urge as the modern scientist, or, the philosopher and theologian of all ages. Treading the tempting road of metaphysics and logic, he went a long way from the mood of Prophet, Rabbi and Psalmist. They, viewing totality through personaltiy, could only see a God who is near to all those who call on Him, who is near in every kind of nearness, who bends His ear from His lofty throne to the humblest of petitioners. Maimonides, though believing in the same God, in every way just as the Rabbis and Prophets, in his terminology came near emptying that belief of all content.

Even philosophers were frightened by Maimonides' rapid and daring strides. As late as the fifteenth century Crescas and Albo were still zealously laboring to restore to God the attributes of existence, unity, omniscience, volition and omnipotence.[69] Maimonides himself takes great pain to persuade the reader that he had in no way removed himself from the Jewish religious *Anschauung*, as was indeed subsequently claimed by a Jewish philosopher. He is most anxious to convince his reader that he is only echoing the true spirit of his people's tradition. He finds a "very expressive remark in the Book of Psalms, 'Silence is praise to Thee,' "[70] and another "recommended by men of the highest culture. . . . 'Commune with your own heart upon your bed, and be still.' "[71] Maimonides literally glories in these phrases. What does this silence imply? Why this silence? The answer is simple. Since God is best comprehended negatively, then the less said the better.

If the reader should still feel that this mass of argument hangs from an extraordinarily thin peg, Maimonides will discover for him a "celebrated passage" in the Talmud. He is so grateful for this extra support that he exclaims, almost, with childish glee: "Would that all the passages in the Talmud were like that!"[72] "A certain person," Maimonides proceeds, "reading prayers in the presence of Rabbi Haninah, said, 'God, the great, the valiant and the tremendous, the powerful, the strong, and the mighty.'—The rabbi said to him, Have you finished the praises of your Master? The three epithets, 'God, the great, the valiant and the tremendous,' we should not have applied to God, had Moses not mentioned them in the Law, and had not the men of the Great Synagogue come forward subsequently and established their use in the prayer; and you say all this! Let this be illustrated by a parable. There was once an earthly king, possessing millions of gold coin; he was praised for owning millions of silver coin; was this not really dispraise to him?"[73]

Is Maimonides satisfied with his intellectual feat? Has the Jew in him completely abdicated to the logician and metaphysician? Has intuition altogether surrendered to reason? Not at all. Already in the Introduction to the Guide he had said: "At times the truth shines so brilliantly that we perceive it as clear as day. Our nature and habit then draw a veil over our perception, and we return to a darkness almost as dense as before. We are like those who, though beholding frequent flashes of lightning, still find themselves in the thickest darkness of the night."[74] "Those who read the present work," he humbly and painfully admits, "are aware that, notwithstanding all the efforts of the mind, we can obtain no knowledge of the essence of the heavens . . . we say that the heavens are not light, not heavy, not passive, and therefore not subject to impressions, and they do not possess the sensations of taste and smell; or we use similar negative attributes. All this we do, because we do not know their substance. What then can be the result of our efforts, when we try to obtain a knowledge of a Being that is free from substance, that is most simple, whose existence is absolute, and not due to any cause, to whose perfect essence nothing can be superadded, and whose perfection consists, as we have shown, in the absence of all defects . . . in the contemplation of His essence our comprehension and knowledge prove insufficient; in the examination of His works, how they necessarily result from His will, our knowledge proves to be ignorance, and in the endeavor to extol Him in words all our efforts in speech are more weakness and failure."[75] Even to Moses so many "gates of perception" were closed.[76] There is, Maimonides reluctantly admits, a boundary set to the human mind which it cannot pass.[77]

Maimonides, then, after making his logical circuit, returns to where the Rabbis usually begin. They admitted, at the very outset, almost, in the words of Maimonides, that our knowledge is ignorance and that all our efforts vain and futile. It was beyond man to understand a Being, omniscient, omnipotent, all wise and good. His essence and His ways are inscrutable. They could of course have taken just one more step and made of God the logical Absolute, icy, forbidding, without any significance to man. But they preferred a personal God, and that personal God was always accommodated by "fancy and imagination."[78] If to make God personal meant to ascribe to Him corporeality, affection potentiality and resemblance to His creatures, the Rabbis took the risk. Even to attribute only mercy to God had worried Schleiermacher. "It were more appropriate," he frowned, "to a poetic manner of speaking than to a dogmatic."[79] The Rabbis preferred to remain poetic, Maimonides chose the path of logic but being a good Jew the twain did meet. "It would be a mistake," writes Professor Husik, "to suppose that his (Maimonides') philosophical deduction represented his last word on the subject (Judaism). As in Philo so in Maimonides his negative theology was only a means to an end. Its purpose was to emphasize God's perfection."[80]

Indeed, in the chapter following the philosopher's confession, like every good Jew before him and since his day, Maimonides takes refuge with Moses and Solomon. It is through them, through these unparalleled personalities that he sees his God. He does not, like Averroes, regard Aris-

totle "as the man whom alone, among all men, God permitted to reach the highest summit of perfection."[81] To
Maimonides that man was only Moses. Like Philo he decidedly believed that the lawgiver "had attained the very
summit of philosophy."[82] Maimonides is, after all his reasoning, not far removed from Yehudah Halevi and his insistence
on the God of Abraham, Isaac and Jacob. He is only more
rigidly logical, seeking to eliminate all contradictions and
to tie up all loose ends. With him everything must submit to
a system, to order, to a syllogism. His basic conceptions,
however, he had imbibed with his mother's milk. The unity
and incorporeality of God, which necessarily implies His
existence, he had had as the foundations of his faith from
his earliest childhood.

His philosophizing made neither Greek nor Aristotelian
of him. Logic and Reason prevailed up to a certain point;
deeply rooted in his whole being was the faith of intuition.
"Maimonides," writes Professor Friedlaender, "at no time
doubted and on many occasions emphatically acknowledged
the divine origin of the Pentateuch in the strictest sense of
the word . . . the belief logically pursued means not the
sovereignty of reason, but the sovereignty of the divine."[83]
Not even his theory of negative attributes could make of
Maimonides but a "Jew in letter" and a "Greek philosopher
in spirit."[84] The mental twist, that might propel a human
being to pursue a theory, does not alter his inner life. Maimonides, we submit, was no less a pious, devout, believing
Jew than was Rabbi pseudo-Jacob Tam.

It is true that historians of Jewish philosophy have overlooked the *Sepher ha-Yashar*, and the remarkable fact that
for centuries the book was without any reservations or mis-
givings attributed to the renowned French scholar. Jewish
philosophy has been given isolated treatment. Its roots are
sought everywhere but in Judaism. If a writer's Hebrew is
foreign, artificial, improvised, the philosophers will think
well of him. Should he pay his respect to Plato or Aristotle

the philosophers will make a Helene of him, and build him a monument. Rabbi pseudo-Jacob Tam betrays no such greatness. His Hebrew style is not hampered by the rigors of logical precision. Of Plato and Aristotle, there is but a faint echo in his work. Yet it should not be difficult to make a Greek of him. "Know," he writes, "that in reality, nothing need be attributed to the Creator, Blessed Be He, neither power, nor life, nor wisdom, nor being, nor unity. He is beyond all these attributes and it is useless to ascribe them to Him. We are, however, compelled to do so for two reasons. In the first place, it is written in Scripture, 'The Lord by wisdom founded the earth,' and there are similar verses. In the second place, we must speak of Him as existing, in order to remove from Him what is ascribed to the non-existent. The non-existent is absent and impotent; neither is it an agent of good or evil. We are, therefore, obliged to speak of Him as existent. For the same reason we must speak of His Unity, to remove from Him every hint of plurality, divisibility, multiplicity, diminution or amplification. . . . After we understand, that His true existence consists in rejecting the possibility of conceiving His existence, then we shall know that He is neither far nor near. . . ."[85]

Not unlike Maimonides, Rabbi Tam continues on the tautly drawn rope: "A thing can only conceive that to which it is in some way related or analogous. If then we could conceive one of the Creator's attributes, there would have to be between us and that attribute relation and likeness. Then again, since God and his attributes are one and indivisible, to say there is relation between us and any of His attributes would of necessity imply that there is relation between us and God. This then is conclusive proof that He is beyond our understanding, and that there is no analogy or relation between our properties and His. He is the Creator and we the created. . . . There is then no way of conceiving God. Now that this is self-evident, it is the proof *par excellence* of His existence. For just as the ability to conceive

His existence would make His existence impossible, even so our inability to conceive Him is proof that He exists. For conceiving Him would make His existence analogous to ours, which is accidental, transitory and perishable; but His existence is the antithesis of ours."[86] In other words "the sum total of what we know of Thee, is that we do not know Thee."[87]

There is nothing to our knowledge more Greek or heretical in Maimonides than the foregoing citation. If we turn the pages of the *opusculum* attributed to Rabbi Tam we shall be treated to more than one surprise. This son of the distinctly Jewish community, grandson of the unphilosophical Rashi, this supreme member of the Tosafist commentators, steeped body and soul in the intricacies of Talmudic discussions, was yet unhesitatingly regarded the author of a work avowedly intellectualistic.

Wisdom and knowledge, he was made to declare eternally imperishable.[88] The worship of God without knowledge of Him cannot endure.[89] Without the intellect indeed there is no proper worship.[90] For it is the *sechel* that is the source of faith.[91] "Therefore," concludes Rabbi Tam, without any assistance from Aristotle, "have I given precedence to intellectual proofs over scriptural, because the heart[92] accepts them more readily and the soul of the listener absorbs them because they are convincing."[93] Perhaps then Rabbenu Tam too, like Maimonides, was no more than a Jew in letter.

XI. Creatio ex Nihilo

How far his early faith and the organic view of the Universe held Maimonides is evident in every page the man wrote, the Guide not excluded. The most important instance might here be considered. In Aristotle, he found a theory which, while not altogether new, was contrary to the climate of opinion in which Maimonides had lived. The Stagirite had assumed the eternity of matter. The opinion was not unknown to the Rabbis. In several sources we read: A philosopher questioned Rabbi Gamaliel saying: "Your God is a great artist but He found good materials which helped Him." "What are they?" said Gamaliel. "Chaos and void," replied the philosopher, "darkness, water, wind and abyss." Rabbi Gamaliel satisfied or dismissed the philosopher by pointing to scriptural verses which speak of the creation of these primordial substances.[1] While Maimonides was acquainted through the Rabbis with the Aristotelian doctrine, he also knew that Jewish tradition affirms the principle of *creatio ex nihilo*.

In this conflict, Maimonides displays not only his great intellectual powers, but gives us a true insight into the *motif* of his work.[2] Other traditionalists at this point either cursed Aristotle or declared reason inferior to theology.[3] Not so Maimonides. To him truth always remains one and this truth has only one source. Therefore, Jewish tradition and Aristotle cannot differ, since both of them have been confirmed by the same Active Intelligence. How then does Maimonides resolve the conflict? Does he humbly kneel before Aristotle? Unlike most medievalists, Maimonides is too conscious of his own great powers to be a slave to authority.[4] The man, who, unceremoniously, jostled generations of *Amoraim* out of his path, could not be overawed by a philosopher even though he be the greatest of his class. Maimonides is impatient with those who follow Aristotle blindly, and "accept all his arguments as conclusive and absolute proof." He goes even further: "I will not," he says, "deceive myself, and consider dialectical methods as proofs; and the fact that a certain proposition has been proved by a dialectical argument will never induce me to accept that proposition, but, on the contrary, will weaken my faith in it, and cause me to doubt it. For when we understand the fallacy of a proof, our faith in the proposition itself is shaken."[5]

Unlike the *Mutakallemim*, Maimonides proceeds to argue, in thoroughly modern fashion, for Creation, as if, temporarily, he accepted Aristotle's view of the eternity of matter. "I do not believe," says he, "in that eternity, but I wish to establish the principle of the existence of God by an indisputable proof. . . . For this reason you will find in my works on the Talmud, whenever I have to speak of the fundamental principles of our religion, or to prove the existence of God, that I employ arguments which imply the eternity of the universe."[6] Later on, Maimonides summarizes: "We have . . . shown that whether we believe in the *creatio ex nihilo*, or in the Eternity of the Universe, we can prove by demonstrative arguments the existence of God, i.e., an absolute Being. . . . The theory that God is One and Incorporeal has likewise been established by proof without any reference to the theory of the Creation or the Eternity of the Universe.[7]

The meat, then, of Maimonides' argument, is independent of the Aristotelian assumption, which proved such a stumbling-block to the other medieval philosophers. "My method," says Maimonides, "as far as I now can explain it in general terms, is as follows: The universe is either eternal or has had a beginning; this is clear to common sense; for a thing that has had a beginning cannot be the cause of its own beginning; another must have caused it. The universe

was, therefore, created by God. If, on the other hand, the
universe were eternal, it could in various ways be proved
that apart from the things which constitute the universe,
there exists a being which is neither body nor a force in a
body, and which is one, eternal, not preceded by any cause,
and immutable. That being is God."[8]

Thus, making no concession to theology, and establishing
the existence of God on the basis of Reason only, Maimonides now more freely examines Aristotle's opinion of the
eternity of the universe. He points out that Aristotle was not
sure of his own mind in this matter. In the first place, he
attacks his opponents a little too severely, ascribing their
arguments to folly and absurdity, a sure indication of resort
to passion where logic had failed the Greek. Then again,
Maimonides continues, the Greek philosopher at this point
was too anxious to quote the opinions of like-minded predecessors. "But," says Maimonides, "a truth, once established
by proof, does neither gain force nor certainty by the consent
of all scholars, nor lose by the general dissent."[9] Further-
more, Aristotle himself betrays the uncertainty in his own
mind. In his *de Caelo et de Mundo* he says: "There are
things concerning which we are unable to reason, or which
we find too high for us; to say why these things have a
certain property is as difficult as to decide whether the universe is eternal or not."[10] It is evident therefore that Aristotle does not bring his theory to definiteness. His difficulty,
interestingly enough, according to Maimonides, was his defective knowledge of astronomy. This science had not yet
developed in Greece "to the height it has reached at present."[11] We are, therefore, neither bound to accept his arguments as conclusive and final nor see a contradiction between
philosophy and revelation.

With Aristotle humbled, Maimonides deploys a brilliant
dialectic against the arguments of his opponents. That is all
to which he aspires. "I think," says Maimonides, "that the
utmost that can be effected by believers in the truth of Revela-

tion is to expose the shortcomings in the proofs of philosophers who hold that the Universe is eternal, and if forsooth
a man has effected this, he has accomplished a great deed!
For it is well known to all clear and correct thinkers who
do not wish to deceive themselves that this question, namely,
whether the Universe has been created or is eternal, cannot
be answered with mathematical certainty; here human intellect must pause."[12]

In some respects Maimonides is anticipating Morgan's
theory of emergent evolution. According to Maimonides,
Aristotle has made the mistake of thinking that the properties of a thing actually existing are completely an emanation
from the thing in potential existence. Therefore, he argued
that the properties of actual matter could not have come
from non-existence.[13] But, says Maimonides, what a process
of genesis and development does every substance go through
before it reaches its final state. How different are its properties "from those which it possessed at the commencement of
the transition from potentiality to reality, or before that time.
Take, e.g., the human ovum as contained in the female's
blood when still included in its vessels; its nature is different
from what it was in the moment of conception, when it is
met by the semen of the male and begins to develop; the
properties of the semen in that moment are different from
the properties of the living being after its birth when fully
developed."[14] Similarly the present properties of matter, say
nothing of the properties of matter at its production, and
since we know nothing of the nature of those properties at
the beginning, there is nothing to prevent us from assuming
that they themselves had come into existence from absolute
non-existence.[15] This is strongly reminiscent of the present-
day theory that evolution as a creative process is continually
engaged in bringing forth something new. New properties,
which did not exist in the "thing" before, emerge and the
future is altogether unpredictable. Life and consciousness,

for example, are qualities which emerged, and were not always characteristic of the universe.[16]

Now, if Maimonides could establish Creation and, at the same time, accept the eternity of matter, why does he engage in such a prolonged battle with Aristotle? Is he merely propelled by the force of logic or metaphysics? One of the most gifted contemporary expositors of Maimonides seems to make such a claim,[17] but Maimonides himself offers us quite a different reason. The traditional opinion regarding *creatio ex nihilo*, he tells us, is a "high rampart erected round the Law, and able to resist all missiles directed against it."[18] This theory, he pleads, is a "fundamental principle of the Law of our teacher Moses; it is next in importance to the principle of God's unity. Do not follow any other theory. Abraham, our Father, was the first that taught it, after he had established it by philosophical research."[19] And again, "The theory of the Creation was held by our Father Abraham, and by our Teacher Moses. . . ."[20] If we were to accept the Eternity of the Universe, as taught by Aristotle, that everything in the Universe is the result of fixed laws, that Nature does not change, and that there is nothing supernatural, we should necessarily be in opposition to the foundation of our religion, we should disbelieve all miracles and signs, and certainly reject all hopes and fears derived from Scripture. . . ."[21] "Many of our co-religionists thought that King Solomon believed in the Eternity of the Universe. This is very strange. How can we suppose that anyone that adheres to the Law of Moses, our Teacher, should accept that theory? If we were to assume that Solomon has on this point, God forbid, deviated from the Law of Moses, the question would be asked, Why did most of the Prophets and of the Sages accept it of him? Why have they not opposed him, or, blamed him for holding that opinion, as he has been blamed for having married strange women, and for other things?"[22] "If," says Maimonides in a clinching paragraph, "philosophers would consider this example well and reflect on it, they would find that it represents exactly the dispute between Aristotle and ourselves. We, the followers of Moses our Teacher, and of Abraham our Father, believe that the Universe has been produced and has developed in a certain manner, and that it has been created in a certain order. . . .[23] "In short, in these questions, *do not take notice of the utterances of any person. I told you that the foundation of our faith is the belief that God created the universe from nothing.*"[24]

We are then back again with Father Abraham and our Teacher Moses. We are again experiencing the Universe intuitively and seeing it organically through the eyes of personality. Aristotle makes of the world an automaton, a view not unknown to the Rabbis.[25] All things proceed from necessity. God is the unintentional cause of the universe, and the universe is nothing more than the necessary effect. The two are inseparable. It is true that Aristotle had considered the necessary activity of God as conscious, but the content of this consciousness had no reference to the universe or man. It was simply the contemplation of God himself and "the act of contemplation is that which is best,"[26] but that, of course, could not satisfy Maimonides. He drew a distinction between conscious necessary activity and unconscious necessary activity, and between the former and design. "Aristotle," says Maimonides, "holds that the Prime Cause is the highest and most perfect Intellect; he therefore says that the First Cause is pleased, satisfied, and delighted with that which necessarily derives existence from Him, and it is impossible that He should wish it to be different. But we do not call this 'design,' and it has nothing in common with design. E.g., man is pleased, satisfied, and delighted that he is endowed with eyes and hands, and it is impossible that he should desire it to be otherwise, and yet the eyes and hands which a man has are not the result of his design, and it is not by his own determination that he has certain properties and is able to perform certain actions."[27]

At this point Maimonides, steeped in Bible and Talmud, in the experience and history of his people, boldly injects into the scheme of things design, choice, desire. Here he is helpless, and can only bend logic to the intuitions of his being, to the experience of his people. "We hold that all things in the Universe are the result of design, and not merely of necessity."[28] Moses constantly looms before his eyes. How can anyone deny purpose or design to the great lawgiver? How then can anyone deny it to Moses' God? Maimonides had no alternative but to devastate Aristotle and accept *creatio ex nihilo*. Not that Maimonides anywhere states dogmatically what God's purpose in the creation of the Universe and man was. To such knowledge he laid no claim, and was perfectly willing to ascribe it to the inscrutable will of God and His infinite wisdom, but a purpose God had, and that made it necessary to reject Aristotle.[29]

Philo and many other Jews, who were enticed by Greek speculation, likewise reject the eternity of the universe and its purposelessness. With characteristic eloquence Philo writes: "There are some people who, having the world in admiration rather than the Maker of the world, pronounce it to be without beginning and everlasting, while with impious falsehood they postulate in God a vast inactivity; whereas we ought on the contrary to be astonished at His powers as Maker and Father, and not to assign to the world a disproportionate majesty. Moses, both because he had attained the very summit of philosophy, and because he had been divinely instructed in the greater and most essential part of Nature's lore, could not fail to recognize that the universal must consist of two parts, one part active Cause and the other passive object; and that the active Cause is the perfectly pure and unsullied Mind of the universe, transcending virtue, transcending knowledge, transcending the good itself and the beautiful itself; while the passive part is in itself incapable of life and motion, but, when set in motion and shaped and quickened by Mind, changes into the most perfect masterpiece, namely this world. Those who assert that this world is unoriginate unconsciously eliminate that which of all incentives to piety is the most beneficial and the most indispensable, namely providence. For it stands to reason that what has been brought into existence should be cared for by its Father and Maker. For, as we know, it is a father's aim in regard of his offspring and an artificer's in regard of his handiwork to preserve them, and by every means to fend off from them aught that may entail loss or harm. He keenly desires to provide for them in every way all that is beneficial and to their advantage; but between that which has never been brought into being and one who is not its Maker no such tie is formed. It is a worthless and baleful doctrine, setting up anarchy in the well-ordered realm of the world, leaving it without protector, arbitrator or judge, without anyone whose office it is to administer and direct all its affairs."[30] In other words, in a pinch, Philo like Maimonides yields the palm to intuition and reverts to the tradition of his childhood.

XII. This Solid Flesh

Maimonides, it would seem, can best be understood as the traditional Jew with a passion for logic. The totality of Jewish experience, the whole qualitative, organic, personality content of Judaism, he was eager to force into the stubborn mold of syllogistic formulation. There was nothing in the gorgeous, variegated, tangled pattern of tradition which he was prepared to discard. He was a rationalist, he had mastered the Aristotelian technique to perfection, but he loved deeply every item in the lore of his people. He does not deviate from the principles enunciated by the Rabbis. He always tries to weave the loose threads of their intuitive thinking into orderliness. The logician and systematizer are much in evidence, but the Rabbi is constantly on guard.

It is asserted that, unlike Homer, Maimonides never nods. He is everywhere lucid, concise, convincing and honest. There is, however, one exception. When he comes to the discussion of the resurrection of the dead, he grows cryptic. He discusses the belief in several places, devotes a whole monograph to it, but nowhere does its presentation display his wonted crystal clarity. In his own generation, he was accused of heresy;[1] in subsequent generations, he was charged with hypocrisy. Both charges are ridiculous and do the man serious wrong. Maimonides was intellectually honest to a fault. He never would have embodied the Resurrection in his Thirteen Articles of the creed, had he disbelieved it. Certainly, skeptical himself, he would not have gone so far as to read others out of the fold[2] who shared his skepticism. The charges of hypocrisy or heresy explain nothing. What happened was that on this point the logician and traditionalist engaged in their severest conflict. Either refused to yield.

There was no escape. Whenever Maimonides returned to the question he was moving between Scylla and Charybdis. The logician was unbending, he resisted tradition mightily. "I tell you" . . . Maimonides writes, "as a general rule that Themistius was right in saying that the properties of things cannot adapt themselves to our opinions, but our opinions must be adapted to the existing properties."[3] He has no patience with the theologians who are guided by their imagination, and flatter themselves to be following the dictates of intellect.

Maimonides the logician attempted to fathom the purpose of man's existence. If there is design in the universe, certainly man is not a mere caprice, or accident. Aristotle was perfectly satisfied to leave the human race without a goal. In Maimonides the traditionalist is stubborn. To all sublunar creatures, he had offered the privilege of serving man. To man himself, he assigned the sublime duty of meditating, knowing and understanding God and his ways.[4] But Maimonides, physician and psychologist that he was, knew human beings and their serious limitations. The Jews of the Orient, with whom he was best acquainted, as well as the Gentiles, were altogether slaves of their passions. They wallowed in ignorance and superstition. They were indolent, and decidedly incapable of sustained intellectual effort. Maimonides would not deceive himself that the multitude could ever ascend to his metaphysical tower. Like another intellectual aristocrat—Schiller—he saw that many would continue "eternally blind." For one man who attained wisdom, ten thousand were destined to remain fools.

Has then the bulk of humanity no purpose in life? No function to fulfill? Are the masses of men less fortunate even, than all the dumb beasts and insects upon earth? Such a probability was inconceivable. Being logical and methodical, and traditionalist to boot, Maimonides found something to keep the swarming millions busy. God, he maintained, had put them upon this earth for two reasons. First, to pro-

vide the few wise men with the meager necessities of life.
It is true that the wise man needs but little, but even that
little, were he called upon to be his own tiller, baker, cook,
shoemaker and tailor, would require endless toil, and pre-
clude him from metaphysical meditation. In the second place,
a world limited to wise men only, would be empty and
lonely. Therefore, God created the masses, to provide com-
panionship for the intellectual few. Thus the one man provides a *raison d'être* for millions, while (his own) purpose
in life remains to penetrate the mysteries of creator and
creation.[5]

Even so, pure speculation remains a large task, even for
the wisest of men. Weariness and sleep for one are enemies
to study.[6] So frequently the body, its needs and desires prove
an obstacle. "All obstacles which prevent man from attain-
ing his highest aim in life, all the deficiencies in the character
of man, all his evil propensities, are to be traced to the body
alone.[7] . . . Some consider . . . all wants of the body as
shame, disgrace, and defect to which they are compelled to
attend; this is chiefly the case with the sense of touch, which
is a disgrace to us according to Aristotle, and which is the
cause of our desire for eating, drinking and sensuality.[8]
Intelligent persons must, as much as possible, reduce these
wants, guard against them, feel grieved when satisfying them,
abstain from speaking of them, discussing them, and at-
tending to them in company with others. Man must have
control over all these desires, reduce them as much as possible, and only retain of them as much as is indispensable.
*His aim must be the aim of man as man, viz., the formation
of ideas, and nothing else.*"[9] This is man's task and purpose.

However, "*the corporeal element in man is a large screen
and partition that prevents him from perfectly perceiving
abstract ideals; this would be the case even if the corporeal
element were as pure and superior as the substance of the
spheres; how much more must this be the case with our dark
and opaque body. However great the exertion of our mind*

*may be to comprehend the Divine Being or any of the ideals,
we find a screen and partition between Him and ourselves.*[10]
Thus the prophets frequently hint at the existence of a partition between God and us.[11] . . ."

"It is . . . the object of the perfect Law to make man
reject, despise and reduce his desire as much as is in his
power. He should only give way to them when absolutely
necessary.[12] . . . *You must know that even if you were the
wisest man in respect to the true knowledge of God, you
break the bond between you and God whenever you turn
entirely your thoughts to the necessary food or any necessary
business; you are then not with God, and He is not with you;
for that relation between you and Him is actually interrupted
in those moments. . . .*"

"*When the perfect man is stricken in age and is near
death, his knowledge mightily increases, his joy in that
knowledge grows greater, and his love for the object of his
knowledge more intense, and it is in this great delight that
the soul separates from the body.*[13] . . . It is (therefore)
clear that all corruption, destruction, or defect comes from
matter. Take, e.g., man; his deformities and unnatural shape
of limbs; all weakness, interruption, or disorder of his actions, whether innate or not, originate in the transient substance, not in the form. All other living beings likewise die or
become ill through the substance of the body and not
through its form. Man's shortcomings and sins are all due
to the substance of the body and not to its form; while all
his merits are exclusively due to his form. Thus the knowledge of God, the formation of ideas, the mastery of desire
and passion, the distinction between that which is to be
chosen and that which is to be rejected, all these man owes
to his form; but eating, drinking, sexual intercourse, excessive lust, passion, and all vices have their origin in the
substance of the body."[14]

We have quoted profusely from the Guide, because it is
important to see how far Maimonides, the logician, advances,

step by step, syllogism by syllogism, in his deprecation of the body. It gradually becomes in his mind the most resistive obstacle to a rationale of man's place in the scheme of things. If only man could rid himself of his body, how nearer his life's goal he could come, *tikkun ha-nephesh b'hurban ha-guph*.[15] Ultimately there is a release. Death overtakes the physical frame, and the "acquired Intellect" is now free to dwell in the glory of the divine presence. Imagine then the discomfort of the logician pledged to the negation of the flesh when the traditionalist in him whispers, "but Jews believe in the resurrection of the body," to have had to account for the Resurrection. After a hard life, in which the wise man has struggled against his body, and after a final victory in death, he had to face the unpleasant thought that this incubus of matter would again, by the Grace of God, be imposed upon the intellect. Here Maimonides was in a *cul de sac*. There was no way out.

Maimonides, however, could not help but yield to the pressure of his inner being, to his deeply imbedded respect and love for the tradition of his people. Immortality of the soul alone had not satisfied the ancients. Like the soul of Moses,[16] every Jew was reluctant to leave his body for ever. His religion was this worldly, and he hoped for a return to this earth with body, garments and all.[17] The great Akiba stormed against those who had the temerity to suggest that the Resurrection was not already implied in the Torah.[18] What an insurmountable difficulty Maimonides faced here. To accede to tradition meant to dismantle his whole philosophic structure. He therefore passed over the vexing conundrum cryptically. The Freudians would say the conflict was repressed into the subconscious.

It is not the only repression that Maimonides had to make. There are other knots in his writings which are not easily unraveled. In the citations from the Guide we have placed before the reader, it is evident that Maimonides had gone over altogether in the direction of extreme asceticism—

an asceticism Platonic and Christian but decidedly not Jewish. The conception of *soma*, as body and prison of the
soul, made its way from Plato to Philo, Paul, Plotinus, Augustine and many other neo-Platonist and Christian thinkers.
"So long as we have the body," Plato wrote, "and the soul
is contaminated by such an evil, we shall never attain completely what we desire, that is, the truth. For the body
keeps us constantly busy by reason of its need of sustenance;
and moreover, if disease come upon it they hinder our pursuit
of the truth. And the body fills us with passions, desires and
fears, and all sorts of fancies and foolishness, so that, as
they say, it really and truly makes it impossible for us to
think at all. The body and its desires are the only cause of
wars and factions and battles; for all wars arise for the
sake of gaining money, and we are compelled to gain money
for the sake of the body. We are slaves to its service. And
so because of all these things, we have no leisure for philosophy. But the worst of all is that if we do get a bit of leisure
and turn to philosophy, the body is constantly breaking in
upon our studies and disturbing us with noise and confusion,
so that it prevents our beholding the truth, and in fact we
perceive that, if we are ever to know anything absolutely,
we must be free from the body and must behold the actual
realities with the eye of the soul alone. And then, as our
argument shows, *when we are dead we are likely to possess
the wisdom which we desire and claim to be enamoured
of, but not while we live.* For, if pure knowledge is impossible while the body is with us, one of two things must follow,
either it cannot be acquired at all or only when we are dead;
for then the soul will be by itself apart from the body, but
not before. And while we live, we shall, I think, be nearest
to knowledge when we avoid, so far as possible, intercourse
and communion with the body, except what is absolutely
necessary, and are not filled with its nature, but keep ourselves pure from it until God himself sets us free. And in
this way, freeing ourselves from the foolishness of the body

and being pure, we shall, I think, be with the pure and shall know of ourselves all that is pure—and that is, perhaps, the truth. For it cannot be that the impure attain the pure."[19]

In Judaism this view never thrived. There is hardly any relation between the Christian and the Jewish ideas of Holiness. To the Christian, Holiness often implied the annihilation of the body, the negation of civilized living. The attitude of many of the Church Fathers toward marriage the Rabbis could never understand.[20] St. Jerome pleaded with Christians to abandon civilization and seek religious fulfillment in the cell or desert. The Rabbis advised scholars against the making of their homes in cities which were not provided with a court, community chest, synagogue, bathhouse, lavatories, physician, scribe and elementary school. Rabbi Akiba would insist even on a variety of good vegetables.[21] Extreme self-denial and habitual vow-making the Rabbis discouraged.[22] Some even allowed the natural desires of men considerable latitude.[23] When after the destruction of the Temple by the Romans in the year 70, many Jews despised this earthly life, and took refuge in ascetic practices, Rabbi Joshua ben Hananiah, renowned scholar and saint, led his contemporaries back to normal living. You abstain, he said, to the extremists, from meat and wine because they remind you of the Temple sacrifices and oblations, why not then give up bread because of the shew-bread; figs and grapes too because of the first-fruit offering? Of course, not to mourn our national catastrophe is inconceivable, but to mourn overmuch is imprudent. Let us then symbolize our sorrow by means of some minor deprivations.[24]

There is, we need hardly assure the reader, in the Talmud vigorous emphasis on the cultivation of the higher human faculties. The mind was exalted above the body. Israel's teachers were no epicures or gourmets. Self-indulgence, they were wise enough to know, leads only to indolence, vice, cruelty and disintegration. What Xenophon relates of Socrates is most true of the Sages. Whenever he accepted an invitation to dinner, he resisted without difficulty the common temptation to exceed the limit of satiety; and he advised those who could not do likewise to avoid appetizers that encouraged them to eat and drink what they did not want: for such trash was the ruin of stomach and brain and soul. "I believe," he said in jest, "it was by providing a feast of such things that Circe made swine; and it was partly by the prompting of Hermes, partly through his own self-restraint and avoidance of excessive indulgence in such things, that Odysseus was not turned into a pig. This was how he would talk on the subject, half joking, half in earnest."[25]

The Rabbis were not only half in earnest. The scholar, they said, who overindulges in feasting indiscriminately, in the end destroys his home, widows his wife, orphans his children, forgets his knowledge, causes much dissension, loses his authority, desecrates the Name of God, the names of his teacher and his father, and brings evil upon himself and his posterity to the end of his days.[26] It is wise then to sanctify oneself and restrain even from things permitted by law.[27] It is prudent not to advance too close to the forbidden; transgression dulls the soul.[28] To yield to desire, they declared, was tantamount to the worshiping of idols.[29] On its path one crossed the road to murder.[30] Of normal human desires, however, and the human body they rarely spoke as evil and impure. In the final analysis this frame of flesh and blood was the only instrumentality for the performance of *Mizvot*.[31] Were it not for the evil *Yezer* no man would build a house or marry a wife.[32] The world then stands as much in need of the tempter as of rain.[33] The intention of the *Mizvot* is the propagation of life and not death.[34] The statement of Rabbi Simeon ben Lakish that the Torah can be preserved only by him who offers his life for it, refers only to the assiduity with which one should pursue knowledge.[35] Without the body there is no knowledge, no life and no *Mizvot*.[36] To Hillel the body was for this very reason a sanctuary.[37]

How far removed then is Maimonides from tradition, when he tells us to feel "grieved when satisfying" physical wants, or that it is the object of the Law to make man reject and despise the body, or when he declares: "You break the bond between you and God whenever you turn entirely your thoughts to *necessary* food,[38] or any necessary business; you are then not with God and He is not with you." It follows, of course, since one should prefer God all the time, not even to attend to necessary food. Maimonides, were we to know nothing more of him than the foregoing citations, would here be at variance with the spirit of his tradition.

What is even more puzzling is that the contradiction is not only between Maimonides and Hillel, but in Maimonides himself. In his well-known Eight Chapters there are sentences which differ in their implications, *toto coelo,* from the opinions we saw expressed in the Guide. "It is only fools," we are there told, "who think that God hates the body and seeks its destruction. Those early Hasidim who are known to have practiced rigid asceticism did it only as a "cure," to rid themselves of some evil propensity or to escape the effects of social contacts. The Torah countenances no such extremes. It ordains man to eat, drink and mate. So many of the prohibitions aimed at nothing more than to keep man from overindulgence, but not to impose useless denials and abnegations." With enthusiasm he quotes the reproach of Rabbi Isaac against the habitual vow-maker, "are not the biblical prohibitions enough for you, must you add to their number?"[39] Indeed, Maimonides has heard nothing more marvelous than this *bon mot* of the sage.[40]

As a matter of law, Maimonides records that to pursue asceticism, to abstain from meat, wine, marriage, a beautiful home and fine clothes is to be a sinner.[41] Care for the body is very important; its health must be maintained with the utmost diligence.[42] How is it then that "in great delight the soul separates from the body," and old age is so dear to Maimonides? Why, if the body is so useless, does he give attention to the details of the Law, the discussions of Abaye and Rava concerning things permitted and things forbidden? Why does he make them a prerequisite to entering the *Pardes*, i.e., to the study of metaphysics?[43]

Maimonides is involved in yet another contradiction. To assure the leisurely contemplation of the metaphysician, he was ready to make the multitude his servants. It is true the philosopher will require but enough to keep life and soul together, but that little Maimonides asks the world to provide for him. Everywhere else, however, Maimonides prizes the labor of one's hands. He does not allow the scholar to accept any service from any human being, except from his pupils.[44] How are we to get around this difficulty without becoming involved in hair-splitting casuistry? "He who decides to devote himself completely to study," Maimonides again legislates, "and live on charity is desecrating the Name of God, disgracing the Torah, extinguishing the light of Judaism, bringing evil upon himself, in this world, and forfeiting his share in the world to come. To derive material benefit from the Torah is strictly forbidden."[45] Self-support is an inescapable duty and, at the same time, a distinction.[46] Maimonides' opposition to the salaried scholar is well known. The distinguished men in Israel, he pointed out, engaged in the most menial labor, but refused to accept assistance from others. There is nothing, he storms, in the Bible or Talmud urging us to lend support to those who give themselves entirely to study.[47] If all this is true, what shall our metaphysician do? Shall he devote himself completely to metaphysics, live on charity and desecrate the Name of God, disgrace the Torah, etc.?

There is to our mind but one solution to these difficulties —viz., the limitations of logic and metaphysics. It is beyond the tenuity of rationalism to contain the fluidity of life. Maimonides makes a heroic attempt, puts forth Herculean strength, but the task is too much even for his matchless equipment. Logic and metaphysics occasionally win a contest, but in the end tradition and intuition remain in possession of the field.

XIII. THE ORTHODOXY OF MAIMONIDES

W HEN MAIMONIDES LEAVES
metaphysics, and enters upon the discussion of religio-ethical
questions, he is in every way a Biblico-Talmudic Jew.[1] Here
we see him virtually live upon the words of the Prophets
and Rabbis. His pages teem with quotations from their
writings. All the religious, ethical and social problems Maimonides raised had already been adumbrated by the Prophets,
and had been discussed by the Rabbis for centuries. Maimonides weighs them invariably in the scales of logic, but dis-
poses of them in the spirit of Jewish tradition.[2] When, here
and there, he does seem to deviate, we find, as a rule, that
he already had a predecessor. He leans heavily, as was prev-
iously noticed, on the Jewish rationalists of the century immediately preceding his.

When Maimonides is explaining the visions of the
Prophets as dreams of the night, he is only following ibn
Ezra,[3] as indeed he does in several other instances.[4] It is
with ibn Ezra that he concludes that God knows the species
only but not the individual.[5] The stimulus to search for reasons of the laws, Maimonides also could have derived or
perhaps did derive from ibn Ezra who declared that all the
commandments have a purpose.[6] Every *maskil*, says ibn
Ezra, understood that to know God was the final aim of
man and his highest good and that was the purpose (of
the commandments).[7] The other great Jewish "Aristotelian"
ibn Daud anticipated Maimonides' theory of negative attributes,[8] and in many other important ideas as well. Guttmann goes as far as to maintain that ibn Daud's work served
as the model for the Guide. "Indeed," says Dr. Guttmann,
"the renowned author of the *Moreh* did not disdain to appropriate from time to time the conclusions of his predeces-

126

sor, in details as well as in main principles. It is decidedly not impossible, that the structure of the *Emunah Ramah* was not without influence, even on the method of presentation, and the distribution of material found in the *Moreh*. We do not, at any rate, regard it as a mere coincidence that both the work of Maimonides and Abraham ibn Daud take the form of an epistle to a young friend, and that both are divided into three main parts . . . The supposition of a certain external dependence upon ibn Daud's work will gain probability after we are convinced, in what follows, how numerous and important are the suggestions which Maimonides owes to it in the real subject matter."[9]

In many instances, Maimonides followed Saadia, even though he does not mention him by name.[10] The assumption that man was not the whole purpose of creation had been entertained by Jewish scholars before Maimonides.[11] His insistence on causation and the laws of nature is decidedly not in antithesis to Judaism. It is true, that in the Bible and the Talmud, there is no such conception as Nature or natural law. The very word is not to be met with before medieval times,[12] but there is ample evidence to prove awareness of order in the universe, and of a uniformity of occurrence. God was of course regarded omnipotent who could at any time interfere with nature, but it was part of the Divine Wisdom that He never did. Miracles were rare and even those recorded in Holy Writ required, as it were, a special agreement with primordial nature. It should not be forgotten that Maimonides himself struggled against a rigid acceptance of nature and natural law, and, in the end, in the spirit of the Rabbis did make room for miracles.[13] What we regard as the constancy of nature, he attributed, even like the Bible and the Talmud, to the Will of God. In the spirit of this literature he perceived natural laws and order "as the condition for excellence," but not as "stifling the freshness of living."[14]

Maimonides' conception, as against *Kalam*, that "this Uni-

verse, in its entirety, is nothing else but one individual being,"[15] is not altogether new. The analogy from man, the
Olam Katon—microcosm, to the universe was known to the
ancients.[16]

Throughout, the differences between Maimonides and historic Judaism are only on the surface. The rationalism and
skepticism ascribed to him, by foes and admirers alike, have
their decided limitations.[17] In the consideration of such matters as Prophecy, Omniscience, Providence, Freedom of the
Will and Evil, Maimonides is careful to pile up scores of
Biblical and Talmudic parables, incidents and dicta, to assure, as it were, himself and his reader that he is standing
on the *terra firma* of Judaism. His training in science and
philosophy was naturally bound to provide him with a vocabulary and a method unwelcome to the Rabbis.

Those who maintain that Maimonides was the pure metaphysician, completely dominated by Reason, Aristotelian to
the finish, have much to explain.[18] Nowhere in Maimonides
does one discover any deviation from the fundamentals of
Judaism as taught by the Rabbis. In his scheme of thought
Revelation remains paramount and central. "Know," he
writes to a correspondent, "that there is a stage in knowledge
superior to the philosophic, namely, the prophetic . . . only
the prophet can gain knowledge of the supernatural. . . .
Only he who denies that Moses was a prophet will ask for
proof of the unattainable. . . . It is the foundation of our
faith to rely on the Mosaic revelation. . . . To discuss the
supermundane philosophically will lead nowhere. It is like
trying to gather all the waters of the world into one small
ladle."[19] Is it surprising to find, after such a *confessio fidei*
that there are instances in Maimonides' work where the intellect executes the most humble salaam to tradition? "He
who obligates himself," he puts down as a law, "to observe
the seven Noahidic laws and is careful in their observance,
such a one is counted among the pious Gentiles, and is
assured a share in the world to come. That assurance is his,

provided he observed these laws, as coming from God
through Moses, together with the information, that they had
been revealed to the Noahides of yore. If, however, he observed them only because he finds them reasonable, he belongs . . . neither to the pious Gentiles nor to their wise
men."[20] No wonder then that, even, in the minutest details,
his mind shows itself thoroughly conditioned by rabbinic
teachings. Despite the controversies which raged about his
work, he was nevertheless hailed *ha-Rav ha Maamin*, the
believing Rabbi.[21] His *Yad ha-Hazakah* is the master code of
Judaism. When Maimonides finished the gigantic opus,
Moses himself, legend will have it, appeared to him in a
dream to marvel and to praise.[22]

It would take us too far afield, to gather all the sub-
stantiating data, to prove how closely Maimonides follows
the minutest traditions. A few instances will have to suffice.
He believed in the recorded longevity of the antediluvians.[23]
He accepts the Midrashic accounts of Abraham's iconoclasm,
missionary activity and gift of prophecy as historic facts.[24]
The biblical accounts of the lives of the Patriarchs, he regarded as "a perfect proof that Divine Providence extends to
every man individually."[25] The "generation of the desert" he
credited with the gift of prophecy, so that the least of its
women equaled Ezekiel.[26] He believed that the writing on
the Tables of the Law were produced by God's Will. It is
not more difficult, says Maimonides, to believe this than in
the creation of the stars in the spheres.[27] How, indeed, could
he deny it, when the Mishnah explicitly lists the "writing"
among the ten things created on Friday, in the twilight of
the evening.[28] The very arrangement of paragraphs and lines
in the Torah is of such vital concern to him that he goes to
the trouble of giving a detailed description of such an arrangement in a carefully edited Asherite manuscript he had
observed in Egypt.[29] On the other hand, the Book of ben
Sira, following a Talmudic opinion, he dismisses as being
"without taste or value, and only a waste of time."[30]

He did not question but that the "water of bitterness taken by the suspected woman, if guilty, would produce the effect as described in the Bible."[31] He regards Moses as the greatest of mortals,[32] who like Elijah ascended on high alive.[33] He declared, that while ordinarily the occurrence of leprosy in inanimate objects was contrary to the laws of nature, nevertheless, such inflictions were visited on houses and clothes in Palestine, to wean their owners from indulging in slanderous gossip.[34] He never doubted but that Moses, Elijah and Isaiah were reprimanded and punished for speaking ill of Israel.[35] The fifteenth day of Ab, he was sure, was observed as a day of merrymaking because it witnessed the halting of the plague in the desert.[36] He codified a benediction for the tourist who might, in his travels, come across the lion's den of Daniel, or the furnace of Hananiah, Misha'el and Azariah.[37] It is needless to add that he regarded both the written and oral law in all its details as absolutely Sinaitic.[38] All ritual measures came from Moses.[39] It was Moses, too, who embellished the Hebrew letters with the crownlets.[40] Therefore, the Law was permanent and unchanging. No prophet could introduce any reforms into it.[41] The test of the true prophet is the fulfillment of his predictions to the last detail.[42] He expected the final return of the Davidic Dynasty to power.[43] Elijah, of course, as was predicted by Moses, would herald the coming of that moment.[44]

There are verses in the Bible, such as Genesis, ch. 35, v. 22, which the Rabbis for certain reasons maintained should be read in the Synagogue, but not translated into the vernacular. Maimonides here implicitly follows the Rabbis.[45] It never occurred to him to make the suggestion to omit such verses altogether. The laws of *Mezuzah* and *Tephillin* he begins without any prefatory remarks, assuming that, in all their details, they are Sinaitic.[46] He expected the order of the Temple service to be restored exactly to what it was before the destruction.[47] He does not reject the Hanukah story of the flask of oil as legendary.[48] If he repudiates the mythical size of Og, he already had authority for it in *Targum* and *Midrash*.[49] Despite all his conjectures about the origin of sacrifices, he, nevertheless, believed that in the days of the Messiah they would once again be offered at the Temple of Jerusalem.[50] He is certain that both Samson and Solomon converted the foreign women to Judaism before they married them.[51] He believed implicitly in the effectiveness of the *Urim* and *Tumim*.[52] *Gan Eden* he was certain was a place of extraordinary peace and beauty, the location of which God will make known to man in the end of days.[53] He repeats, with enviable naïveté, the Talmudic belief that the place upon which the altar of Adam, Cain and Abel stood was the very place upon which Noah built his, after he left the Ark. It was on the same spot that Abraham bound Isaac, and it was there too that David and Solomon had erected their altars. He knows of their exact height, and confidently expresses the conviction that the altar of the future will be of the same altitude.[54] In the Guide he says: "I do not doubt that the spot which Abraham chose in his prophetical spirit was known to Moses our Teacher, and to others; for Abraham commanded his children that on this place a house of worship should be built."[55] The column of smoke, that would rise during sacrifices, Maimonides records, was neither deflected nor dispersed by the wind.[56] David, he assures us, was frequently vexed by idolators and infidels with questions concerning the inexplicable statutes of the Law, such as *Shaatnez*, the red heifer, etc.[57]

This list could be augmented *ad infinitum*; enough has been offered to prove that Aristotle may have provided Maimonides with a method, but certainly not with the ideology. His ideology is thoroughly rabbinic. He reminds his readers again and again of the greatness of the Sages. He examines their every utterance with concentration and reverence. "You must know," he remarks, "that their words . . . are most perfect, most accurate and clear to those for whom they were said."[58] "Note . . . and remember . . . *it is im-*

possible for any person to expound the revelation on Mount Sinai more fully than our Sages have done. . . .[59] After these remarks of mine listen to the following useful instruction given by our Sages who in truth deserve the title of 'wise men'; it makes clear that which appears doubtful, and reveals that which has been hidden, and discloses most of the mysteries of the Law."[60]

Every word of the sages must be carefully interpreted, their meaning thoroughly searched. Every chance of misunderstanding must be removed. Maimonides will go to the greatest length to guard the Rabbis against the least misrepresentation. Rabbi Eliezer the Great, of the first century, evidently a poet by the Grace of God, once gave rein to his imagination and composed the following homily: " 'Whence were the heavens created? He took part of the light of His garment, stretched it like a cloth, and thus the heavens were extending continually, as it is said: He covereth Himself with light as with a Garment, He stretcheth the heavens like a curtain.'[61] 'Whence was the earth created? He took of the snow under the throne of glory, and threw it; according to the words: He saith to the snow, Be thou earth.' "[62] Thus mused the Rabbi. Maimonides is deeply concerned, lest we be misled into thinking that Rabbi Eliezer believed in *materia prima.* He cannot adequately explain this passage in terms of *creatio ex nihilo.* He is unhappy about it. He is dealing here with Rabbi Eliezer, an inspired sage and not with a mere Aristotle. After some effort, Maimonides finds at least some science in the passage, viz., that it is the opinion of Rabbi Eliezer that the celestial substance differs from the sublunar.[63] Maimonides is pleased. He has saved the Rabbi from the least suspicion of heresy.

XIV. WISDOM AND CONDUCT

MAIMONIDES' GOLDEN MEAN IS
easily traced to the *Bible and Talmud*.[1] Extremes we have
noticed were not countenanced in Judaism. The Torah had
always urged that man choose life. "See, I have set before
thee this day life and good, death and evil. . . ."[2] "I call
heaven and earth to witness against you this day, that I have
set before thee life and death the blessing and the curse;
therefore choose life. . . ."[3] The Torah, say the Rabbis, is
like two paths, one of fire and one of snow. Incline to the
one and you freeze, to the other and you burn; it is better
then to walk in the middle.[4] Those who can see, walk in the
center, it is the blind who take to the sides.[5] In the desert,
Jewish folklore suggested, only those were punished who
asked for meat to satisfy their gluttony, but not they who
needed it for their sustenance.[6]

To label Maimonides' ethics Greek because of the measure and balance he urges, is absurd. Virtue in Greece was
synonymous with efficiency.[7] Its validity was guaranteed by
success. The ethical concepts lacked the deep moral coloring
which monotheism and the whole course of Jewish history
lent to Jewish practice. The various Greek attempts to purify
morality and spiritualize custom failed. They could not give
their gods a new past. They remained licentious and impotent. It was too much then to expect the average Athenian
to be better than his favorite deity. "Who," asks Lucretius,
"is strong enough to rule the sun, who to hold in hand and
control the mighty bridle of the unfathomable deep? Who
to turn about all the heavens at one time and warm the
fruitful worlds with ethereal fires . . .?"[8] Of course not
the wretched deities of Olympus or the Forum. The God of

Israel, on the other hand, was so loftily envisaged that nothing could be conceived beyond His power.

> "Who hath measured the waters in the hollow of his hand,
>   And meted out heaven with the span,
>   And comprehended the dust of the earth in a measure,
>   And weighed the mountains in scales,
>   And the hills in a balance?"[9]

Of course the Holy One of Israel! He was omnipotent, omniscient, merciful. Any wonder, then, that sin meant little more than the "departure from the divinely revealed rule of life, whether in the field of morals, or of religious observance."[10] Every page of Maimonides emphasizes this concept. To him the Torah, the source of Law, is definitely holy, and holy because it is the revealed word of the One God.

Greek ethics was essentially intellectual and theoretic. The will was practically ignored. The Greek had a horror of applying his theories. It was as true in his philosophy as it was in his science. Had the Hellene taken to experimentation, the contemporaries of Archimedes might have anticipated the twentieth century; but they did not experiment. The Greeks trained the mind, but failed to discipline the will. There were many who could hang on the words of Socrates or Plato with enthusiasm, but who like Alcibiades lacked the will to achieve virtue. They could define it with skill and defile it with zest. Jewish youth on the other hand was warned that it were better not to have been born than to study or theorize without practice as an aim.[11] Maimonides' devotion to the Law was not to theory. He was deeply concerned with its implementation. If he did philosophize about the Law, it was only to make its observance more of a privilege and a joy.

Ethics to the Greeks forever remained a branch of philosophy. Maimonides made his philosophy a part and a small part, at that, of a legal code. His philosophy of ethics meant little more than finding the *Ta'ame ha-Mizvot*. It is un-

deniable that in his investigation of the "reasons for the commandments" he went beyond all his predecessors; but it is
sufficient to know that he had predecessors. Disinclined as
the ancients were to probe into origins, they yet frequently
searched for the why of the *Mizvah*. But whether Maimonides theorized more than ben Zakkai, Rabbi Simon ben
Yohai, Rabbi Meir, Abba Arika or not, is not quite as important as the fact that his attitude to the living Law of his
people differed in no way from theirs.

Because Greek ethics was only discussion it lacked heart;
it knew no pity or mercy. In Judaism the "quality of mercy"
was repeatedly emphasized. It was present at the very creation of Adam.[12] Whoever has no mercy for his fellowmen is
not of the seed of Abraham.[13] God extends his sympathy
only to the compassionate.[14] Always the Merciful One sets
the example. Let but a man be ill and He hastens to his bed-
side.[15] His Torah then, the Jew's Law, without loving-kind-
ness was inconceivable.[16]

The Greek was not conscious of his responsibility for the
conduct of other Greeks. He could be neither prophet nor
martyr—the Jew was both. What Greek could have created
the image of the suffering servant?[17] What Greek would lie
430 days on one side or another and eat by weight, drink by
measure, and consume barley biscuits baked with "the dung
that cometh out of man"—all this only to symbolize the
iniquity and punishment of his people.[18] Such self-sacrifice
and love for one's people the pagan mind could not comprehend. "Your God is a jester," they ridiculed, "to tell a man
to lie on his side."[19] In the Talmud a deep sense of social
responsibility finds noble expression. Let a man consider,
the Rabbis urged, carefully each deed he is about to perform, as though the fate of the whole world depended upon
his one deed. Happy he who does the good deed, and tips
the scale of merit for himself and his fellowmen. Woe unto
him who does wrong, and tips the scale of guilt for himself
and his fellowmen.[20]

Jewish ethics was social and decidedly national. Maimonides' approach to the Law, allowing for all his syllogisms, was the same. He felt a deep sense of pride in the Law, that it was the Jewish Law, the Law as he so affectionately puts it, of *ha-Goy ha-Tahor ha-Zeh*, this pure people.[21] Like Plato, Maimonides shows a decided aversion to those arts which prove seductive and lead man to sin. Maimonides, however, rules them out because, says he, the end that we are seeking is that we should be a holy people.[22]

The good life with the Jew was not optional, it was a most serious obligation. It was not the luxury of a few fine spirits; it was the duty of a whole people. Among the Greeks ethical systems are identified with individuals or schools. Not so among the Jews. To them there was but one Torah, God its author, and it was the *Morashah Kehillat Yakob*, the inheritance of the congregation of Jacob.[23] "Individual men," says an unknown ancient author, "thou mayest find who have Thy precepts; but nations thou shalt not find."[24] Without the Torah, Israel was inconceivable.[25] And to this Torah Jews showed a loyalty which no government could ever impose. Cicero reports that Xenocrates, when asked what his disciples were learning, replied: "To do of their own accord what they are compelled to do by the law."[26] In Israel this was not a luxury for the few but an ideal, often achieved by the many. The law did offer reward and promises of resurrection, but the Rabbis discouraged such expectations as a stimulus for conduct. The law for its own sake, *al menat shelo lekabbel peras,* was the ideal.[27] Maimonides' ethics, his philosophy of conduct, is deeply rooted in this human, noble Jewish tradition. His pages overflow with a keen sense of responsibility and a profound sense of sympathy for his fellowmen. How the aloof, theorizing Aristotle can be brought forward as the fountainhead of Maimonides' ethics is somewhat difficult to comprehend. He may have borrowed a few terms from the Greek, but never his spirit.

It has, however, been argued that insofar as Maimonides

intellectualized and placed contemplation above everything, the very foundation of his ethics is, therefore, Aristotelian.[28] It is true that no Jew, perhaps, has given as much emphasis to pure thought as the end and aim of man's life as has Maimonides. The important question for us, however, is— did Maimonides have to go for such emphasis to Aristotle? Couldn't he, didn't he, find the impetus in that direction in his own tradition? Anyone acquainted with Jewish history knows that in every age the most respected member of the community was the *Hacham*, or *Lamdan*. There is no doubt that from his earliest childhood, Maimonides had seen his father and grandfather, as well as his teachers, spend every spare moment of their lives in study. When he grew older and was introduced to the Bible, he could not help but be deeply impressed with the emphasis given there to study, knowledge, wisdom.

The greatest hope, Moses held out to his people, was to be regarded wise and understanding.[29] Solomon's deepest wish was for an "understanding heart."[30] Hosea in his day was convinced that Israel was perishing for lack of knowledge. "Because thou hast rejected knowledge, I will also reject thee, that thou shalt be no priest to Me."[31] The ideal ruler, Isaiah had pictured as endowed with wisdom, understanding and knowledge.[32] The ideal age, according to the same prophet, would come only after "the earth shall be full of the knowledge of the Eternal, as the waters cover the sea."[33] The only man entitled to praise, Jeremiah had said, was he who knew God understandingly,[34] a statement which, it will be recalled, Maimonides utilized to the utmost advantage. What the Wisdom literature prized as the highest good is too well known to require any reference.

In the writings of the Rabbis, the love for learning finds, if possible, only more fervent expression. Abraham, they report, was the head of a *Yeshibah* and Eliezer poured out to overflowing the master's wisdom for the benefit of the nations.[35] Shem, Eber and Jacob too occupied themselves as the heads of academies.[36] God himself, according to the Rabbis, spends three hours each day in study.[37] The Torah was an emanation from God's wisdom.[38] Why, asked the Rabbis, were the Jews not brought into Palestine by the shortest road? Their answer is characteristic. "God said: If I bring Israel into the land (Palestine) directly, then immediately all of them will give themselves to the fields and vineyards, and neglect the Torah. I will, therefore, make them circle about, in the desert, for forty years, supplying them with manna and water from the (miraculous) well, study will then be their sole pursuit."[39]

It was through wisdom that Moses ascended to heaven and defeated the angels in argument.[40] So great is knowledge, that Holy Writ put it between the names of God.[41] Study was preferable to a thousand sacrifices.[42] It excels in importance the building of the Temple, respect for parents or even the saving of lives.[43] To fail to educate one's son is to make an idol of him.[44] To Deborah it was revealed that only those who spend their days and nights in study are entrusted with the mission to save Israel.[45] Indeed, with all their emphasis on conduct, the Rabbis not unfrequently declared it secondary to study.[46] It was to it that David owed the Kingdom and Aaron the priesthood.[47] David, in their opinion, was victorious over Absalom, only because he had devoted himself to learning.[48] Even sin cannot extinguish Torah.[49] Torah, on the other hand, will lead the sinner back to righteousness.[50] If a man finds nothing reproachful in his conduct, and is yet overwhelmed by misfortune, let him attribute it to the neglect of learning.[51] The great source of joy for the pious, in the world to come, is that they study Torah in the academy of God.[52] The *Bet ha-Midrash* was declared greater and holier than the synagogue, and it is reported that the scholars, despite the numerous synagogues in their cities, would pray only where they studied.[53] God, the Father of mercy, finds it hard to destroy men who master the Torah and Mishnah, even though they be defiled and stained by ugly conduct and unworthy deeds.[54] Before the Jew prays in the morning for his human needs, he petitions his God for knowledge, understanding and intelligence.[55] For these are of the ten precious things of the world;[56] it is with them that the world was created.[57] It was particularly with wisdom that God fashioned everything.[58] On the day of judgment a man's cross-examination will begin with his scholarship.[59]

The verse in Proverbs,

> "The Lord made me as the beginning of His way,
> The first of His works of old."[60]

suggested to the Rabbis the notion that the Torah contained the plan of creation. Evidently they were of the opinion that thought precedes action.[61] Without the Torah heaven and earth could not subsist.[62] Such verses as "Whoso loveth knowledge loveth instruction; but he that hateth reproof is brutish,"[63] suggested to the Rabbis the intimate relation between conduct and wisdom.[64] Indeed, the wise man was essentially the good man. Without conduct a man could not possibly attain wisdom. A wicked man, philosopher or scholar, the Rabbis would have regarded as a contradiction in terms.[65]

"The Jewish people," remarks Professor Ginzberg, "as one of the oldest of the cultural races of the world, place a high estimate upon intellectualism—indeed sometimes too high an estimate. The older and the more deeply rooted the culture of a nation, the more strongly it is impressed with the truth that 'knowledge is power,' not only material but also spiritual power."[66] Rabbi Johanan ben Zakkai went as far as to declare that man was created for the purpose of study.[67] He himself certainly acted on that belief. Even though he lived in one of the most trying periods of his people's history, he remained aloof, deeply absorbed in learning and meditation.[68] So have thousands of other Jews in all ages.

It cannot be seriously maintained that the Rabbis were only concerned with practical wisdom embracing conduct which had no reference to pure knowledge or speculation. For one thing, the injunction not to teach cosmogony publicly already implied that in private such study was neither prohibited nor rare.[69] There is a Talmudic tradition to the effect that ben Zakkai, Joshua ben Hananiah, Eleazer ben Arach, Akiba, Hananiah son of Hachinai had devoted considerable time to esoteric studies.[70] It is told of ben Zakkai that he was once so impressed with the exposition of the *Chariot* by one of his pupils that, kissing him, he exclaimed: "Blessed be the Lord God of Israel who gave unto Abraham our Father a son, able to penetrate and expound the glory of his Heavenly Father."[71] Tradition has it that Father Jacob, before his death, came near revealing to his sons the divine mysteries.[72] The *Sepher ha-Yashar*, decidedly not Aristotelian, makes the meditation of God the highest good and best proof of the perfection of man.[73]

However, no matter what the general conception of wisdom or knowledge in Biblical and Talmudic literature may have been, Maimonides was decidedly of the opinion that the Prophets and Rabbis were great metaphysicians. What was Maimonides' attitude toward an Abaye? Did he regard him unworthy of immortality? There was certainly no difference in kind between Rabbi Akiba and any of the other Talmudic scholars.[74] And Akiba, Maimonides declared, had attained the highest degree of human perfection.[75] The Sages we learned an instant ago were the unsurpassed expositors of Scripture, the very storehouse, according to Maimonides, of metaphysics. The small verse, "In all thy ways acknowledge Him, and He will direct thy paths,"[76] upon which the Rabbis made all the essentials of the Law depend,[77] would unquestionably suggest to a Maimonides the primacy of metaphysical studies. In a well-known passage in the Guide, he argues: "It was not the object of the Prophets and our Sages . . . to close the gate of investigation entirely, and to prevent the mind from comprehending what is within its reach, as is imagined by simple and idle people, whom it suits better to put forth their ignorance and incapacity as wisdom and perfection, and to regard the distinction and wisdom of others as irreligion and imperfection, thus taking darkness for light and light for darkness. The whole object of the Prophets and the Sages was to declare that a limit is set to human reason where it must halt."[78]

Maimonides was not the only Jewish thinker who had this opinion of the ancients. Don Isaac Abravanel, for instance, remarks that of the forty days Moses spent in heaven, the first twenty he devoted to the study of the "natural sciences" and in the second twenty days he went up to heaven and attained what was possible of the Divine, namely, he studied metaphysics.[79]

Citations on this point could be multiplied endlessly. Enough has been offered to show that placing wisdom and the wise man on the top rung was not limited to Aristotle. As a matter of fact, the Rabbis went beyond Aristotle. No Greek completely emancipated himself sufficiently from the admiration of the beautiful to put anything above it. Even Aristotle maintained that no man can be happy "who is absolutely ugly."[80] The Rabbis suffered from no such inhibitions. There was nothing that they would have placed in their hearts beside study. Of course the Rabbis never would have approved the sentiment expressed by Homer and reiterated by Plato that, "one learned leech is worth the multitude,"[81] but neither would Maimonides.

XV. PHILOSOPHY AND FOLKLORE

THE RABBIS WERE NOT ALWAYS consistent. It would not be difficult to cite considerable evidence that frequently they gave preference to conduct. Surely the goal of study was practice[1] and the end of wisdom repentance and good deeds.[2] Consistency, so aptly remarked Dr. Schechter, was not one of the Rabbis' weaknesses. For our purpose, it was enough to know that from his earliest childhood, Maimonides found in Judaism sufficient stimulus to regard the thinker as the chosen man. That here, as well as elsewhere, his logical, orderly mind led him to rigid conclusions, in no way makes an Aristotelian of him. Aristotle had primarily provided Maimonides with an organon —an instrument regulative of all sciences—but his content and spirit remained Jewish.

Aristotle, as a matter of fact, predominated through the Middle Ages, despite his "heresies," only, because it was comparatively easy to abstract from him a method and to discard his philosophy.[3] From him the medievalists had learned the "five words"—genus, species, difference, property and accident; and the ten categories—substance, quantity, quality, relation, place, time, position, possession, action and passion. With these for a start they could juggle endlessly. Plato, Gibbon opines, did not fare quite as well with the Arabs because he "wrote for Athenians, and his allegorical genius is too closely blended with the language and religion of Greece."[4] A typically brilliant observation by the great historian.[5] Already, in ancient times, Plato had appeared too fond of myths.[6] In him, Professor Caird remarks, "the poet generally spoke before the philosopher."[7] On the other hand, the medieval vogue of Aristotle is unquestionably a triumph of method over matter. Averroes who accepted from him the eternity of the universe and denied immortality was a noted exception, among medieval philosophers. The Stagirite, too, was preferred because his "Form" was more congenial to men raised on the Bible than Plato's Ideas. Knowledge to the latter was wholly independent of the senses. That of course, as we have noticed, was contrary to the best tradition of scholasticism. Aristotle, on the other hand, rejected the notion that ideas existed apart from things,[8] and by means of his "entelechy" made it easier for the scholastics to speak of creation as the potential actualized.

What Maimonides then takes from Aristotle is an argot. In his philosophy he remained the Talmudic Jew, continuing in the climate of opinion in which he had grown to maturity. The peripatetic cast of thought was only incidental, a matter of temperament, a mental habit rather than a total world view. The substance of Maimonides' thought was determined in advance; the datum to which he applied his tools of logic was Biblical and Talmudic.[9] In a paragraph, that leaves little room for doubt, Maimonides gives us an insight into the working of his mind. Aristotle, he tells us, attributed the motion of the spheres to the existence of Intelligences. "Although this theory," Maimonides continues, "consists of assertions which cannot be proved, yet it is the least open to doubt, and is more systematic than any other, as has been stated by Alexander in the book called 'The Origin of the Universe.' "[10]

What makes Maimonides particularly lean towards this theory, he avers, is not the mere assertion of it by Aristotle. His confession is revealing. "It includes maxims which are identical with those taught in Scripture, and it is to a still greater extent in harmony with doctrines contained in well-known genuine Midrashim, as will be explained by me. *For this reason I will cite his views and his proofs, and collect from them what coincides with the teachings of Scripture, and agrees with the doctrine held by our Sages.*"[11]

Does not Maimonides here give us the very secrets of his

inmost thoughts and do we not see that Aristotle is only incidental, a mere logical scaffolding? Maimonides remains
in the climate of opinion in which he was nurtured. To be
sure, he was no exception in this. Philosophers in all ages,
but for a few modern thinkers, built their systems on the
vague speculations and accepted dogmas inherent in their
environment. *Fides praecedens intellectum.* Philosophy has
not unfrequently been "a reflection of temperamental presuppositions of exceptional personalities."[12] It was rationalization carefully concealed.[13] Pure reason was rarely absolute
dictator. It was swayed by emotional predispositions, by
deeply rooted beliefs, for which the philosophers seldom
made any allowances. To quote Professor Whitehead again:
"The chief danger to philosophy is narrowness in the selection of evidence. This narrowness arises from the idiosyncrasies and timidities of particular authors, of particular
social groups, of particular schools of thought, of particular
epochs in the history of civilization. The evidence relied upon
is arbitrarily biased by the temperaments of individuals, by
the provincialities of groups, and by the limitations of
schemes of thought."[14] Even the great scientists who are
considered absolutely impersonal recognize the subjective
element in their labors. Planck does not hesitate to speak of
science as a work of art, expressing a certain side of man's
nature.[15]

Quidquid recipitur secundum modum recipientis recipitur
—everything is received according to the manner of the recipient—was the scholastic dictum. Our philosophy is the
handmaid of our inclinations. If we will to believe, it will
supply us with logical support. "Almost all philosophic arguments are invented afterwards, to recommend or defend
from attack, conclusions which the philosopher was from
the outset bent upon believing, before he could think of any
arguments at all."[16] In Maimonides we find no discussion of
transubstantiation. To him it was no problem at all. The
Trinity he dismisses with one sentence.[17] To Aquinas, how-

ever, raised as a Christian, the credo *haec tria esse unum et idem* is a fortress impregnable, mocking all the assaults of logic, metaphysics, or reason. To him all the problems of faith peculiarly Christian, Transubstantiation, Incarnation, the Trinity are as vital as Unity and Incorporeality are to Maimonides, and Aquinas solves them with as much display of profound reasoning and logical acumen as Maimonides applies to *creatio ex nihilo*.

Early in the *Summa Theologica*, Saint Thomas devotes an entire treatise to the discussion of the origin, or procession and relations of the divine Persons of the Trinity.[18] Catholic philosophers and historians testify, that in Aquinas, the Trinity and Incarnation find the most complete and best attestations from Scripture. We face, then, the alternative of concluding that either *creatio ex nihilo* is no more inherent in the mind than transubstantiation, or, that transubstantiation is as inherent as *creatio ex nihilo*.[19] Many would prefer another alternative, namely, the recognition that philosophers are merely the children of their environment.

In Maimonides himself we find a remarkable awareness of this truth. In chapter twenty-three of the second part of the Guide he writes in remarkably modern terms. "If you are predisposed in favor of one of them (theories), be it on account of your training or because of some advantage, you are too blind to see the truth. For that which can be demonstrated you cannot reject, however much you may be inclined against it; but in questions like those under consideration you are apt to dispute (*in consequence of your inclination*). You will, however, be able to decide the question, as far as necessary, if you free yourself from passions, ignore customs, and follow only your reason." So far so good. But hearken again. "I mention this lest you be deceived; for a person might some day, by some objection which he raises, shake your belief in the theory of Creation, and then easily mislead you; you would then adopt the theory (of the Eternity of the Universe) which is contrary to the fundamental principles of our religion, and leads to 'speaking words that turn away from God.' *You must rather have suspicion against your own reason, and accept the theory taught by two prophets (Abraham and Moses) who have laid the foundation for the existing order in the religious and social relations of mankind.*"[20]

What is even more interesting is the manner in which Maimonides recognized that both he and Aristotle are mentally the children of their predecessors. "You will not find it strange," he remarks, "that I introduce into this discussion historical matter in support of the theory of Creation, seeing that Aristotle, the greatest philosopher, in his principal works, introduces histories in support of the theory of the Eternity of the Universe. In this regard we may justly quote the saying: 'Should not our perfect Law be as good as their gossip?'[21] When he supports his view by quoting Sabean stories,[22] why should we not support our view by that which Moses and Abraham said, and that which follows from their words?"

How far Aristotle was influenced by these "Sabean" stories we learn fortunately from himself. "A tradition," he says, "has been handed down by the ancient thinkers of very early times, and bequeathed to posterity in the form of a myth, to the effect that these heavenly bodies are gods, and that the Divine pervades the whole of nature. The rest of their tradition has been added later in a mythological form to influence the vulgar and as a constitutional and utilitarian expedient: they say that these gods are human in shape or are like certain other animals, and make other statements consequent upon and similar to those which we have mentioned. Now if we separate these and accept only the first, that they supposed *the primary substances to be gods, we must regard it as an inspired saying;* and reflect that whereas every art and philosophy has probably been repeatedly developed to the utmost and has perished again, *these beliefs of theirs have been preserved as a relic of former knowledge.* To this extent only, then, are the views of our forefathers and of the earliest thinkers intelligible to us."[23] The great Catholic philosopher makes a similar admission: "Custom, and especially custom to which we have been born, acquires the force of nature; whence it happens that tenets with which the mind has been imbued from childhood are as firmly held as if they were self-evident by nature."[24]

Indeed, the gap between the Homer-Hesiod tradition and Aristotelian philosophy is not as wide as it is generally imagined to be. "Aristotle everywhere attaches himself to tradition, to popular opinion, to the conceptions contained in language.[25] His system is to some extent a rationale for the Greek myth, even as Homer's epic is a humanization of the Greek or Cretan folktale. The *materia prima* and the Eternity of the Universe were not, as the medievalists believed, concepts emanating from Aristotle's pure reason, but were rather imbedded in the mythology of the Greeks. Professor Nilsson in his History of the Greek Religion, calls attention to the fact that in Homer, Oceanos is given as the origin of the gods, thus foreshadowing Thales' primeval water and Aristotle's eternal matter.[26] In Diodorus Siculus, Oceanus is still credited as being the source of the gods.[27]

In the Greek myth, creation is not attributed to the gods, or to a Maker. The gods are younger than the world. The Greeks, Professor Murray tells us, never claimed that their gods created the world.[28] It is assumed to have proceeded automatically, or by necessity, a view which survives in Aristotle.[29] The gods are only "departmental powers" and had no share in designing, or willing the Universe into being. The fundamental distinction between matter and force, or matter and form, idea, concept, was already dimly perceived by Hesiod.[30] Aristotle's denial of design in the Universe can be traced back to the mythological *Moira, Tychei,* and the incurable fatalism of the Greeks. So many things in the old tales had happened *hyper theon,* contrary to the will of the gods. "Even the gods," said Plato, "do not fight against necessity."[31] Certainly the Intelligences as we have seen were not put into the cosmic spheres by Aristotelian logic or metaphysics. It cost Anaxagoras his freedom to declare that the sun was a lifeless, glowing mass.[32] Xenocrates, a more cautious philosopher, spoke of the heavenly bodies as the eight gods of Olympus, an opinion which was not unknown to Maimonides.[33] It is evident, that here, Aristotle's Intelligences and Maimonides' angels found their origin.[34]

Professor Nilsson says: "We have only to strip off the mythological disguise to have natural philosophy, and indeed natural philosophy for a long time called its principles by mythological names."[35] It was not uncommon for the philosophers to equate Reason, for example, with Zeus.[36] Aristotle, then, no less than Maimonides, was remolding the imaginative accounts of the universe of his people into rational discourse.[37] Even like Maimonides, he frequently reminds us that "there are things concerning which we are unable to reason, or which we find too high for us."[38] "Philosophy," Professor Dewey laconically remarks, "inherited the realm with which religion had been concerned."[39]

XVI. THINKING IN A CIRCLE

WE HAVE MADE CLEAR, WE HOPE, in the preceding chapters that Maimonides' philosophizing in no way divorced him from the Jewish view of the Universe. At the close of the last chapter we noticed, interestingly enough, that the Stagirite had not altogether escaped the traditional Greek view of things. In other words, Aristotle's philosophy owed as much to Greek mythology as Maimonides' did to the prophetico-rabbinic tradition. Neither man escaped the imprints of his childhood training, reflection and experience. Each built his system on the beliefs current among his people for centuries. Hellenic philosophy, no less than medieval scholasticism or the more recent absolute idealism, reared its structure on the foundations of inherited myth and folklore. For the legends long rehearsed on the farm, or at the fireplace, a new vocabulary was devised. The grandiose terminology, however, did not always successfully hide the lowly primitive origin of its contents. Let this be writ large over the portals of every attempt made to expose the "tenderness" of organic world views, of systems such as the prophetico-rabbinic is. The "toughness" of metaphysicians and logicians has rendered them no more immune to daydreaming and wishfulness. There is a poetic core in the most abstruse thinker. Like the poet, he gathers up in the folds of his imagination the tale, the humble adage or aphorism to clothe it with the sublimity of thought and the elegance of expression. Memory and fancy are primary, reason a willing acolyte. The intellectualizing of the philosopher and even the scientist is "largely guided and sustained by their delight in the sheer beauty of the rhythmic relation between law and instance, species and individual, cause and effect."[1] In other words, it is largely a matter of temperament, and temperament is wayward. It will consort with *Nous* as readily as with *Pathé*.

The Peripatetic, Platonic, neo-Platonic or Scholastic systems of thought are no more free from folklore than is the "naïve" prophetico-rabbinic view of the Universe. Basically, one is no more logical or "pure" reason than the others. All of them, in so far as they deal with matters that are beyond sense experience, are out of their depths. Sooner or later they catch for a straw. Once the problems become ontological, cosmological or cosmogonic the solutions are in the end *à priori*, all circumlocution notwithstanding. A skillful logician, an experienced abstractionist will of course display a finer array of prepositions and demonstrations. However, a little probing beneath the surface will reveal, that concerning the substance or stuff, the constitution, and origin of the Universe, he is only guessing. He is projecting reason beyond sense experience, and the result is intellectual vertigo from which he sobers down by leaning on the age-old "immutable" truths.

The ablest of all these thinkers was Aristotle. Yet his treatise *tā metā tā physika* was really a theology—a name which Aristotle himself often applied to his metaphysics.[2] It was the speculative science *par excellence*[3]; a study in the science of absolute being or *nóēsis noēseōs*, thought of thought.[4] "If," says Aristotle, "there is not some other substance besides those which are naturally composed, physics will be the primary science; but if there is a substance which is immutable, the science which studies this will be prior to physics, and will be primary philosophy, and universal in this sense that it will be primary. And it will be the province of this science to study Being *qua* Being; what it is, and what the attributes are which belong to it *qua* being."[5] Therefore Aristotle's metaphysics was really little else than the study of God and His attributes, the science of being "eternal and immutable and separable from matter"[6]; of Being *qua* Being, what it is and the attributes are which belong to it, *qua* Being."[7] With Bacon the same distinction prevailed. "Physic," he says, "should contemplate that which is inherent in matter, and therefore transitory; and metaphysic that which is abstracted and fixed." And again "that physic should handle that which supposeth in nature only a being and moving; and metaphysic should handle that which supposeth further in nature a reason, understanding and platform."[8] "Metaphysics," still insists a modern French thinker, "is essentially super-rational, and that it must be so or not be it at all."[9]

Aristotle's metaphysics was so deftly manipulated that for centuries it passed for Pure Reason. It was recognized as *Prote philosophìa*, the *perì àpchàs epistéme*.[10] In the end it is but a theology. His physics never ceased to be anthropomorphic. The logical premises upon which Aristotle rests his world is nothing more than the vague beliefs, tales and speculations of many predecessors, only more finely spun, more delicately abstracted. It is one of those successful major operations which leaves the patient, Pure Reason, breathing but lifeless. Aristotle's *Noumena*, contends Professor Lange, are "cobwebs of the brain" and his "pure reason" is fabulous.[11] His philosophy became the inexhaustible source of self-delusion.[12] "It is the standing type of perverted method, the great example of all that is to be avoided, in its mingling and confusion of speculation and inquiry, and in its pretension not merely to comprehend but to dominate positive knowledge."[13]

Plato's Idealism is never really rejected by Aristotle. The distinguished disciple was simply twisting the master's theories out of their beautiful artistic settings. If it is true that Plato was never able to bring his ideal and the particular together, it is equally true that Aristotle never escaped the difficulty. He discovered a kind of verbal relation between the idea and the phenomenon, conception and perception, but how the form becomes particularized he nowhere explains. The adaptation of body to soul and the organization of body are as much of a mystery to him as to most of us. When hard pressed to account for the differentiation of species, he offers us the assurance that nature works to a purpose and does "nothing at random." On what scientific grounds Aristotle makes that commitment in behalf of Nature is not quite clear, unless we bear in mind some tales from Homer and Hesiod.

Aristotle even as Plato, and all the scholastics as well, makes the immutable, the perfect—endowed with higher value than that which varies. This assumption though purely arbitrary persists nevertheless as the rockbed of their thought. With some slight manipulations it becomes the very "physis" of most philosophic systems, the matrix of concepts, ideas, form, Prime Movers and First Causes. That change and imperfection are synonymous is stated with the conviction of mathematical certainty. And where does change most prevail? Of course where man's opportunities for observation are best. Here on earth where the flower fadeth and the grass withereth, alteration is incessant. This sublunar region is the very cesspool of corruption. We might as well abandon any attempt to learn anything about this region. "For there can be no knowledge of things in flux."[14] We dare not even hope for as much as a general definition of sensible things.[15] Were there nothing in the Universe that is eternal, separate and permanent there could be no order in it.[16] Fortunately, "it is only the realm of sense around us which continues subject to destruction and generation, but this is a practically negligible part of the whole."[17] It would be absurd to waste our time forming our opinion of the truth from the appearances of this quicksilver environment. It is to heaven, to the starry skies above, that we must direct our gaze, and, with reference to them, prosecute our search for the truth. "For these do not appear to be now of one nature and subsequently of another, but are manifestly always the same and have no part in change of any kind."[18] If by some miracle Aristotle's parents had, while he was yet a child, moved for a number of years to Mars the good old earth might have attained to some reputation with the philosopher. As it is he was only repeating with more semblance of logic, of course, the calumnies Greeks had been believing for centuries.

Aristotle's Prime Mover cannot claim to be the favorite first-born son of Logic. It is only Plato's Idea of the Good re-incarnated. Aristotle describes his *deus ex machina* in the very words that Plato had described his. Both are eternal, unchangeable, immovable, wholly independent, incorporeal, etc. Why this unmoved mover particularly appealed to logicians, it is hard to tell. The difference between it and the first verse of Genesis, "In the Beginning God created Heaven and Earth," is not very obvious. At any rate, David Hume and Immanuel Kant, no mean logicians themselves, did not find the *protôn kinoûn akinēton* too impressive.[19] It is inherent in man, metaphysicians postulated, to regard every effect as the result of a cause. He is driven by curiosity to a prolonged series of causes, until he comes to the *causa prima*, and then suddenly his thirst is slaked and the search abandoned. Since motion is not self-imparted, there must be always a mover preceding, until we perforce come to one unmoved, then we are pleased, and the First Cause, unmoved, in transcendental solitariness reigns supreme.[20]

The difficulty with this so-called cosmological proof is simply that it is not logic but a pious wish. It bases itself on the psychological necessity of finding a cause, and then contradicts itself by saying that an infinite series of causes is impossible. Aristotle's argument, that "without a first cause there would be no other cause," can be parried with, "since every cause is an effect there would be no first effect without a preceding cause." "You ask me," ridicules Hume, "what is the cause of this cause? I know not, I care not; that concerns not me. I have found a Deity; and here I stop my inquiry."[21] To shove off the difficulty for a moment does not satisfy Hume. For in the next moment he is stung by implacable curiosity to know the cause of the First Cause. Kant rejected the First Cause as "a false self-satisfaction of the human reason."[22]

A distinguished modern biologist suggests that the "argument from contrivance to contriver gets one nowhere, it leaves the origin of things just where it was."[23] Professor Planck not only devastates Aristotle but Kant as well. "The simple fact," he writes, "that there exists a whole literature whose scenes are laid in wonderland is proof that the concept of strict causality is not an inherent necessity of human thought."[24] It is the causal laws grounded in experience and observation that give us the right to infer a cause, but when we seek to transfer the causal series beyond observation it ceases to be operative. At any rate, whatever the philosophers may or may not regard as inherent in the human mind, Aristotle's Prime Mover is an arbitrary assumption. The causes that logic and science can discover are only derivative. A final cause to account for the origin of the totality of the world lies outside their ken. No wonder the cautious theist today strongly hesitates to lean on cosmology or on ontology.

The unmoved movent was not the only *à priori* assumption of Aristotle. There still had to be called into existence a something which always moves that which is moved, since the Prime Mover itself was tied hand and foot.[25] In other words the Prime Mover had a hard time getting down and starting operations in the sublunar world. Aristotle out of the generosity of his Logic provides him with a number of unmoved movents,[26] either for the purpose of corrupting man's habitation, or to keep the First Cause from loneliness. For some inexplicable reason the whole material universe is charmed by this Prime Mover and his companions, and to display its *affaire de coeur* starts on a circular jig. Why *phora kuklophoria* are particularly acceptable to the movents was incomprehensible even to one so expert in the matter of dynamics as Galileo.[27] As a matter of fact, he denied that circular locomotion was the characteristic amatory technique of the spheres.[28] Hume could not understand why the sub-

lunar world needed a charmer to start it off. Why wasn't it,
he asked, just as easy to assume the beginning of motion in
matter itself as its communication from mind and intelligence?[29]

The medieval thinkers were disturbed that their master,
Aristotle, had neglected to record the Prime Mover's birth-
day. According to Aristotle the First Cause did not become
active at any particular time. Logically he decided there can
be no first moment in time, since every particular moment
of time must lie between two others. Medievalists were
therefore constrained to admit that "that the world had a
beginning, was an article of faith."[30] But how far is this
question of time removed from a causal series. If you posit
a First Cause, why not a first moment or creation in time?
Kant to be consistent showed that he could both prove and
disprove that the world had a beginning in time. The medievalists were especially troubled, that they could find no logical reason, why the world was created at the particular moment that it was, and not before. The difficulties raised and
the solutions proffered need not concern us here. It was
nothing less than an attempt to read the mind of the Creator,
a stupendous undertaking. But logicians and metaphysicians
were not lacking in temerity. Their suggestions are scintillat-
ing, brilliant, but in the final analysis, subjective. They have
no more claim to pure reason than the arguments advanced
by two famous Rabbis. On the verse in Koheleth, "He hath
made everything beautiful in its time,"[31] Rabbi Tanhuma
comments as follows: The world was created in its time,
before that it was not worthy of creation. To which Rabbi
Abuha adds: "The Holy One Blessed Be He was creating
universes and destroying them, until He created the present
world. Then, He said, 'this pleases (Me), the others
didn't.' "[32]

The groundwork of Aristotle's metaphysics is evidently no
less *à priori* than rabbinic speculation. To accept his conclusions logic alone will not do. One must exercise the will

to believe. To give the spheres particular intelligences, to assume a distinction between sublunar and celestial stuff; to posit that God is mind, that mind is selfishly preoccupied with itself, that the other unmoved movents are the thoughts of the prime unmoved movent, or that the world should have only one movent which even Aristotle can establish only by analogy[33]—all this we say may be very noble and pious, but it has no more claim to finality than the God of Abraham, Revelation, Angels, the Messiah to come, Design or Purpose. Why such a great mover should have no purpose at all, but only to obey some logical caprice of an Aristotle is incomprehensible. Plato was much more consistent when he boldly spoke for his God: "Let me tell you why the Creator made a world of generation. God is good; and the good can never have any envy or jealousy. Being thus far removed from any such feeling, He desired that all things should be as like Himself as it was possible for them to be. This is the sovereign cause of the existence of the world of change, which we shall do well to believe on the testimony of wise men. God desired that everything should be good and nothing evil, so far as this was attainable. Wherefore, finding the visible world not in a state of rest but moving in an irregular and disorderly fashion, out of disorder He brought order, thinking that in every way this was better than the other."[34]

As far as religion is concerned the net result of all this hard speculation of the centuries was almost useless even to men like Schleiermacher and Kant. Both of them, after extraordinary mental exertion, came to positions not wholly removed from that of the Rabbis. The former in his famous Lectures on Religion makes our knowledge of God intuitive and immediate. We do not, according to Schleiermacher, reach God climbing on the ladder of dialectics, but are instantly aware in the depths of our consciousness, of our absolute dependence upon Him. We know God not because we think Him, but because we are innerly drawn to Him as steel is to the magnet. We cannot help ourselves.[35] Kant, on the other hand, dismisses the attempt to formulate a religious philosophy on the basis of Reason as completely beyond our water. Man is denied, by the very limitations of his faculties, such luxury. The matrix then of religion becomes for Kant the moral conscience of man.[36] In his incomparable discussion of the nature of religion, Hume poignantly states: "I shall venture to add an observation, that the argument *à priori* has seldom been found very convincing, except to people of a metaphysical head, who have accustomed themselves to abstract reasoning. . . . Other people, even of good sense and the best inclined to religion, feel always some deficiency in such arguments, though they are not perhaps able to explain distinctly where it lies. A certain proof that men ever did and ever will derive their religion from other sources than from this species of reasoning."[37]

Neither philosophy nor science has been able to do more with Beginnings and Ends than has common sense or intuition. Galileo, Bacon and Descartes dismissed final causes as unscientific. Philosophic investigations insofar as they have concerned themselves with origins have been moving in a circle. According to Newton, the planets move from west to east because such is the inscrutable will of God. The pious Englishman was too meek to search His mind. But the more astute Leibnitz and the rebellious Voltaire thought it preposterous not to find sufficient reasons for God's actions. Locke argued it was godless to maintain that God could not create thinking matter. Voltaire found the thinking in the matter. Leibnitz thought ideas were innate and the universal a hereditary privilege. Locke found the new-born brain a perfect vacuum. Thus, systems come and systems go, the problems remain the same, only solutions multiply.

"What are the main results reached by the philosophers?" asks Professor Sheldon. "A superficial inspection reveals a goodly number of them, many displaying remarkable acumen, many dull and barbarously expressed, many profoundly interesting. But what is our amazement when, looking a bit deeper, we find that each system denies the fundamental principles of the rest! . . . Let any professional philosopher be asked to name *one* doctrine that is by his compeers generally accepted, if he is disingenuous enough to name one, it will be found that others name a different one."[38]

After a lapse of centuries it still holds good among philosophers, *si Thomas aliquid affirmat, nittitur eius argumenta infirmare Scotus*—if ever Thomas affirms anything, Scotus tries hard to disaffirm it. Unfortunately what was in the middle ages and in antiquity only true of metaphysics has of late become equally applicable to science. "There is scarcely an axiom," complains Professor Planck, "that is not nowadays denied by somebody." Even within the province of physics itself "the spirit of confusion and contradiction has begun to be active."[39]

Even the tyro cannot be unacquainted that Neoscholasticism, the New Realism and the New Physics have reopened all the old problems. We are again floundering in the midst of speculative uncertainty. So much so that Professor Dewey, too, comes near siding with the Rabbis. At any rate he is unwilling to base human happiness and associative living on the "quest for certainty." Perhaps then the rabbinic view is not quite so naive, and Aristotelian metaphysics not altogether rational.

XVII. The Quest for Freedom

It is not only in the realm of metaphysics that our thinking has been circular. In matters ethical or psychological we have been no more fortunate. The Jewish view of the Universe, being organic and intuitive, fails to harmonize its contradictions here as well as elsewhere. How about the speculative logical approach? Does it offer anything more permanent and convincing? In an earlier chapter we showed the great difficulties the Rabbis had with the human will. Its freedom was postulated as axiomatic. With justice as the groundwork of all Jewish thinking, a passionate demand for freedom was inevitable. But often the will to believe oneself free faltered. The dice against a human being are so heavily loaded, that for him ever to win seemed to require a miracle. The Rabbis, of course, believed in miracles and held on to human freedom. Have the philosophers anything more positive to offer? We know that we are free, Kant said, although we do not know how it can be so. Under the influence of materialism in the past century, this subject was for a short while dismissed, like so many others in those halcyon days, as strictly theologic and not worth any bother. Has the twentieth century remained equally dogmatic and adamant? Or does here, too, our thinking continue circular?

Only recently one of the world's foremost scientists felt called upon to make the discussion of free will the central thesis of a book.[1] Only, it is to be regretted that Professor Planck really does not get very far. "Our own consciousness tells us," he says, "that our wills are free.[2] . . . The profound depths of thought cannot be penetrated by the ordinary intellect. And when we say that spiritual happenings are determined, the statement eludes the possibility of

proof."[3] Allowing for the lapse of centuries and for con-
comitant changes in the linguistic idiom, such an opinion
could well be ascribed to an Isaiah or an Akiba.

Professor Planck, it is understood, even like a Maimonides
will not be satisfied with vague expressions. As an exact
scientist he is seeking a formulation that will not be self-
contradictory. "How can the independence of human volition," he asks, "be harmonized with the fact that we are
integral parts of a universe which is subject to the rigid
order of nature's laws?"[4] The distinguished scientist takes
a long time answering the question. He first labors hard to
deny that the new physics has shown any tendency to question causation. "Of course it may be said that the law of
causality is only, after all, an hypothesis like most of the
others, but it is a fundamental hypothesis because it is the
postulate which is necessary to give sense and meaning to
the application of all hypotheses in scientific research."[5]
The validity of this law is as yet unshakable. Of course,
this is beyond demonstration. We are still in the days of
Kant or for that matter of Maimonides, and causation is a
category of the mind, independent of experience, therefore,
naturally beyond proof, but valid nevertheless.

Professor Planck holds his ground with all the vigor of
his long scientific training. To negate causation, he pleads,
is to make science impossible. We analyze, search and syn-
thesize only on the assumption of causal interrelations. This
postulate of complete determinism applies to psychological
research as well as to biological. How then about human
conduct? Are man's action determined by causes, influenced
by motives in accordance with this inflexible determinism?
Read what Professor Planck has to say: "The fact is that
there is a point, one single point in the immeasurable world
of mind and matter, where science and therefore every
causal method of research is inapplicable, not only on practical grounds but also on logical grounds, and will always
remain inapplicable. This point is the individual ego. It is a

small point in the universal realm of being; but in itself it is a whole world, embracing our emotional life, our will and our thought. This realm of the ego is at once the source of our deepest suffering and at the same time of our highest happiness. Over this realm no outer power of fate can ever have sway, and we lay aside our own control and responsibility over ourselves only with the laying aside of life itself."[6] How far have we advanced beyond the Talmud?

Of course, Professor Planck does not solve what is an apparent contradiction, with the citation of a verse from Scripture. He makes a more heroic effort. Theoretically, he argues, there is no reason why we should not discover the causal series leading to our conduct. Practically, we confront the difficulty of having the observer and the thing observed in one. If we could get out of ourselves, if we were vouchsafed a kind of prolonged shadow, composed wholly of mind, that mind looking at us would clearly discern the casual law operating in our conduct. "If," continues Professor Planck, "there be a Supreme Wisdom whose celestial nature is infinitely elevated above ours, and who can see every convolution in our brains and hear every pulse beat of each human heart, as a matter of course such a Supreme Wisdom sees the succession of cause and effect in everything we do."[7]

After all his labors, then, the father of the Quantum Theory returns to Aristotle or to the Middle Ages. It is not difficult to point out that Professor Planck is rapidly approaching a logical absurdity. Our Freedom, according to him, is due to our ignorance. Our future conduct is to us undetermined, because we cannot see all the preceding interrelations in our past. If, however, we were so fortunate as to have that knowledge, our actions to us would be determined. Our blissful freedom then is due to our abysmal ignorance. Professor Planck would also have his difficulties with his Supreme Wisdom. He says nothing about *its* freedom. How could that Wisdom, without a lengthened shadow of mind, know itself, and if it couldn't how would it be free. Or would Professor Planck suggest that its knowledge is *sui generis*? What progress have we made?

Professor Planck's book closes with a Socratic dialogue in which the cautious Einstein makes his appearance. The suggestion, that physical science is disturbing the law of causation, he impatiently dismisses not merely as nonsense but as "objectionable nonsense."[8] "Indeterminism is an illogical concept."[9] In this he agrees heartily with Planck. To the suggestion from Mr. Murphy, the translator of the book and interlocutor in the dialogue, that certain distinguished English scientists have nevertheless drawn such conclusions from the Heisenberg principle of indeterminacy, the ready retort is: "You must distinguish between the physicist and the *litterateur* when both professions are combined into one. In England you have a great English literature and a great discipline of style. What I mean is that there are scientific writers in England who are illogical and romantic in their popular books, but in their scientific work they are acute logical reasoners."[10]

Einstein, however, is evidently not at one with Planck in his discussion of the freedom of the will. "Honestly," he says, he cannot understand what people mean by it. Neither does Mr. Russell. He dismisses the "will" either as observable phenomenon or as metaphysical superstition.[11] The two best known schools of modern psychology—Behaviorism and Psychoanalysis, as we have seen,[12] make human actions determined either by external stimuli, or, by fortuitous upthrusts from the unconscious. Under the circumstances man's actions are, of course, not free. Pavlov's experiments on the conditioned reflexes have certainly not made the problem any simpler.[13] Professor Eddington on the other hand affirms: "Our purposes, our volitions, are genuine; and ours is the responsibility for what ensues from them. It seems necessary to admit this, for we are scarcely likely to accept *a theory which would make the human spirit more mechanis-*

tic than the physical universe."[14] In this universe, contrary to Professor Einstein and Planck, Schroedinger has discovered some capricious atoms characterized by a spontaneity most enviable. It leads Professor Schroedinger to conclude: "Fortuitousness is the primary state for which there is no plausible explanation, whilst lawfulness only appears in the microscopic world owing to the cooperation of numerous accidental operating molecules."[15] The determinists, then, and the freewillists are still at loggerheads.

Maimonides differs but little in the discussion of the problem, or at any rate in his conclusions from Professors Planck and Eddington, or for that matter from Spinoza who, in his own behalf, executed, with unmatched dexterity, a number of somersaults to save freedom. In the Code Maimonides writes: "Allow not to cross your mind the statement of Gentile fools and many Jewish blockheads, viz., that the Holy One Blessed Be He decrees at a man's creation whether he is to be a *zadik* or a *rasha*. That is not so. Each man is fit to become as righteous as Moses our Teacher or as wicked as Jeroboam. . . . This is a fundamental principle and the pillar of the Law. . . . If man were determined by the decree of God . . . how could God then command him through the Prophets—do this and do not do this? . . . By what law would the wicked be punished and the righteous rewarded?"[16] So far so good, but Maimonides, not unlike Professor Planck or for that matter the Rabbis, is troubled by a logical difficulty. How about the foreknowledge of God? Does not that predestine a man to act in accordance with God's knowledge? Where then is his freedom? How much paper, time and effort were not consumed in the discussion of this problem, the numerous solutions offered being equally wanting.

Maimonides more boldly than Professor Planck advances the familiar view, viz., that the knowledge of God is unique, which, of course, answers all questions since that knowledge is beyond man.[17] "We know without doubt that man is mas-

ter of his own conduct and that God neither prompts him
nor decrees that he is to act in a certain way. We know this
not only on the basis of our religious tradition but with
convincing philosophic proof,"[18] into which Maimonides
does not enter because of the uniqueness of God's knowledge. All this makes Maimonides' severe critic, Rabbi Abraham ben David, charge him with conduct unbecoming the
wise. Why, asks he, begin that which you cannot finish?
Why all this philosophical circumlocution only to return to
faith?[19]

Ben David could have been even more critical of Maimonides. Maimonides we may recall had consigned the majority of mankind to ignominious slavery because "many
men are naturally so constituted that all perfection is impossible; e.g., he whose heart is very warm and is himself
very powerful is sure to be passionate, though he tries to
counteract that disposition by training; he whose testicles
are warm, humid and vigorous, and the organs connected
therewith are surcharged, will not easily refrain from sin,
even if he makes great efforts to restrain himself. You also
find persons of great levity and rashness, whose excited man-
ners and wild gestures prove that their constitution is in disorder, and their temperament so bad that it cannot be cured.
Such persons can never attain to perfection; it is utterly
useless to occupy oneself with them on such a subject (as
Metaphysics)."[20] If so where then does every man have the
opportunity to become like unto Moses? If their "natural
constitution" militates against them, is not their will hampered by external causes?

Unlike the writers of the Declaration of Independence,
Maimonides finds human beings are not equal. "He (man)
is, as you know, the highest form in the creation, and he
therefore includes the largest number of constituent elements;
this is the reason why the human race contains such a great
variety of individuals, that we cannot discover two persons
exactly alike in any moral quality, or in external appearance.

The cause of this is the variety in man's temperament, and in accidents dependent on his form; for with every physical form there are connected certain special accidents different from those which are connected with the substance. Such a variety among the individuals of a class does not exist in any other class of living beings; for the variety in any other species is limited; only man forms an exception; two persons may be so different from each other in every respect that they appear to belong to two different classes. Whilst one person is so cruel that he kills his youngest child in his anger, another is too delicate and faint-hearted to kill even a fly or worm. The same is the case with most of the accidents. This great variety and the necessity of social life are essential elements in man's nature."[21] Did not Maimonides fully realize what the effects of such natural differences would have on the conduct of the individual? Did he not realize how the will would be urged or impeded by wealth, poverty, deformity, or handsomeness? Was he not a good enough sociologist to understand how far environment influences behavior? Did he not urge man to run away into the desert, forsake wife and children to escape contamination?[22] Isn't there evidence scores of times in his writing that "wisdom is not acquired . . . but implanted by nature?"[23] Did he not so frequently imply that "You can no more order anyone to be wise than to live or exist"?[24] Alas, even the Holy One Blessed Be He bestows wisdom only on him who already has it.[25] Ben David could have asked Maimonides if the purpose of the *Mizvot* is to prepare man for the ultimate contemplation of the divine presence,[26] and if that comprehension ultimately comes only to one in millions, then why bother about the commandments? Of what good is freedom of the will to the horde of humanity circumscribed and limited?

But whether contradictions can be pointed out in the logical armor of Maimonides is not as important, at the moment, as the fact that in his conclusions he adopts the general

prophetico-rabbinic view. It is true that Maimonides attempts
to explain why man's will is necessarily free. . . . "It was
clear," he tells us, "that this was the case—it was impossible, according to the wisdom of God, that substance should
exist without form, or any of the forms of the bodies without substance, and it was necessary that the very noble form
of man, which is the image and likeness of God, as has been
shown by us, should be joined to the substance of dust and
darkness, the source of all defect and loss. For these reasons
the Creator gave to the form of man power, rule, and do-
minion over the substance; the form can subdue the substance, refuse the fulfillment of its desires, and reduce them,
as far as possible, to a just and proper measure."[27]

Such an explanation the Rabbis would have readily accepted. The idea that the soul redeems the body was not
foreign to them. But how far does it get Maimonides in the
exposition of man's freedom? He fares no better than Professor Planck. Whether we view the problem theologically as
a conflict between God's omniscience and man's responsibility; or, metaphysically on the basis of predetermination
emanating from a First Cause; or scientifically as a question
of the universal validity of the law of causation we are, in
either case, no nearer a solution.

The problem has received numerous new formulations,
profound, stimulating to be sure, but not conclusive. In the
mass of modern literature the contradictions are as apparent
as in the Bible and Talmud. There wells up from the human
consciousness the feeling that "a deliberate appetition of
something is within our power," thus making goodness and
badness too within our power.[28] *Ha-Reshut Netunah,* conscience urges, but suddenly we are aware that man is a fragile
potsherd, a passing shadow. What strength can there be in
him?

XVIII. Conclusion

The millennia of stupendous efforts, in the direction of metaphysics, have not brought either enlightenment or salvation. Like the motion of Aristotle's sphere our reasoning has been circular. We always meet ourselves, as it were, coming back. After eras of Logic and Epistemology, the New Realists bring us the very distressing information that the crucial problem in philosophy today is the problem of Knowing. Forsooth, New Realism claims nothing more for itself than that it is "primarily a doctrine concerning the relation between the knowing process and the thing known."[1] Professor Perry is so heartless as to bring us the sad tidings that substance is no longer as it once was, something dark, rigid, inert and passive stuff, or "that which is extended in space and persistent in time," but rather that it is nothing more than a name, an identification label,[2] a way of cataloguing a thing and knowing it, at least, by name only.

The fundamental problems of Reality remain locked with seven locks.[3] The solving of any one problem reveals only a more baffling mystery in the solution. Were we to depend on absolute knowledge our lot would be unenviable. The truth is man cannot live by reason alone, even though he cannot get very far without it. He evidently needs must limp on both intuition and reason. The universe for him must be envisaged qualitatively as well as quantitatively. Too frequently the claims of reason have been altogether pretentious. Attacks on the intuitivist were coupled with the warning that the revolt against reason spells the breakdown of civilization. Yet Reason has not infrequently wrought its own ruin. For one thing it has been the fashion in Europe to limit Reason to the consideration of half a dozen problems in epistemology and metaphysics.

In the Middle Ages, we have seen, theologians and philosophers claimed that the Bible was the storehouse of esoteric truths. "If," says Spinoza, "one inquires what these mysteries lurking in Scripture may be, one is confronted with nothing but the reflections of Plato or Aristotle, or the like. . . ."[4] Is it unkind to level the same criticism against the devotees of Reason? Aren't they, on the whole, stating and restating the ancient differences between Plato and Aristotle? Did not, for example, Spinoza himself convert the scholastic distinction between material and immaterial, which in Aristotle was distinguished as the subject matter of physics and metaphysics respectively, into a distinction in his own philosophic system between the finite and infinite?[5] "But," said old Thomas Moore, "the change of the word does not alter the matter."[6]

Aside from the limitation of scope, has not reason so frequently been a willing accomplice to blind passion? Has German pure Reason really been such a great boon to mankind? Has the fact, that in Germany the "apothecary cannot make a prescription without being conscious of the relation of his activity to the constitution of the universe,"[7] either influenced the conduct of the apothecary, or made a wiser man of him? Did Treitschke and Bernhardi find it difficult to bend the categorical imperative, the *Ding an sich* and the whole of the Absolute Idea, to the imperialist ambitions of the Hohenzollerns? What did a Bismarck do with Kant's abstract law of reason but substitute the German state for it, and demand loyalty to it?[8] How far was Hegel himself removed from a police conception of government? Were not Hegel and his followers responsible for the notorious cleavage throughout the nineteenth century between science and philosophy? Did not the apostle of Reason vehemently and acrimoniously attack Sir Isaac Newton and all the scientists because the distinguished scientific men regarded his Philosophy of Identity as "crazy."[9] In our day and age have not winners of the Nobel Prize for physics attacked Albert Einstein with equal vehemence but deeper hatred? Have the scientific training and achievement of Prof. Philipp Lenard, discoverer of "Lenard's rays," and of Prof. Johannes Stark, discoverer of "the Stark effect" prevented them from dismissing the Theory of Relativity as "characteristically Jewish"? Did not these distinguished men join hands with some obscure Willi Menzel and declare that physics is "conditioned by race and blood"?[10] How easily is abstractionist thinking perverted and abused when removed from all social, qualitative context. How frequently does mere rationalism lose itself in the sands of superficiality without freeing itself from untenable dogma?[11]

It is true that intuition, too, goes mad. The evidence is writ large in all the histories of magic, astrology and the numerous mystic cults. Human beings are easily swayed by the irrational and intrigued by the uncanny. Men ever prefer the marvelous to the simple.[12] Kant notwithstanding, there is little, that seems to be as deeply ingrained in the mind of man, as the desire to see a break in the causal series, and to celebrate the birth of some kind of an effect generated without a cause. Methinks it was much easier for Athenians to acquiesce in Aristotle's First Cause, the uncaused one, than in his long series of causes and effects. It is here that reason renders its greatest service to mankind. When it projects itself beyond *ta physika* it does not discover new truths but detects old errors. It checks the idle vagaries of intuition; puts its myriads of notions to the test and rejects the abnormal and fantastic. It detects and at times routs the stupidities and superstitions buoying up from the subconscious depths of our being.

Without the aid of reason human advance is as conceivable as the progress of a helmless ship on the high seas. True the vessel does not stand still, it is perpetually moving, but getting nowhere. Even so without reason man flounders in the rapids of delusion and hallucination. But the helm is not the ship and, steering the wheel, is not sailing. Even so abstract speculation, divorced from the whole qualitative content of man's experience, is not thinking. It is an idler's luxury if it is not related to life. Its influence need not be immediate. Reason may, if it can, think in terms of centuries, it may envisage conclusions which will require millennia to implement, but life, the individual, society must be its ultimate aim. Such an aim will direct the philosopher's attention to empirical evidence without which all his vexation is vain. Wise men therefore will for the present or perhaps for all time not divorce Reason from intuition even if they should occasionally have to risk contradiction. They will perhaps with a slight loss of logic attempt to serve their fellowmen by blending the two, in an effort to obtain a world view comprehensive and qualitative, but free from aberration, and secure against a maudlin romanticism with its wayward offsprings, naziism and fascism.

Such, we think, was the effort of Maimonides. In this wise he was the unbending rationalist; the sworn, almost natural enemy of benighted obscurantism and vulgar superstition. He engaged the weight of his mighty intellect and wide erudition against the many-headed monster of human folly. He slashed at it dexterously and mercilessly. He breathed but scorn for the foibles and extravagances of the imagination. *Stultea delenda est* was a deeply rooted conviction with him. It was more. It was to him an inescapable obligation. For his insight into the working of the mind was keen and of its numerous pitfalls he was forever aware.

His attitude to astrological beliefs and practices is most revealing. Astrology was a sinister goddess whose hypnotic eye bewitched mankind. Anxiously the devotees sought the knowledge of their destiny in the twinkling of a star. Jews it is true never yielded altogether to astral fatalism.[13] The opportunity to shape one's moral being they could not, if their religion were to have any meaning, quite entrust to the whims of comets. The beliefs and practices of Egypt and Babylon could make but small headway against the ridicule and irony of the prophets. "The signs of heaven" failed to dismay a Jeremiah,[14] or his fellow prophets. To many, however, the witchery of astrology was irresistible. The cultured Josephus,[15] as well as the devout apostles,[16] made much of celestial portents. Even the Rabbis seriously discussed the influence of the stars on the affairs of men.[17] In the Middle Ages the Jews were certainly no less susceptible. The astronomer and mathematician Abraham bar Hiya, the encyclopedist Judah b.Solomon ha-Cohen ibn Matkah, the erudite and widely traveled ibn Ezra, to mention but a few out of many, could not escape the contagion.[18]

It was Maimonides who sought to eradicate the belief, root, branch and all. He charged against it with all the force of reason at his command. Despite his reverence for the Talmud he did not include in his Code any of its rules or practices astrological in character.[19] He gave the Rabbis of Southern France no quarter. In his famous letter to them on the subject he is ruthless in his condemnation of this "baseless, ridiculous foolishness."[20] In the *Yad* he sweeps away the whole rubbish of witchcraft, star-gazing, magic, sciomancy, psychomancy, rhabdomancy and pessomancy with a typically Maimonidian paragraph: "All these things," he writes, "are false and fabulous, a wretched legacy of a credulous heathenism. Jews, endowed as they are with superior intelligence, should not be drawn to such follies, neither regard them advantageous. Is it not written: 'For there is no enchantment with Jacob, neither is there any divination with Israel'?[21] Were we not warned: 'For these nations, that thou art to dispossess, hearken unto soothsayers and unto diviners; but as for thee, the Lord thy God hath not suffered thee so to do'?[22] He then who believes in such absurdities, and sees in them truth and wisdom, despite unequivocal biblical injunctions, belongs with fools and imbeciles. . . . Wise and understanding men are convinced beyond a doubt that the

Torah has prohibited these things because they are void and vain, and therefore a ready temptation to the weakminded who gladly forsake the paths of truth for any hokus-pokus."[23] Can we not see from such a passage whence Maimonides' vigorous attack on corporeality would emanate? Was it not motivated by the desire to remove from the God Idea every vestige of superstition, every trace of the irrational, the least compromise with the vagaries of heathen mysteries?

In his discussion of the *Ta'amei ha-Mizvot* Maimonides shows himself again the persistent rationalist. He is most insistent that all the commandments and prohibitions have a rational basis. If any of the *Hukkim*, or ordinances seem groundless to us, it is due only to the weakness of our knowledge or the limitation of our intellect.[24] Many of the laws, he argues, have for their purpose the inculcation of truths and the removal of erroneous opinions.[25] At the heart of the Torah Maimonides sees the opposition to idolatry which was characterized by abominable practices as well as abysmal folly.[26] The law aims to save Israel from these evil and pernicious doctrines. It seeks to implant a reasonable attitude toward life, an understanding of cause and effect. The multitudes are prone to disregard rational causation and to seek success and comfort in one delusion or another. Why, asks Maimonides, does the Torah prohibit any benefit whatever from an idol? His answer is penetrating. "A person may be successful and make a good profit on the business in which he employed the money received for the idol; he might then think that the idol was the cause of his success, and that the blessing of the money received for it brought him the profit; he would then believe in the idol."[27]

Neither could the mystic fancies so common in his day delude Maimonides. He had no more patience with kabalistic than with magic jugglery. In his discussion of Divine Names Maimonides writes: "When bad and foolish men were reading such passages, they considered them to be a support of their false pretensions and of their assertion that they could, by means of an arbitrary combination of letters, form a *shem* ('a name') which would act and operate miraculously when written or spoken in a certain particular way. Such fictions, originally invented by foolish men, were in the course of time committed to writing, and came into the hands of good but weak-minded and ignorant persons who were unable to discriminate between truth and falsehood, and made a secret of these *shemot* (names). When after the death of such persons those writings were discovered among their papers, it was believed that they contained truths; for, 'The simple believeth every word.' "[28]

It is clear that Judaism was to Maimonides the acme of reason. He surveyed the whole realm of human wisdom and discovered nothing that might challenge the foundations of Judaism. Quite the contrary. The philosophies and sciences of the nations only offered invincible proof for the generalizations of Torah and Talmud. Therefore, Maimonides, though he loved the lore of his people with a great love, yet drank with quenchless thirst from the culture of all peoples. The catholicity of his intellectual interests proved most beneficial to his people. In every age men who sought secular knowledge found in the example of Maimonides support and justification for their own inclinations. The pious R. Isserels, the emancipated Mendelssohn, the wayward Maimon, the apologetic Levinsohn, each appealed to Maimonides against the obscurantists of his day.

The rationalism of Maimonides then is an indisputable fact. But he exercised Reason and applied it within the spirit and scope of his tradition, a tradition deeply rooted in experience and intuition. True he checked the vagaries of faith and dissolved the mists of intuition by the application of disciplined thought. But he also clothed cold reason with the warm accoutrements of a living Judaism. And yet Maimonides may have realized that both intuition and reason need supplementation. Society, he perhaps surmised, cannot

be built either on the hypothesis of the one or on the musings of the other. Judaism, Maimonides guessed, was a living
entity only because and insofar as its Law lives. This Law,
observation had convinced him, was a mightier weapon with
which to check and combat the aberrations of Reason and
the mummeries of intuition than ever Reason could itself.
Of this Maimonides was fully cognizant, and, therefore, ex-
pended his major efforts not in primary philosophy but on
the exposition, codification and application of the Law, not
the theoretic Law of some imaginary Republic but the laws
affecting the Jew's daily life, making for the continuity of
the Jewish people, for the preservation and enhancing of
specific Jewish values.

Here he brooked no compromise. He was confident, that
in their Law, the Jews had a legacy precious beyond rubies.[29]
All ideologies, no matter how lofty, must find their means
of implementation. The value of ideals lies in their impatience to find form. The vigor of a religion emanates not
from vague generalization but from concrete application.
The speculation of the few does not convert the many into
philosophers. Judaism saw that more clearly than the other
religions and philosophies. It alone had carefully elaborated
a method of application,—the all-embracing, comprehensive
law. Indeed Judaism has made the application of this law
more essential than all theory. For with every *mizvah* there
is increased holiness.[30] It was with this in mind that Maimonides drew the severe contrast between Judaism and the
other religions. Only a child, says he, can confuse God's
masterpiece with the feeble efforts of men. The difference is
between a living human being and the sculptor's statue.[31]
The statue has exquisite form and beauty. Something indeed to be admired. But it remains removed from life and
is limited to some corner in a museum or street. Occasionally
a gleam of it gives birth to inspiring thoughts only to be
soon dissipated. Judaism, *per contra,* was a living religion
reaching out into every nook and crevice of the life of the

community and the individual, infusing men with vigor and vitality.[32] It took nothing for granted and under all circumstances insisted on discipline by means of the Law.[33] To this Law, Maimonides gave his major strength.

With this in mind, the attack on Maimonides as an intellectual aristocrat becomes ludicrous. To say that Maimonides was concerned only with the metaphysician and indifferent to the brutish multitude is to disregard the man's life-work. To contrast severely the democratic spirit of Judaism with the aristocratic temper of Maimonides is to misinterpret both. The undisputable fact is that the whole life of Maimonides is just one long day of the profoundest interest in all his fellowmen. He spent his lifetime toiling for the mass.[34] He knew of no joy more deeply stirring, more glorious than to gladden the heart of the poor, the orphan, the widow, or the stranger. He, states Maimonides, who brings a little happiness into the lives of these miserable people is like unto the Divine Presence.[35]

As a physician he waited on patients until he could no longer stand on his feet.[36] As a writer on medicine he diffused homelike advice in the simplest language for the benefit of the most ordinary mortals. As a Jew he gave every indication of his deep interest in the people as a whole. He expounded the Mishnah, codified the Law, befriended the Karaites, comforted the Yemenites, and encouraged every community on the Jewish horizon that sought his counsel and aid.[37] Readers of his Responsa will recall that the least communal or congregational problem was not dismissed by him as trifling, but received his meticulous attention.[38] No one unless it be the Hasid Hillel himself has ever shown a finer understanding of, or deeper sympathy for, the convert to Judaism. The humble *ger* who, in his humiliation, wrote to the master was drawn to the very heart of the Jewish community with the assurance that he is now one of the people, indivisible and inseparable.[39] How could a man have devoted his whole life to serve those he spurned?

On the other hand, it is the rankest perversion of Judaism to maintain that its democracy made no room for, or did not encourage the individual. It is the most malicious of all the libels invented against Judaism. If the "one" was revered anywhere more than in Israel then it was in Utopia. If it is assumed that Judaism tolerated pious popular ignorance then no greater injustice can be done to it. Both in the Bible and Talmud the ignorant man finds but reproof. What could not a Maimonides make of the verses—

> "How great are Thy works, O Lord!
> Thy thoughts are very deep.
> A brutish man knoweth not,
> Neither doth a fool understand this."[40]

Had not the Rabbis echoed the sentiment numerous times? Did they not appreciate that it is only the Torah which sets Nahman bar Abba apart from the multitude?[41] A Moses equals the whole of Israel, or the whole of mankind.[42] Had not Hillel himself with all his deep love for the common folk declared: "A rude man does not fear sin nor is an ignorant man a saint"?[43] A later generation cautioned, should there be found an exception, viz., the pious ignoramus, shun him as neighbor.[44] To marry one's daughter to an *am ha-arez* was tantamount to throwing her bound before the lion.[45]

It is true that without genuine reverence wisdom was under suspicion in Israel, but wisdom was made a prerequisite to reverence.[46] To Rabbi Akiba every human being was beloved because he saw in it the image of God.[47] In the shedding of any man's blood he saw the diminution of the divine image.[48] He had selected the "golden rule" as the most significant in the Pentateuch.[49] Yet, the same Rabbi Akiba had but little patience with the ignoramus and boor.[50] It was he, too, who was most happy that his "portion" was among the scholars, and not the traders and idlers.[51] Though he would gladly promise immortality to any man even for one good deed,[52] yet, was he ready to exclude from a share in the world to come those who did not "wait upon scholars."[53] The patient Hillel himself had declared that he who does not "wait on the scholars" was guilty of death.[54] The man without knowledge or intelligence they hardly thought worthy of pity.[55]

Even as the ignoramus and boor were despised, even so was the outstanding individual prized. Impatiently God himself waits for the semen from which the *zaddik* is to be born.[56] To show one of the great in Israel a kindness was equal to caring for the whole community.[57] Everything and everyone can be replaced but not the scholar.[58] Therefore his death is as grievous to God as the breaking of the Tablets of the Law.[59] He was ever the aim and hope of the Jewish Community. It always aspired to raise supermen—cedars and Leviathans.[60] Without them a community was considered drab and uninteresting. In their absence, the glory and prestige of a city fled.[61] They were as important as the ministering angels.[62] Because they are so few God distributes them through the generations[63] and guards their honor more jealously than His own.[64] There is no atonement for him who treats the elect lightly.[65] God's own greatness depends upon their honor and prestige.[66] It is they who are the molders and builders of society.[67] Therefore, they must in every way set the example for the community. If only a speck be found on their garments they are guilty of death.[68] Careful as the scholar must be of his honor, so too must the community guard it zealously. Jerusalem was destroyed because it maltreated its scholars and did not distinguish the excellent from the commonplace.[69] Very few of its inhabitants resembled the laundryman of Rabbi Judah the Prince.[70] Resurrection, the Rabbis long before Maimonides taught, is only for the righteous.[71] Their souls are hidden under the Throne of Glory.[72] In the future the Eternal Himself will be the crown of their heads.[73]

Judaism then was mindful of the individual but not unmindful of the community. They fail to understand Israel who do not see this remarkable interlinking between the one and the many, the *yahid* and the *zibbur*. Beware, said the Rabbis, of neglecting fellowship,[74] for only in company is culture acquired.[75] The Divine Presence Itself prefers to dwell only with the multitudes.[76] Every tribe could be counted on raising men of note, Judges and Prophets.[77] To advance the one and help the many, withdrawal and disassociation from the life of the community were discouraged.[78] The life of the recluse was depicted as intolerable. Death was preferable to solitude.[79] The greater the individual the more he was urged to participate in the life of the community, exert over it his influence and shed over it his glory. A genuine superman, a Moses would not escape but gladly share the burdens and sorrows of his fellowmen.[80] For even a Moses was reminded that he owed his greatness to his people.[81]

This interrelatedness of the community—the aristocrats of mind and heart with the common folk—has been the source of Jewish strength and continuity.[82] All Jews were responsible for one another.[83] The righteous were created only for the redemption of the many.[84] There is a marked contrast to the state of affairs among the Greeks. They knew of no such harmony in Athens between the *hoi poloi* and the *aristoi*. One generation of patricians barren could spell the doom of Attica. In Judea they always looked forward to the time when prophecy, wisdom, knowledge would be the gift of all.[85] There men came up from the pasture grounds of Tekoa to be the boldest spokesmen; they rose from the shoemaker's last to weigh the nation's spiritual destiny in the consuls of the august Sanhedrin. One could never tell whence the great would issue forth. The descendants of such vile men as Haman, Sisera and Sennacherib were distinguished teachers in Palestine[86] Rabbi Simon ben Lakish is the author of a delightful parable in which he masterfully depicts the solidarity of Jewish society. "This people," he says, "is like unto the vine. Its shoots represent the men of affairs; its clusters of grapes are the scholars;

the leaves are the peasantry; the rods are the vain idlers.[87] Let no one then say I will hate the wise and despise the ignorant, but love all."[88]

What brought pauper and prince, foolish and wise, poor and rich, slave and master together? What was the magic spell that chased away all distinction? It was the Law. Nobody could live outside or above it. It was because of the Law that Jewry was never a fertile field for sects. Sectarians could not disregard the Law. Those who did were soon expunged from the community; those who lived the life of the people were, in the course of time, reabsorbed into the main body. It was the Law that spared to Judaism the gruesome inhumanities of religious madness. The Law, more effectively than Reason elsewhere, impeded the spread of repulsive asceticism, sex orgies, physical mutilations and weird mysteries.[89] Frankists and Sabbatai Zevites could not remain in the fold, because the Law would not tolerate their license. No man, no matter how saintly or inspired, could in the name of a thousand visions affect one rule of conduct. God himself, though exempt from the observance of the Law, nevertheless practiced it, if only to set a good example.[90]

Rabbis Isaac Luria,[91] Hayyim Vital,[92] Israel Besht,[93] Nahman Breslauer[94] were men of most captivating personality, of the widest popular appeal. They were religious figures of extraordinary beauty and magnetic power, endowed with imagination rich and mystic. Yet all of them bent their visions to the discipline of the Law. The least rumor or suspicion of deviation might otherwise rouse, indeed on one occasion did, the threatening ire of so peaceful and recluse a soul as an Elijah Gaon.[95] When he rose in implacable fury to challenge the Hasidim, he did so as the recognized spokesman of the Law. For it brooks no reckless deviations that lead to unchecked sectarianism and division. This Torah, the conviction was deep, no one of the seed of Jacob can ever escape, consciously or unconsciously.[96] No prophet, no matter how distinguished can invalidate any of its laws. He lies, who seeks to deny the prophecy of Moses. Even if he performs miracles without number, Maimonides taught, disregard them, and make him pay for his impudence with his life.[97]

What the philosophy of Aristotle and Democritus could not achieve for Greece, the Law of Moses, Hillel, and Akiba achieved for the Jew. Indeed, Plato's Pure Reason fathered so much bastard folly. It easily mated with all the wayward practices and mysterious rites of the putrid religions of the crumbling East. Nothing reflects quite as much on the civilization of Greece as the ease with which the oriental mystagogue gained mastery over its citizens and émigrés. Culture, metaphysics, ascetic mysteries, sensuality were boon companions. If the Jew remained aloof it was not because Reason in Israel did not go astray. The imagination of the heart of man is weak everywhere, but in Israel the imagination found a fortress which it could not easily storm.

Maimonides' great service to his generation, as well as to our own, was that he linked Reason to the Law and subjected the Law to Reason. By syncretizing the gifts of thought with the bequests of tradition, he provided us with the clearest, most comprehensive presentation of the totality of Judaism. The extent of his knowledge and retentiveness of his memory are past understanding. One might almost say that he knew the whole of the Britannica by heart, except that he remembered equally well all the cross references.[98] Thus, for example, Maimonides knows the Talmudic tractate dealing with vows, but in addition, he has indexed in his mind every important and unimportant dictum, every cursory reference bearing on the subject, scattered in the remotest nooks and recesses of the whole field of Jewish literature.[99]

It is wrong, however, to conclude that Maimonides merely recapitulated and synthesized the work of his predecessors. All his books bear the stamp of profound originality.[100] He brought to masterful logical conclusion the numerous implications in Biblical and Rabbinic writings, viz. that the universe is a unified whole governed by the will of the one unchanging, incorporeal God. In the field of philosophy, Professor Wolfson tells us, "within the limited range of twenty-five propositions, he contrived to summarize in compact and pithy form the main doctrines of Aristotle."[101] Elsewhere Professor Wolfson adds: "His (Maimonides') work is the most excellent depository of medieval philosophic lore, where one can find the most incisive analyses of philosophic problems, the most complete summaries of philosophic opinions, the clearest definitions of terms, and all these couched in happy and quotable phrases."[102] In addition, he was one of the greatest clinicians of his age. His *Fusul Musa*, better known in the Hebrew as *Pirke Mosheh*, does not fall short of the famous Canon of Avicenna in the same field.[103] Maimonides was a voluminous writer on medicine, and was equally versed in all natural sciences, mathematics, logic and philosophy, and possessing a fair acquaintance with general folklore.

Whether the present philosophic and scientific upheaval will help the Maimonides system is unimportant. We venture to suggest that his metaphysics cannot be rescued nor can it serve as a support for religion. Even the offerings of Jeans and Eddington, so generously distributed in the modern pulpit, will be found to be a broken reed. The roots of religion have their origin in other soil—in man's quest for the good life. Both its ideology and technique, its dogma and ceremonial have a long history. They are not the immediate gifts either of intuition or of reason, but the offshoot of man's persistent quest. Maimonides was too much bereft of a historic sense to perceive this. We doubt therefore whether his philosophy of religion can maintain itself in the face of the religious sciences. But, whether his philosophy stands or falls, those who will go to him will make contact with a consummate genius, a patient teacher, a cautious and eager guide, a great humanitarian, and withal, a humble man. Whether his premises are right or wrong, his ethico-moral system remains deeply impressive, appealing both in its grandeur and simplicity, in its earnestness and aloofness. The whole man emerges from the dim past as a ray of light, or, to use his own language, as the Active Intellect, searching out the abyss of our miseries and revealing the sanctuary of our hopes.

LIST OF ABBREVIATIONS

AE.—Agadat Esther
AR.—Aichah Rabba
ARN.—Abot d'Rabbi Nathan

B.—Buber
b.—The Babylonian Talmud
B.B.—Baba Batra
B.K.—Baba Kama
B.M.—Baba Mezia

CR.—Canticles Rabba

Deut.—Deuteronomy
DEZ.—Derech Erez Zuta
DR.—Deuteronomy Rabba

ER.—Esther Rabba
ExR.—Exodus Rabba

GR.—Genesis Rabba

Hil.—Hilchot
HUC.—The Hebrew Union College

j.—The Jerusalem (Palestinian) Talmud
JAOS.—The Journal of the American Oriental Society
JE.—The Jewish Encyclopedia
JQR.—The Jewish Quarterly Review

KR.—Kohelet Rabba

LR.—Leviticus Rabba

M.—Midrash
MEx.—Mechilta Exodus
MGWJ.—Monatsschrift fuer Geschichte und Wissenschaft des Judentums

MHag.—Midrash ha-Gadol
Mish.—Mishnah
MK.—see KR.
MPr.—Midrash Proverbs
MPs.—Midrash Psalms
MS.—Midrash Samuel
MT.—Midrash Tannaim

NR.—Numbers Rabba
Numb.—Numbers

PK.—Pesikta Rabbi Kahana
PR.—Pesikta Rabbati
PRE.—Pirke Rabbi Eliezer

RAA.—The Rabbinical Assembly Annual
RR.—Ruth Rabba

SD.—Sifre Deuteronomy
SER.—Seder Eliyahu Rabba
SEZ.—Seder Eliyahu Zuta
SN.—Sifre Numbers

TEx.—Tanhuma Exodus
TG.—Tanhuma Genesis
TL.—Tanhuma Leviticus
TN.—Tanhuma Numbers
Tos.—Tosefta

YCh.—Yalkut Chronicles
YD.—Yalkut Deuteronomy
YE.—Yalkut Esther
YEx.—Yalkut Exodus
YG.—Yalkut Genesis
YH.—Yalkut Hosea
YI.—Yalkut Isaiah
YJ.—Yalkut Joshua
YJb.—Yalkut Job
YK.—Yalkut Kohelet
YKs.—Yalkut Kings

YL.—Yalkut Leviticus
YN.—Yalkut Numbers
YPr.—Yalkut Proverbs

YPs.—Yalkut Psalms
YREx.—Yalkut Reubini Exodus
YS.—Yalkut Samuel

NOTES

NOTES

CHAPTER I

1. *Confessio Judaica*, 256, ed. Bieber, Berlin, 1925.
2. *SD.*, 306, 131^a, ed. Friedmann, Vienna, 1864.
3. The whole of nature is only an illustration of man. *ARN.*, 33, 91; *KR.*, 1, 9. Only God is personality. *b. Sotah*, 42^b. Great is the courage of the Prophets who compare the likeness of God to the likeness of man. This man whom I want to create excels you all in wisdom, says God to the angels. It is from man that I received my very name. *PR.*, 14, 9 & 10; *GR.*, 27, 1, ed. *Theodor*, 255-6; *NR.*, 19, 3; *TN.*, 110-16; *PK.*, 36 & 37; Maimonides, *The Guide of the Perplexed*, I, 45, trans. M. Friedlaender. We believe, says Rabbi pseudo-Jacob Tam, in the immortality of the soul for Reason compels us to believe that the soul of Moses could not possibly perish. *Sepher ha-Yashar*, 5, 29, Lublin, 1873. The wisdom of the Creator, says Abraham bar Hiya, man can comprehend through the form of his body and the perfection of his limbs. *Hegyon ha-Nephesh*, 2^b, Leipzig, 1860. *Cf.* also H. Zeitlin, *Ketavim Nivharim*, I, *ha-Tov veha-Ra*, 23, Warsaw, 5671; H. A. Wolfson in *JQR.*, vol. II, 297-9; J. Bergmann in the *Adolph Schwartz Festschrift*, 100-104. In *MGWJ.*, vol. 78, 397, Lothar Lubasch writes: "*Die Beziehung zwischen Gott und Welt erhaelt durch den Begriff der Persoenlichkeit ihre Aufhellung.*" The absence in Judaism of what the Occident regards as biography in no way contradicts our contention. The "personality" quality of Moses, David, Akiba is vividly presented in our literature, even where *Tendez* predominates. *Cf.* I. Rabin, *Dubnow Festschrift*, 46-9.
4. Louis Ginzberg, *The Legends of the Jews*, vol. V, 64, n. 3; 69, n. 12, Philadelphia, 1925.
5. *GR.*, 8, 6, 61 & note *a.l.*; *RR.*, 2, 3.
6. *Idem.*
7. *Proverbs*, 10, 4; *b. Gittin*, 61^a. *Cf.* also *MPs.*, 34, 245, three *Zaddikim* were the foundation of the world, Adam, Noah & Abraham.
8. *b. Yoma*, 38^b; *b. Kiddushin*, 72^b; *GR.*, 58, 2, 619; *KR.*, 1, 10; *MS.*, 8, 9, 30.
9. *b. Sanhedrin* 103^b.
10. *b. Yoma, loc. cit.*
11. *MPs.*, 1, 15.
12. *SD., loc. cit.*
13. *GR.*, 35, 2. In *Theodor* 330 the reading is slightly different; *idem*, 56, 9, 602 reads: There is no generation in which the like of Abraham, Jacob, Moses, or Samuel is not found; *cf.* also *GR.*, 49, 7, 501-2, & note *a.l.*; *b. Hullin*, 92^a where the numbers 45 & 30 are given; in *Sanhedrin* 97^b, the number is 36; *NR.*, 10, 2. In *b. loc. cit.*, 89^a we read: The world exists only because of Moses and Aaron.
14. *GR.*, 60, 11, 650. In heaven Eliezer imparts the Torah of his master to multitudes. *Cf. b. Yoma*, 28^b; *b. Nedarim*, 32^a. Another tradition lists Eliezer among nine who entered Paradise alive. *DEZ.*, 1.

15. *GR.*, 53, 12, 563, & note *a.l.* for variants & additions; *TG.*, Buber, 107; *PR.*, 22.

16. Amos warned God that without the presence of a man like Jacob the world is doomed to destruction. *SER.*, 6, 32, 33.

17. The Holy One Blessed Be He says to His world: "My world, My world, who created thee, who fashioned thee? Jacob is thy creator, Jacob is thy fashioner." *LR.*, 36, 4; *TG.*, 135; Ginzberg, *Legends*, V, 274, 35.

18. Ginzberg, *idem*, 290, 134.

19. *SD.*, 355, 148ᵃ; *cf.* however n. 44, *a.l.* & Professor Ginzberg's note in Geiger's *Kobez Ma'amarim*, 393-4.

20. *PR.*, 4, 1.

21. MhaG., 59.

22. *GR.*, 8, 1, 56; *cf.* also *idem*, 1, 2, 17 where it is identified with the spirit of the Messiah.

23. *Idem.*, 4, 7, 30.

24. *b. Sanhedrin*, 111ᵇ; *cf. Tosafot, a.l.; j. Taanit*, 2, 1, Krotoschin, 65ᵇ.

25. "And David went forth and took seven stones and wrote upon them the names of his fathers, Abraham, Isaac, and Jacob, Moses and Aaron, his own name and the name of the Most Mighty." *The Biblical Antiquities of Philo* (ps.-Philo), LXI, 5, ed. James, 234.

26. *b. Sanhedrin*, 98ᵇ.

27. *Tosefta Berachot*, 1, 16, ed. Zuckermandel, 3; *b. Menahot*, 53ᵇ; *ARN.*, 43, 121.

28. God does not interfere with the order of the universe. *b. Abodah Zarah*, 54ᵇ. Miracles were not welcome as proof; *cf. b. B.B.*, 59ᵇ.

29. *Cosmos.*, trans. E. C. Otté, Bohn's Scientific Series, 1882.

30. *SD.*, 306, 131ᵃ reads: "Observe heaven and earth which I have created to serve you. Have they changed their nature? Does the sun not rise from the east and shed its light over the whole world. Even as it is written, 'The sun also ariseth, and the sun goeth down.'" "The Israelite conception of Divine Righteousness meant that God was dependable throughout all His activities; and such a conviction has assisted, however unconsciously the growth of the scientific outlook." Stanley A. Cook, *Ethical Monotheism in the Light of Comparative Religion*, 21, Lecture delivered before The London West Synagogue Association, 1932.

31. *MEx.*, ed. *Weiss*, 35ᵇ, 36ᵃ.

32. *Tos. Sotah*, 10, 1, 313.

33. With something else in mind Professor Eddington writes: "It is . . . of the very essence of the unseen world that the conception of personality should dominate it. . . . After exhausting physical methods we return to the inmost recesses of consciousness, to the voice that proclaims our personality. . . . We have to build the spiritual world out of symbols taken from our own personality." *Science and the Unseen World*, 82, The Macmillan Co., 1930.

34. Renowned Tosafist, grandson of Rashi, known as Rabbenu Tam. *Jew. Enc.*, vol. VIII, 36-9.

35. *Sepher ha-Yashar*, 1, 6. See *infra*, p. 213 n. 85.

36. From an address by Manilal Ni Dvivedi of Bombay before The World's Parliament of Religions, quoted in *The Open Court*, vol. 47, 222.

37. *Religion in the Making*, 50, Lowell Lectures, 1936. "Already in the New Testament," writes Edward Caird, "it (Christianity) is not only a religion, but it contains, especially in the writings of St. Paul, the germs of a theology." *The Evolution of Theology in the Greek Philosophers*, I,

7, Glasgow, 1923; *cf.* also E. Hatch, *The Influence of Greek Ideas and Usages upon the Christian Church,* 116-38, 4th ed. The Hibbert Lectures, 1888.

38. Quoted in *JAOS.*, vol. 51, 292.

39. R. A. Nicholson, *The Idea of Personality in Sufism,* 2, Cambridge, 1923.

40. The view was not unknown to the Rabbis. *j. Hagigah,* 2, 1, 77ᵃ.

41. It is true that the Milesian thinkers were not altogether materialists. Thales spoke of the universe as alive, as having soul (*ēmpsychon*). On the other hand, it is equally true that speculation in Ionia and Elea had as its main object nature (*physis*) and not man or society. Most of the writings of their philosophers bear the title, *peri phýseos. Cf.* L. Robin, *La Pensée Grecque,* 43-56, Paris, 1923; F. M. Cornford, *From Religion to Philosophy,* 7, Longmans, Green & Co., 1912. The earliest occupants of the Greek Pantheon were the nature gods, envisaged not as personalities, but as functionaries created by human needs. M. P. Nilsson, *A History of Greek Religion,* 118, Oxford, 1925.

42. S. Schechter, *Aspects of Rabbinic Theology,* 37, 38, New York, 1910.

43. Note how Aristotle depersonalizes the famous dictum of Protagoras that man is the measure of all things. *Metaphysics,* X, i. 1053b, 1-3.

44. *GR.,* 74, 9; *cf.* Maimonides, *The Guide,* III, 43.

45. *Tos. Sotah,* 4, 1-6, 293-9; *b. BM.,* 86ᵇ. *Cf. SER.,* 27, 132, where the redemption from Egypt is credited to the Matriarchs.

46. *Tos. idem,* 11, 1-2, 314 & 315 for gifts due to Joshua and Samuel.

47. A. N. Whitehead, *Process and Reality,* 513, The Macmillan Co., 1929.

48. *The Decline and Fall of the Roman Empire,* vol. II, ed. Bury, 321.

49. *Cf.* I. Epstein in *JQR.*, vol. 25, 207.

50. *Kuzari,* IV, 3, Hirschfeld trans., 212.

51. Emerson, *Essays,* 2nd series.

52. "Inquire," wrote Erasmus to the Archbishop of Palermo, "if you will but do not define." *Epistolae,* 613, *Opera Omnia,* III, i, 691, 1703. Mr. Maurice Samuel in a letter to the author writes: "Referring to the successive refinement of definitions into something which approaches the meaningless, a recent writer says: 'At every changing of the guard the password becomes more subtle.' C. D. Broad, trying to escape from the impossible attenuations of 'scientific' definitions without lapsing into the grossness of vulgar simplicity coins the phrase 'on the level of enlightened commonsense'—an attempt to make the best of both worlds."

53. W. H. Sheldon, *Strife of Systems and Productive Duality,* 105, Cambridge, 1918.

54. Maimonides quotes R. Meir's dictum from a *Baraita. Responsa,* 347, 7, 312, ed. A. Freimann, Jerusalem, 1934. Freimann did not know the source of the *Baraita.* Professor Ginzberg (orally) is of the opinion that Maimonides had in mind a statement in *Baraita deMazalot,* 6, ed., Wertheimer. *Supra* note 3 for reference to the praise given the Prophets because from the form they see the Creator.

55. *b. Erubin,* 13ᵇ, 53ᵃ; *b. Kiddushin,* 81ᵃ where we learn that the scholarship of R. Meir is respected even by Satan; *b. Sanhedrin,* 24ᵃ, where we learn of the extraordinary impression he made in the academy; *j. Baiza,* 5, 2, 63ᵃ where a scholar attributes his learning to a glimpse he had caught of R. Meir's back.

56. A. Kaminka in *Moznaim,* vol. IV, 47-9.

57. *Mish. Sotah,* end; *b. Gittin,* 67ᵃ; *KR.,* 2, 22.

58. The evidence for this conjecture the author hopes to offer in his work on the Pharisee, Rabbi Judah b. Illai.

59. Thomas Aquinas, *De Veritate*, q. 10, a. 6, ad 2. In the *Summa Contra Gentiles*, I, 3 Leonine ed., vol. 13, 8ᵃ, he writes: *Cognito a sensu incipiat.* Cicero, *De Finibus*, I, 19, 64, writes: *Quidquid porro animo cernimus, id omne oritur a sensibus.* Every mental presentation has its origin in sensation. It is there criticized as an Epicurean doctrine. *Cf.* Ph. H. Wickstead, *The Reaction between Dogma and Philosophy*, etc., 360-405, London, 1926. M. C. Darcy, *Thomas Aquinas*, 84-8, London, 1930; P. Rousselot, *L'Intellectualisme de S. Thomas*, 94, Paris, 1924.

60. *"Dass alle unsere Erkenntnis mit der Erfahrung anfange, daran ist gar kein Zweifel; denn wodurch sollte das Erkenntnisvermoegen sonst zur Ausuebung erweckt werden, geschaehe es nicht durch Gegenstaende, die unsere Sinne ruehren. . . ."* Opening words of Kant's *Kritik der Reinen Vernunft.*

61. Ruskin, *Modern Painters*, vol. III, ed. Everyman, 321.

62. *Kuzari*, IV, 5, 213; *cf.* Saadia Gaon, *Emunot v'Deot*, Introduction, 47-8 Bialystok 1913.

63. *Essays*, II, 5.

64. Cornford, *op. cit., passim.*

65. F. A. Lange, *History of Materialism*, vol. I, 76, trans. E. C. Thomas, Harcourt, Brace & Co., 1925.

66. *b. Sabb.*, 75ᵃ. Note also the interesting statement of R. Johanan (Jonathan): What is wisdom and understanding in the eyes of the nations? The science of cycles and planets.

67. Diogenes Laertius, X, 85; *cf.* Cicero, *De Finibus*, I, 19, 63-4; E. Zeller, *Die Philosophie der Griechen*, writes: *"Die Erkenntnis der natuerlichen Ursachen ist das einzige Mittel, um die Seele von den Schrecken des Aberglaubens zu befreien; dies ist aber auch ihr alleiniger Zweck; wenn uns der Gedanke·an die Goetter und an den Tod nicht belaestigte, sagt Epikor, so beduerften wir keine Naturforschung."* Vol. III, i, 396, also 409-12, Leipzig, 1923.

68. *Religio peperit scelerosa atque impia facta.* Lucretius, *De Rerum Natura*, I, 83.

69. *Tantum religio potuit suadere malorum. Loc. cit.*, 101.

70. *Religionum animum nodis exsolvere pergo. Loc. cit.*, V., 7. Lange, *op. cit.*, 130, n. 61, writes: "The really original element in Lucretius is the burning hatred of a pure and noble character against the degrading and demoralizing influence of religion. . . ."

71. Cicero, *De Republica*, I, 10, 15. In the *Memorabilia*, IV, 7, 6, Xenophon writes: In general, with regard to the phenomena of the heavens, he deprecated curiosity to learn how the deity contrives them; he held that their secrets could not be discovered by man, and believed that any attempt to search out what the gods had not chosen to reveal must be displeasing to them."

72. "We have Socrates to thank for the phantom of definitions which presuppose an altogether imaginary agreement of name and thing . . . we find in the Platonic dialogues quantities of logical tricks, ambuscades and sophisms of all kinds on the side of the always victorious Socrates." Lange, *op. cit.*, vol. I, 53 & 68-9.

73. Erasmus in his letter to the Archbishop of Palermo of January 5, 1522 (quoted *supra*), writes: "Let us have done with theological refinements. There is an excuse for the Fathers, because the heretics forced them to define particular points; but every definition is a misfortune, and for us

to persevere in the same way is sheer folly." Quoted in J. A. Froude, *Short Studies on Great Subjects*, 55.

74. *Yesode ha-Torah*, 15, Przemysl—Lemberg, 1880.

CHAPTER II

1. See his excellent study of *The Theology of Seder Eliahu*, 17-32, Bloch Publishing Co., 1932.

2. *Magnitudinem dei qui se putat nosse, minuit; qui non vult minuere, non novit.* Minucius Felix, *Octavius*, XVIII, 9. "Whoever is brazen enough to expostulate on matters metaphysical before his teacher, out of his own loose and weak mind without basing himself on tradition, is guilty of a thousand deaths." J. Yaabetz, *Ma'amar ha-Ahdut*, 2, 3[b], Altona, 1793.

3. *Aspects*, 12 & 146.

4. Caird, *op. cit.*, vol. I, 33.

5. H. Hoeffding, *The Philosophy of Religion*, 129, Macmillan Co., 1914.

6. *GR.*, 38, 19, 361-4, notes *a.l.*; *NR.*, 14, 7.

7. M. Planck, *Where is Science Going?*, 139, trans. Murphy, W. W. Norton & Co., 1932.

8. Caird *op. cit.*, vol. 1, 46.

9. *b. B.B.*, 16[a].

10. *b. Sabb.*, 30[b]; *LR.*, 28, 1; *cf.* also *b. Rosh ha-Shanah*, 21[b].

11. *At hic tacere nequeo Rabinorum audaciam, qui hunc librum (Proverbs) cum Ecclesiaste ex canone Sacrorum exclusos volebant. Tractatus Theologica-Politicus*, X, *Opera*, vol. II, 214 & 222.

12. Ginzberg, *Legends*, V, 168, 6.

13. *GR.*, 1, 12, 8 & note *a.l.* for further references. For the discussion of the origin of light *cf. idem*, 3, 1, 18-19; for the world as an emanation from light *idem* 3, 4, 20; *LR.*, 31, 6; *ExR.*, 15, 22, 50, 1; *MPs.*, 27, 221.

14. Ginzberg, *idem* V, 3, 5. For the view that the world was created *ex nihilo cf. MhaG.*, 13.

15. *GR.*, 68, 10; *PR.*, 21, 180, Warsaw, 1893. *Makom*, of course, originally signified a holy place and was later extended to designate its occupant. *Cf. Ephemeris*, III, 292. I owe this reference to my teacher Professor Ginzberg.

16. *GR.*, 68, 10; *MPs.*, 90, 390; *YG.*, 117; *Guide*, I, 70; *cf.* however *ExR.*, 46, 6; *TEx.*, 116; See also Bacher, *Agadot ha-Tannaim* II, i, 127, trans. Rabinowitz, *Devir*, 5682.

17. *GR.*, 46, 4, 461. Albo, *Sepher ha-Ikkarim*, IV, 10, 7, trans. Husik, 83, The Jewish Publication Society, 1930.

18. *GR.*, 12, 1, 97; *KR.*, 2, 14; A. Marmorstein, *The Old Rabbinic Doctrine of God*, vol. I, *The Names and Attributes of God*, 162-3, Oxford University Press, 1927. Language quite similar Xenophon puts in the mouth of Socrates: "Mark even the sun who seems to reveal himself to all permits not man to behold him closely but at any attempt to gaze recklessly upon him blinds their eyes." *Memorabilia* IV, 3, 14. The same image is found in the Talmud *b. Hullin*, 59[b] & 60[a]. Another Greek whose language is strongly reminiscent of the Rabbis was Pindar, "For man is not able with his human mind to search out the counsels of the gods, but he was born of a mortal mother," *Dithyrambs*. David Hume, more modern and more sceptical nevertheless admitted that he had no great knowledge of God. *Dialogues con-*

cerning Natural Religion, 10, Edinburgh & London, 1907. Spinoza, despite all his attacks on the Rabbis and the medievalists, is forced to conclude: *ejus essentia universalem non possimus formare ideam,* we can form no general idea of His Essence, *Epistola* 50, *Opera,* vol. III, 173. Let us then not dismiss the modesty of the Rabbis either as ignorance or intellectual ineptitude.

19. *Lephi ma'asai ani nikra.* ExR., 3, 6. Zeno who was a Semite and whose thinking seems to bear the stamp of his native land spoke of the Deity in similar terms: "They give (to God) the name *Dia,* because all things are due to him; *Zeus* insofar as he is the cause of life or pervades all life; the name Athena is given because the ruling part of the divinity extends to the ether; the name Hera marks its extension to the air; he is called *Hephaestus* since it spreads to the creative fire; *Poseidon* since it stretches to the sea; *Demeter* since it reaches to the earth." Diogenes Laertius, VII, 1. Note carefully the different attributes considered by the Hellenized Phoenician and the Rabbis.

20. *b. Sukkah,* 5ᵃ.

21. *GR.,* 4, 4, 27.

22. *Masechet Temurah* in *Sepher ha-Pardes,* 287, ed. Ehrenreich, Budapest, 1924; *MS.,* 13, ed. B.; *cf.* also Isaac Beer Levenson, *Teudah b'Yisrael,* 66, Warsaw, 1901.

23. *Guide,* III, 17.

24. *Idem.*

25. *Nicomachean Ethics,* III, v. 7.

26. Albo, *op. cit.,* I, 1, 3, 4.

27. *Deut.,* 30, 15.

28. *Idem* 30, 11-14.

29. *Jeremiah,* 7, 3.

30. *Idem,* 6, 16.

31. *Mish. Abot,* 3, 15.

32. R. Travers Herford, *Pirke Aboth,* 89, Bloch Publishing Co., 1925.

33. "*Ha-kol biydei shamayim hutz mi-yir'at shamayim,*" b. *Niddah,* 16ᵇ; *b. Berachot,* 33ᵇ; *b. Megillah,* 25ᵃ; *cf.* also *b. Sabb.,* 31ᵇ & R. Samuel Edels on *Berachot, l.c.;* also MPs., 103, 436; YPs., 859.

34. *Cf.* Saadia Gaon, *op. cit.,* IV, 6, 133-5.

35. *Jeremiah,* 10, 23.

36. *Psalms,* 144, 4.

37. *Ezekiel,* 18, 20.

38. *Idem.,* 36, 25-6.

39. *b. Berachot,* 28ᵇ.

40. *b. Sotah,* 5ᵃ.

41. *b. Sabb.,* 156ᵃ; *b. Moed Katon,* 28ᵃ. *Cf.* the very interesting comments of the Tosafists on *b. Niddah,* 16ᵇ & *b. Megillah,* 25ᵃ. They go as far as to say that astrological predestination is out of the hands of God, i.e., God does not want to change the course of the planets.

42. *j. Kidd.,* 1, end; *j. Sanhedrin,* 10, 5, 27ᶜ; *b. Sabb.,* 104ᵃ; *b. Yoma,* 38ᵇ; *b. Menahot,* 29ᵃ; *cf. also b. Makkot,* 10ᵇ; *NR.,* 20, 11; paraphrased in *Zohar Tazria,* 93, ed. Vilno. *Cf.* Aristotle, *loc. cit.,* III, 5, 10.

43. *Propter hoc enim dominus, cum de fructu iustitiae loqueretur, ait discipulis suis: Sine me nihil potestis facere. John* XV, 5; *Ep.,* CCXIV, 2.

44. *j. Hagigah,* 1, 7, 76ᶜ; *Petiha AR.,* 2 where the wording is somewhat different.

45. *b. Sabb.,* 31ᵃ; *ARN.,* 15, 60ᵃ.

46. *j. Sabb.*, 6, 1, 7ᵈ; *j. Sotah*, 9, 16, 24ᶜ; *b. Sabb.*, 59ᵇ; *b. Ketubot*, 62ᵇ, 63ᶜ; *b. Nedarim*, 50ᵃ; *ARN.*, 6, 5, 30ᵃ. Appendix B., 162-3. Of Rabbi Akiba's first marriage, before he began his studies little is known, except that there remained a young boy from that marriage, *idem*.

47. *b. Sabb.*, 67ᵇ. The name of the son is not mentioned here and it may of course refer to his son Joshua, a distinguished scholar, whom some have identified with Rabbi Joshua b. Korhah. *b. Pesahim*, 112ᵃ & *Tosafot*, *a.l.* In that case it was the son from the first marriage.

48. *Semahot*, 9; *cf.* also *Moed Katon*, 21ᵇ.

49. *Mish. Abot*, 4, 1.

50. Hillel was a carpenter; Joshua b. Hananiah a smith; Johanan a shoemaker, Huna tilled the soil; Oshia & Hanina were shoemakers in the harlots' district. *b. Yoma*, 35ᵇ; Maimonides on *Abot*, 4, 5; *j. Berachot*, 4, 1, 7ᵈ; *b. Ketubot*, 105ᵃ; *b. Pesahim*, 113ᵇ.

51. *NR.*, 20, 10.

52. *b. Yoma*, 20ᵃ; *b. Sukkah*, 52ᵃ.

53. *GR.*, 48, 11, 489.

54. *ARN.*, 16, 64, & note 23.

55. *j. Kidd.*, 4, 11, 66ᶜ.

56. *j. Yoma*, 6, 4, 43ᵈ; *j. Nedarim*, 9, 1, 41ᵇ.

57. *Mish. Abot*, 2, 4; *j. Sabb.*, 1, 3, 3ᵇ; *b. Berachot*, 29ᵃ.

58. *b. Hagigah*, 5ᵃ.

59. *b. Berachot*, 61ᵃ; *b. Erubin*, 18ᵃ; *cf.* also *b. Kidd.*, 81ᵃ.

60. *b. Nedarim*, 32ᵇ.

61. *j. Sabb.*, 14, 3, 14ᶜ. *GR.*, 22, 11, 210, where the reading is slightly different; also *Zohar ve-Ethhanan*, 534-5.

62. *b. Sukkah*, *loc. cit.*; *cf.* also *b. Sanhedrin*, 107ᵃ.

63. *b. Idem*, 107ᵃ, let no man ever bring himself to temptation, for David, King of Israel, did and stumbled.

64. *b. Kidd.*, 81ᵃ&ᵇ.

65. *b. Sanhedrin*, 91ᵇ; *ARN.*, 16, 62ᵃ, 63ᵃ; *cf.* also *MK.*, 9, 22; *Guide*, III, 22.

66. *j. Nedarim*, *loc. cit.*

67. *b. Sukkah*, *loc. cit.*

68. *Idem.*

69. *b. Kidd.*, 30ᵇ.

70. *b. Sukkah*, *loc. cit.*

71. *Idem*; *GR.*, *loc. cit.*; *b. Sanhedrin*, 99ᵇ.

72. *Jeremiah*, 12, 1-2.

73. *Habakkuk*, 1, 13-14.

74. *Psalms*, 10, 1-2.

75. *Idem*, 94, 3.

76. *Job*, 21, 7.

77. *Idem*, 31, 6.

78. *Psalms*, 103, 15-16.

79. *b. Yoma*, 76ᵃ; *b. Sotah*, 11ᵃ; *b. Sanhedrin*, 100ᵇ. *Cf. Tos. Sotah*, *loc. cit.*

80. *b. Idem*, 104ᵇ.

81. The reference to *za'ar ba'alei hayyim* in the Talmud and Codes are numerous. *Cf.* Hamburger, *Real-Enc.*, *verbum Thierquaelerei*.

82. He is reported to have said: *deus aut vult tollere mala non potest; aut potest et non vult; aut neque vult neque potest aut et vult et potest. Si vult et non potest, imbecillis est; quod in Deum non cadit. Si potest et*

non vult, invidus; quod neque alienum a Deo. Si neque vult, neque potest, et invidus et imbecillis est; ideoque neque Deus. Si vult et potest, quod solum deo convenit, unde ergo sunt mala? aut cur illa non tollit? Lactantius, *de ira Dei*, 13, in *Migne, Patrologia,* Latin series, vol. 7, col., 121; *Nam quamvis rerum ignorem primordia quae sint, hoc tamen ex ipsis caeli rationibus ausim confirmare aliisque ex rebus reddere multis, nequaquam nobis divinitus esse creatam naturam mundi, quanta stat praedita culpa.* Lucretius II, 177-81. For although I might not know what first beginnings are, this nevertheless I would make bold to maintain from the ways of heaven itself, and to demonstrate from many another source, that the nature of the universe has by no means been made through divine power, seeing how great are the faults it stands endowed with. Zeller, *Die Philosophie der Griechen,* III, 1, 443, n. 1, 5th ed., Leipzig, 1923.

83. Cicero, *De Natura Deorum,* I, 16, 42-3.

84. Cicero, *De Finibus,* I, 17, 60.

85. Lucretius, *op. cit.,* I, 62, 3.

86. *Idem* I, 78-9. Cf. *supra,* p. 188, notes, 68-70.

87. Even when the conception of deity is purified, their indifference to mankind is stressed. Under the influence of Epicurus, the poet Ennius wrote: "I have always said, and I shall always say, that the gods of heaven exist, but I believe that they have no care for what the race of man does. For if they had such care, it would be well with the good and ill with the wicked, which is not the case now." Quoted in C. H. Moore, *Religious Thought of the Greeks,* 238, Harvard University Press, 1925.

88. Even if you see that the Holy One Blessed Be He justifies the wicked and accuses the righteous, He is a God of faithfulness and without iniquity. *Deut.,* 32, 4; *MPs.,* 92, 4. The Rabbis preferred to attribute all the afflictions of humanity to the perversion of justice on the part of the judges. *b. Sabb.,* 193[a].

89. *GR.,* 51, 3, 535.

90. *TL.,* 39.

91. *GR.,* 3, 6, 23.

92. *TL.,* 41.

93. *b. Sabb.,* 104[a].

94. *b. Berachot,* 31[b], 32[a]; cf. *Rashi, a.l.; b. Sukkah, loc. cit.*

95. *b. Berachot,* 7[a].

96. *b. B.B.,* 14[b].

97. *Habakkuk,* I, 2-3; *b. Taanit,* 23[a]; *MPs.,* 7, B., 70, 71; *YH.,* 562.

98. *MEx.,* 10, 80; *SD.,* 32, 73[b]; *j. Berachot,* 9, 5, 14[b]; *b. idem,* 5[a]; *b. Sanhedrin,* 101[a]; *MPs.,* 94, 417. See however *Guide,* III, 17. Cf. also A. Marmorstein, *op. cit.,* 186-7.

99. *GR.,* 32, 3, 290 & note, for further references.

100. *Mish. Abot,* 6, 4; *b. Berachot, loc. cit.; b. Hagigah,* 9[b]; *GR.,* 94, 5, where we read: God does not confer His Name on a living human being unless he be a sufferer.

101. *b. Menahot,* 53[b].

102. *b. Taanit,* 8[a].

103. *TG.,* 47.

104. *j. Ketubot,* 5, 8, 29[c]&[d]; *b. Sukkah,* 52[a]&[b]; *b. Sanhedrin,* 106[a].

105. *YD.,* 850.

106. *LR.,* 30, 1.

107. *b. Berachot,* 60[b].

108. *GR.,* 9, 5, 70.
109. *Mish. Berachot,* end.
110. *b. Idem,* 5[b].
111. *GR.,* 22, 14, 217; *cf.* also *b. Sanhedrin,* 101[b].
112. *GR.,* 39, 6, 368-9.
113. *GR.,* 1, 14, 9.
114. *b. Yoma,* 69[b].
115. *b. Sabb.,* 56[b]; *cf.* also *Guide,* III, 17, 116.
116. *b. Menahot,* 29[b]; *cf.* also *b. Berachot,* 61[b], when God reviewed the generations and came to the generation of R. Akiba, He rejoiced at his Torah and grieved at his death. *b. Sanhedrin,* 38[b]; *Aboda Zara,* 5[a]. *Cf. MPs.,* 9, 88.
117. *NR.,* 14, 4, for the interesting manner in which the Rabbis dispose of the problems of resurrection, the effectiveness of repentance, God's concern for the barren woman, the rescuing of Daniel, etc. The Shammaites and the Hillelites decided the priority of heaven and earth in creation, on the basis of a verse. *b. Hagigah,* 12[a]; *j. idem,* 2, 1, 77[c]; *GR.,* 1, 15, 13.
118. Reference escapes me. Believe it is from Yaabetz, *Ma'amar ha-Ahadut.*
119. The Supreme Mathematician capitalized and deified by anxious theologians and for whose discovery they showed such gratitude to Jeans has quite a history. Already Leibnitz had made of God a mathematician spending His infinite leisure on a problem in the calculus of variations, which of course Leibnitz worked out in a few brief years. Du Bois Reymond, *Leibnitz'sche Gedanken in der Modernen Naturwissenschaft,* 17, Berlin, 1871, quoted in Lange, *op. cit.,* II, 131, n. 97. For another mathematician equally gracious to God *cf.* J. J. Baumann, *Lehre von Raum, Zeit u. Mathematik,* vol. I, 135-9, 231-47, vol. II, 269-86, 332-6, 477-80, Berlin, 1868-9.
120. Hume, *The Natural History of Religion,* sects. 4 & 15. "The only point of theology, in which we shall find a consent of mankind almost universal, is that there is an invisible, intelligent power in the world. . . . Though the stupidity of men, barbarous and uninstructed be so great, that they may not see a Sovereign Author in the more obvious works of nature to which they are so familiarized; yet it scarcely seems possible that anyone of good understanding should reject that idea when once it is suggested to him."

CHAPTER III

1. *b. Erubin,* 13[b]; *cf.* also *j. Hagigah,* 2, 1, 77[c]&[d]; *b. idem,* 12[a]; *GR.,* 14, 5, 129.
2. *ben Sira,* 3, 21-2. The verses are widely quoted in Hebrew literature. *Cf.* Schechter and Taylor, *The Wisdom of ben Sira,* 39, n. 21; Cambridge, 1899; *GR.,* 8, 2, 58 & *n.a.l.*
3. G. F. Moore, *Judaism,* I, 115, Cambridge, 1927; Ben Zion Rappoport, *Hakkarah u'Meziut,* 213, Berlin-Vienna, 1924.
4. Planck, *op. cit.,* 84. "To analyze," says Bergson, "is to express a thing as a function of something other than itself." *Introduction to Metaphysics,* 7. G. P. Putnam's Sons, 1912. In 1887 Ernst Mach was already warning scientists that they were only dealing with phenomenalism and could not touch ultimate reality. *Die Mechanik,* etc., trans. T. J. McCormack, The

Open Court, 1907. Two decades later Lord Balfour urged upon British scientists that the physicist must seek "for something deeper than the laws connecting possible objects of experience." It was non-experimental reality which was "the unalterable faith of science." Quoted in *The Monist*, 1905, 162.

5. Diogenes Laertius, VI, 1.

6. C. H. Moore, *Religious Thought of the Greeks*, 179-81.

7. Diogenes Laertius, III, 37 reports that when Plato read his dialogue *de Anima*, Aristotle alone stayed to the end; the rest of the audience got up and went away.

8. Hume, *Dialogues, etc.*, X, 136. How well Aristotle knew that, *see* Nicomachean Ethics, II, iv, 6.

9. Already in the days of Aristotle the complaint was heard that philosophy had become mathematics. But in those days mathematics was yet a means to an end. Aristotle, *Metaphysics*, I, ix, 992a, 33, 992b, 1-2.

10. *Space, Time and Deity*, 2nd ed., Preface, vi, London, 1927.

11. *The Scientific Outlook*, 98, W. W. Norton & Co., 1931.

12. Of the efforts of Maimonides, in this direction Munk reluctantly admits: *"Les solutions proposées laissent peu satisfaits le théologien et le philosophe de nos jours."* Munk wrote this well-nigh a century ago. *Le Guide des Égarés*, II, Préface, v., Paris, 1861.

13. *Op. cit.*, I, 83.

14. Plato, *The Republic*, VII, 533c, 3-5.

15. The following quotation from Cicero is significant: *"Ut rite ab eo dicendi principia capiamus, quem unum omnium deorum et hominum regem esse omnes docti indoctique pariter consentiunt.* It is proper for us to begin our discussion with that god who alone is admitted by everyone, learned and unlearned alike to be king of all gods and men." *De RePublica*, I, 36, 56.

16. The father and maker of all this universe, writes Plato, is past finding out; and even if we found him, to tell of him to all men would be impossible. *Timaeus*, 28c, 3-5.

17. *Harvard Theological Review*, vol. XIV, 268. Though this may sound somewhat sanguine in the mouth of a twentieth century professor.

18. "If thou knowest," says Albo, "thyself, thou wilt know thy Creator." *Op. cit.*, III, 6, 54; *cf.* Prof. Husik's note *a.l.*

19. *Science & Religion*, a symposium, 136, London, 1931.

20. *Op. cit.*, I, 73, n. 48.

CHAPTER IV

1. Hoeffdings, *op. cit.*, 3.

2. Lange, *op. cit.*, I, 30.

3. *Metaphysics*, III, ii, 997a, 7; iv, 1006a, 9.

4. *Apodeìchēos gàr archē ouk apódeichìs estin.* Idem, IV, v, 1010b, 14.

5. *Idem*, III, ii, 997a, 32.

6. III, v., 1002a, 29.

7. XII, iii, 1070a, 4.

8. I, ii, 982b, 29.

9. II, iii, 995a, 11-13.

10. Caird, *op. cit.*, I, 272.

11. *Idem*, 270.

12. Not even by Kant, although Prof. Lange, following Hermann Cohen, would have it so. *Op. cit.*, I, 247.

13. The cautious C. Lloyd Morgan writes: "I accept as a going concern such a physical world as may afford a basis for that which has been disclosed in the course of scientific research. But, as I shall have occasion to confess, I regard the independent existence of such a physical world in its own right as not susceptible of proof under rigid philosophical criticism." *Emergent Evolution*, 24, *The Gifford Lectures*, 1922, published in New York, 1931. Professor Russell is of the opinion that "Belief in the existence of things outside my own biography exists antecedently to evidence. . . . For purposes of sciences it is justified practically by the simplification it introduces into the laws of physics. But from the standpoint of theoretical logic it must be as a prejudice, not as a well-grounded theory." *The Analysis of Mind*, 132-3, The Macmillan Co., 1924.

14. Diogenes Laertius, I, 17.

15. The sophist runs away into the darkness of not-being, in which he has learned by habit to feel about and cannot be discovered because of the darkness of the place. . . . And the philosopher always holding converse through reason with the idea of being, is also dark from excess of light. *The Sophist*, 254a, 4-10.

16. Grote, *Greece*, vol. VIII, 347, 353, 356, 361-70, New York, 1900; Lewes, G. H., *The History of Philosophy*, vol. I, 106, 107, Longmans, Green, 1867.

17. *Metaphysics*, IV, ii, 1004b, 27-8.

18. Diogenes Laertius, 10, 31; Cicero, *op. cit.*, I, 7, 22 & 19, 63; *cf.* Zeller, *op. cit.*, III, i, 395; Lange, *op. cit.*, I, 107-11.

19. Ruskin, *op. cit.*, III, 322.

20. *Idem*, III, 147.

21. L. Buechner, *Force & Matter*, Eng. trans. Preface vii, New York, 1891.

22. *Op. cit.*, V, 14, Hirschfeld, 268-74; *cf.* H. A. Wolfson, *JQR.*, vol. II, 316-37.

23. F. H. Bradley, *Essays on Truth & Reality*, 246, Oxford, 1914. On page 13, Bradley writes: "Philosophy at its best is but an understanding of its object and it is not an experience in which that object is contained wholly and possessed."

24. Whitehead, *op. cit.*, 521. Spinoza is always interesting as an example of the absoluteness of truth discovered by metaphysicians. From Professor Lange's *History of Materialism* we cull the following two quotations displaying extraordinary unanimity of opinion among philosophers. "The Spinozist is in my eyes a pitiful and deluded creature, whom one must commiserate, and if he is not beyond assistance, attempt to help by two or three not too profound remarks from the 'Theory of Reason' and a clear explanation of what 'one' is and 'many' and what a substance is. He who has clear ideas of these, freed from all prejudices will be ashamed that the deluded notions of the Spinozists have even for a quarter of an hour disturbed him." Professor Hollman, *Lettre d'un Anonyme*, Lange, II, 139. "If the world continues to exist for countless numbers of years, the universal religion will be a purified Spinozism. Reason left to itself leads to nothing else, and it is impossible that it should." Lange, II, 147 from "the acute Lichtenberg."

25. *The Monist*, vol. 15, 171.

26. *Op. cit.*, 108.

27. *Idem*, 76.

28. *See* Professor Alexander's apologetic tone in the Preface to the new impression of *Space, Time & Deity*, vi-vii. Read on the other hand Professor Schroedinger's warning in his *Science and the Human Temperament*, 51, W. W. Norton & Co., 1935: "The old links between philosophy and physical science, after having been temporarily frayed in many places, are being more closely renewed. The farther physical science progresses the less can it dispense with philosophical criticism. But at the same time philosophers are increasingly obliged to become intimately acquainted with the sphere of research, to which they undertake to prescribe the governing laws of knowledge."

29. Despite the acclaim with which this suggestion was greeted in religious circles, and the contempt of scientists, there is really nothing new in it. It was made as early as 1874 by W. J. Jevons in his *Principles of Science*. *Cf.* Preface to 1st ed., and the last chapter. "The hypothetical anticipation of nature," says Professor Jevons, "is an essential part of inductive inquiry." *Loc. cit.*, vii.

30. A. Einstein, *The World As I See It*, 261-8, Covici-Friede, 1934. *Cosmic Religion*, 43-54, Covici-Friede, 1931; J. W. N. Sullivan, *The Observer*, April 13, 1935, 19; *cf.* also *idem*, Jan. 11, when in his interview with Planck, Mr. Sullivan objected that science must be more than an art, since it gives us knowledge of objective reality. Professor Planck countered by asking him what reason he "had to suppose that art and religion did not give us knowledge." *The Observer*, April 13.

31. Diogenes Laertius, IV, 3, 19.

32. "The further," says Professor Lange of Plato, "he was from facts, the nearer he thought himself to truth." *Op. cit.*, I, 75.

33. *Idem*, IV, 2, 53.

34. "I doubt," reports Mr. Sullivan, "whether Schroedinger would think modern physics sufficiently firmly based to have any philosophic bearings of great significance." *The Observer, loc. cit.*

35. *McClure's Magazine*, July, 1930, quoted in Horne, *Free Will and Human Responsibility*, 113.

36. J. Jeans, *The Mysterious Universe*, 146-7, The Macmillan Co., 1931.

37. *Science and the Unseen World*, 37, being the *Swarthmore Lectures* for 1929, published by The Macmillan Co., New York, 1930.

38. *The Observer*, Jan. 25, 1931, 17.

39. Professor Schroedinger in his *Science and the Human Temperament*, 154-5 writes: ". . . The epistemological question: 'Do the electrons really exist in these orbits within the atom?' is to be answered with a decisive No, unless we prefer to say that the putting of the question itself has absolutely no meaning. Indeed there does not seem to be much sense in inquiring about the real existence of something, if one is convinced that the effect through which the thing would manifest itself, in case it existed, is certainly *not* observed."

40. "We all," admonishes Professor Eddington, "share the strange delusion that a lump of matter is something whose general nature is easily comprehensible. . . ." *Science and the Unseen World*, 33.

41. Jennings, *The Universe and Life*, 41. Yale University Press, 1933.

42. Diogenes Laertius, IX. 8, 51.

CHAPTER V

1. Jevons, *op. cit.*, Preface ix.
2. *Système de la Nature*, vol. I, 189, Diderot, ed., Paris, 1821.
3. Dr. James Murphy in his Biographic Introduction to Schroedinger's *Science and the Human Temperament*, ii.
4. Lange, *op. cit.*, II, 302.
5. "The slightest scrutiny of the history of natural science shows that current scientific opinion is nearly infallible in the former case (in its selection of methods), and is invariably wrong in the latter case (formulating judgments of the understanding." Whitehead, *The Function of Reason*, 8, Princeton, 1929.
6. A rabbinic dictum has it, "if all creatures were to come together they could not create a mosquito and endow it with the breath of life." SD., 32, 73ª; *j. Sanhedrin*, 7, 13, 25ᵈ; GR., 39, 14 & 84, 2. For further reference *see Theodor*, 378. *Cf.* also LR., 19, 2, "if all the nations of the earth were to assemble they could not whiten a crow's wing."
7. "Only in opinion," Demokritus had said, "there is sweetness, bitterness, warmth, cold; in truth there is nothing but the atoms and empty space." On which Lange comments: "Atomism is as little able today as in the time of Demokritos to explain even the simplest sensation of sound, light, heat, taste, etc. In all the advance of science, in all the modifications of the notion of atoms, this chasm has remained unnarrowed." Lange, *The History of Materialism*, I, 23. On page 267 the great historian of materialism admits that the weak side of Atomism is its inability to explain sensible qualities and sensation out of atoms and space. . . . Kant denied that consciousness could be derived from material movements. The attempt of New Realists to invent a "neutral" stuff is most unconvincing, despite the approval of the incorrigible skeptic, Bertrand Russell. Wasn't the *logos* after all some kind of a "neutral" stuff? *Cf.* Holt, *The Concept of Consciousness*, 52, The Macmillan Co., 1914; Russell, *The Analysis of Mind*, 25 ff., 1924.
8. Jennings, *op. cit.*, 37.
9. Eddington, *Science and the Unseen World*, 30.
10. Professor Eddington writes: "I am not able to agree entirely with the assertion commonly made by scientific philosophers that science, being solely concerned with correct and colorless description, has nothing to do with significances and values. If it were literally true, it would mean that, when the significance of our lives and of the universe around us is under discussion, science is altogether dumb." *Op. cit.*, 61.
11. Ruskin, *op. cit.*, I, 55.
12. *Idem*, Preface, 2nd ed., XLVI.
13. *Illa tibi est . . . verborum copia cassa omnis quae contra sensus instructa paratast.* Lucretius, IV, 511-12.
14. *Detractis de homine sensibus reliqui nihil est.* Cicero, *De Finibus*, I, ix, 30.
15. "*Humanas actiones atque appetitus,*" says Spinoza, "*considerabo . . . ac si quaestio lineis, planis, aut de corporibus esset.*" *Ethics*, III end of Foreword, *Opera*, I, 121.
16. "*Mea quidem sententia, nihil praeter magni sui ingenii acumen ostendit.*" *Idem*.

17. "The truth is," says Professor Schroedinger, "that arithmetic cannot be applied to matters of the mind any more than to any other manifestation of life." *Science and the Human Temperament,* 34.

18. "It is not real," says Kant of geometrical figures applied to things, "but formal. . . . It is quite different when a number of *things* are presented as without me and enclosed within well-defined limits, as, for example, trees, flowers and walks disposed in regular order in a garden; for these are actually existing things which must be known empirically, and not merely an idea of my own which is determined *à priori* according to a principle. The adaptation in this case is empirical or *real,* and presupposes the conception of an end." *Selections from Kant,* trans. Watson, 323-4, Glasgow, 1927.

19. *Ad naturam substantiae pertinet existere. Idem,* I, Prop. 7, *Opera* I, 40.

20. *Idem, Prop.,* 14, 47.

21. *Lo yihyeh lecho Elohim aherim al panai. Exodus,* 20, 3; *Deut.,* 5, 7.

22. *Deus ex solis suae naturae legibus, et a nomine coactus agit., loc. cit., Prop.,* 17, 51.

23. *"Non aliter scilicet, quam inter se conveniunt canis, signum coeleste, et canis, animal latrans."*

24. *Isaiah,* 40, 18.

25. *Quicquid intelligimus tertio cognitionis genere, eo delectamur, et quidem concomitante idea Dei tanquam causa. Idem* V, Prop. 32.

26. *Amor Dei intellectualis, qui ex tertio cognitionis genere oritur, est aeternus, idem, Prop.* 33.

27. "Were the passion towards God not already lit," admits Professor Alexander, "no speculative contemplation or proof of the existence of attributes of a metaphysical God would make him Worshipful." *Op. cit.,* II, 342; *cf.* M. Waxman, *JQR.,* vol. XIX, 430. Note the remarkable insight of Goethe. He protested against those who conceived of Spinoza's God as an abstract idea. "He was most real who says to Himself, I am that I am, and in all forms in which I may appear shall be what I shall be." Quoted from a letter in Lange, *op. cit.,* II, 148.

28. *Song of Songs,* 3, 5.

29. Locke, *An Essay on Human Understanding,* II, 25, 8. The reader will pardon our common man's acquaintance with Locke. It is only superficial. There is much in the philosopher that he knoweth not.

30. *The Nature of the Physical World,* 342, Cambridge, 1928.

31. Heraclitus of Ephesus, *Fragments,* 41. Greek text by Bywater, Eng. trans. by Patrick, 94; quoted by Aristotle, *Metaphysics,* IV, v., 1010a, 10-15; *cf.* also Plato, *Cratylus,* 402a.

32. Readers of Dante's *Paradiso* may recall what happens to Logic and Metaphysics in the hands of a poet.

33. Renan, *Histoire générale et système comparé des Langues Sémitiques,* I, 3-4, Paris, 1855.

34. See the Introduction to his *Hobat ha-Lebabot*; in Albo, *op. cit.,* I, 10, Husik, 63, we read: "We find no clear pronouncement upon this matter in the discussions of the Talmudic Rabbis. And yet they should have treated of those principles which are the bases and foundations of divine law, seeing that human happiness and spiritual reward are based upon them, as they have treated of torts and contracts which have to do with material interests merely, and are the basis of political and social order." *Cf.* also Klatzkin, *Antologia shel ha-Pilosophiah ha-Ivrit,* I, Preface 8-9.

35. Italics mine.

36. *Op. cit.,* II, 343.

37. *Idem*, 344.

38. *Op. cit.*, 4-5.

39. Albert Lewkowitz, *Religion und Philosophie im juedischen Denken der Gegenwart*, in *MGWJ.*, vol. 79, 8.

40. C. E. M. Joad, *Guide to Modern Thought*, 75, New York, 1933.

41. *Idem*, 120.

42. Sir Wm. Dampier, *A History of Science*, 446-77. *Das religioese Weltbild uebersteigert zwar fuer Bergson das philosophische Weltbild*, Lewkowitz, *loc. cit.*, 9. Of Spinoza, Royce says: "his fundamental personal interest in philosophy lay rather more in its bearing upon life than in its value as a pure theory."

CHAPTER VI

1. The present volume is an expansion of a lecture delivered at the University of Illinois, April 16, 1935.

2. *Epistle to the Jews of Marseilles*, II, 26^b, bottom, quoted in Friedlaender, *Past and Present*, 168-9.

3. The reference escapes me.

4. For Saadia Gaon, as *the* philosopher rather than theologian *cf.* Neumark's Review *of Malter's Saadia* in *HUC Annual*, I, 504-73.

5. This thesis found its classic statement in Achad Ha'am's Essay, *Shilton ha-Sechel. Al Parashat Derachim*, IV, 1-37. An English translation entitled, *The Supremacy of Reason* will be found in Leon Simon's *Ten Essays on Zionism and Judaism* by Achad Ha'am, 162-222, London, 1922.

6. Friedlaender, *op. cit.*, 428.

7. H. A. Wolfson in the *JQR.*, vol. VII, 3.

8. Philo is of course more or less of an exception. Among Christians St. Augustine and the radical John Scotus Erigena should be recalled. The latter, too, made philosophy and religion synonymous—both of which according to him emanated from the same divine Reason. The well-known dictum in some quarter was *veram esse philosophiam veram religionem, conversimque veram religionem esse veram philosophiam. Cf.* E. Gilson, *La Philosophie au Moyen Age*, 14; M. deWulf, *History of Medieval Philosophy*, I, 123-4, 3rd Eng. ed.; H. Bett, *Johannes Scotus Erigena*, 88-149, Cambridge, 1925. Of Maimonides' successors, perhaps only Gersonides went beyond him. The English reader not acquainted with Gersonides will find an intelligent and well-informed guide in N. H. Adlerblum's excellent book, *A Study of Gersonides*, Columbia University Press, 1926.

9. *Deut.*, 4, 6.

10. *Isaiah*, 29, 14.

11. *Guide*, II, 11.

12. L. Roth, *Spinoza, Descartes and Maimonides*, 67, Oxford, 1924.

13. *Guide*, I, 71 & 75.

14. A. Foucher de Careil, *La Philosophie juive et la Cabale*, 2 (2nd part), Paris, 1861. Roth, *op. cit.*, 81; Guttmann, *Moses b. Maimon*, I, 226, Leipzig, 1908.

15. *Guide*, I, 73, under the sixth prop.

16. *AR.*, I, 46-51; *b. Bechorot*, 8^b; *cf.* Professor Ginzberg's article in *JE. verbum* Athenians.

17. Letter from R. Aaron b. Meshullam of Lunel to R. Meir haLevi Abulafia, *Collection of Maimonides' Responsa & Letters*, III, 12^a, Leipzig,

1859; Solomon Duran at the end of his controversial volume *Milhemet Miz-vah*, 30, Leipzig, 1856, speaks of Maimonides as a descendant of David. Abraham b. Yehiya in *Shalshelet ha-Kabalah* (no pagination, top of first page of section designated Rambam) gives Rabbi Judah the Prince as an-cester; *cf.* Azulai, *Shem ha-Gedolim verbum* ha-Rambam, 61ᵉ&ᵈ; *cf.* also Responsa, II, Preface, iii, n. 2. For Hillel as a descendant of David *see j. Taanit*, 4, 2, 68ᵃ; *GR.*, 98, 13.

18. Tradition reports that R. Joseph ibn Megas the teacher of R. Maimon, father of Moses, predicted that the child would become distinguished and that "all Israel from the rising of the sun to the setting thereof would walk in his light." Saadia ibn Danan in the collection of essays *Hemdah Genuzah*, 30ᵇ, Koenigsberg, 1856. At the death of Megas, Maimonides was probably no more than six years old; *cf.* however, Azulai, *loc. cit.*, 61ᵈ.

19. The closing sentences of his *Commentary on the Mishnah*. Yellin & Abrahams, *op. cit.*, 32. The Jewish Publication Society of America, 1903. In another connection Maimonides wrote: "I am the least of the scholars of Spain, whose luster exile has dimmed. Ever I have toiled upward into the night, but ne'er attained the wisdom of my fathers. Hard and evil days over-took me & dragged on without peace." *Iggeret Teman, Responsa*, II, 1ᵇ.

20. Note his endearing *Introduction* to *Tohorot*. Recall his endearing appellation *ha-Goy ha-Tahor ha-Zeh. Cf.* also *Guide*, II, 12, "for our na-tion is a wise nation."

21. In his letter to the scholars of Lunel Maimonides wrote: "In these hard times there are no men left to uphold the ensign of Moses and to study diligently the words of R. Ashi except you and the cities adjoining you . . . but everywhere else . . . Torah has perished in their midst. Most of the larger communities are dead, others are very close to it." *Responsa*, II, 44ᵇ.

22. "You are not an ignoramus," he writes to the humble Joseph ibn Gabbar of Bagdad, a man of little learning, "but our pupil and our be-loved one. So is everyone who wishes to devote himself to study. Even if he understand only one verse or one *halachah*. . . . The important thing is to engage in study. He who neglects study or never studies, of him it is said, 'he hath despised the word of the Lord.'" *Numbers*, 15, 31. Responsa, II, 15ᶜ; found also in Eliezer Ashkenazi's collection, *Ta'am Zekenim*, 73, Frankfurt a.M., 1854.

23. *Responsa*, Introduction, LX, ed. A. Freimann, Jerusalem, 1934.

24. *Guide*, II, 2.

25. Friedlaender, *op. cit.*, 172.

26. In *Ma'amar Tehiyat ha-Metim, Responsa*, II, 10ᵇ, he wrote: "If I could put the Talmud into one paragraph, I would not do it in two." Kauf-man, *Geschichte der Attributenlehre*, 364, Gotha, 1877; Yellin & Abrahams, *op. cit.*, 72-3.

27. *j. Horoyot*, 3, 5, 44ᶜ; *b. idem* & *b. Berachot*, end.

28. *Cf.* his Introduction to *Tohorot* and note the confidence with which he contrasts his knowledge of the obsolete laws, with that of his predecessors.

29. *See*, for example, his *Kiddush ha-Shem, Responsa*, II, 13ᵈ; *Ma'amar ha-Ibbur, idem*, 17ᵃ.

30. "Above all things I prize the teaching of the fundamentals of religion and faith." *Commentary, Mish. Berachot*, end.

31. S. Munk, *Mélanges de Philosophie juive et arabe*, 339-41, Paris, 1859; Malter, *HUC Annual*, 1904, 55-71; DeLacy O'Leary, *Arabic Thought and Its Place in History*, 136-43, London, 1922; *The Legacy of Islam*,

254-5, Oxford, 1931; T. J. deBoer, *The History of Philosophy in Islam*, trans. Jones, 97-106, London, 1933.

32. Munk, *op. cit.*, 352-66; O'Leary, *op. cit.*, 168-80; R. A. Nicholson, *A Literary History of the Arabs*, 360-1; *The Legacy of Islam*, 254-61; deBoer, 131-48.

33. Munk, *op. cit.*, 341-52; *Legacy*, 255-6; Nicholson, 360; O'Leary, 143-56; deBoer, 106-28. L. G. Lévy, *Maimonide*, 45 & n. 10, Les Grands Philosophes, Paris, 1932.

34. Munk, *op. cit.*, 418-58; E. Renan, *Averroès et l'Averroïsme*, 5th ed. Paris; *Legacy*, 275-9; deBoer, *op. cit.*, 187-99; also Ueberweg, *History of Philosophy*, 411, 417, New York, 1885.

35. *Cum fere totius philosophiae consideratio ad Dei cognitionem ordinetur.* Almost every philosophical question tends to the knowledge of God. *Summa Contra Gentiles*, I, 4, 8ᵃ.

36. Rousselot, *op. cit.*, *passim*, particularly 223-9. E. Gilson, *op. cit.*, 161-93; *St. Thomas Aquinas*, C. Lattery ed., chs. 1 & 3, Cambridge-St. Louis, 1924; deWolf, *op. cit.*, II, 3-32; Fr. Olgiat; *The Key to St. Thomas*, trans. Zybura, *passim*, particularly the last chapter, St. Louis-London, 1929.

37. *Guide*, III, 18; cf. H. A. Wolfson, *JQR.*, vol. VII, 1; *see infra* p. 209, n. 31.

38. According to some at the age of 23.

39. It would be interesting to speculate whether Maimonides could have written a work like Anselm's *Monologium*, which was composed at the request of certain monks who wanted proof of the existence of God on the basis of pure reason without any reference to Scripture, *quatenus auctoritate Scripturae penitus nihil in ea persuaderetur. Sed quicquid per singulas investigationes finis assereret, id ita esse . . . rationis necessitas breviter cogeret . . . Monologium* I, 1 & 2, in Migne, *Patrologia*, vol. 158, col. 143.

40. *Guide*, Introduction.

41. *Gesammelte Schriften von M. Steinschneider*, Malter & Marx, eds., 35-89, 375-98; *Enc. Judaica*, II, 33-8.

42. *Psalms*, 119, 126.

43. *Mish. Abot*, 2, 12.

44. *Guide*, Introduction.

45. *See*, ch. 6 of the *Eight Chapters*.

46. A. Weiss, *Moses b. Maimon, Fuehrer der Unschluessigen* I, Introduction, CLXXIV, Leipzig, 1923.

47. *Guide*, Introduction.

48. *Ps.*, 25, 14. *Guide, idem.* Note how Maimonides unexplained leaves the obscure statement of R. Akiba. *Guide*, II, 30; the vision of Ezekiel, III, 1-7; evil not emanating from God, III, 22; *cf.* also his letter to ibn Gabbar, *Responsa*, II, 16ᵇ. He advises him not to delve into these depths. *See* also Munk, *Le Guide*, etc., II, 240, n. 3; III, 7, n. 1 & 162, n. 1.

49. *Guide*, I, 17. In Diogenes Laertius we read: Plato has employed a variety of terms making his system less intelligible to the ignorant. III, 63. Of Heraclitus he reports that he deposited his book *On Nature* in the temple of Artemis and deliberately had made the treatise "the more obscure" in order that none but adepts should approach it. IX, 6. Diodorus Siculus reports that the ancient priests were unwilling to give out the truth to the public, on the ground that perils overhang any man who discloses, to the common crowd, the secret knowledge about God. Maimonides had already stated in his Introduction to *Zeraim* that the sages had veiled great truths in the *Hagadah* to keep them from women and children.

50. *Velo Aristo medaber mi-toch gerono ela torah shelemah she-lanu.* It is not Aristotle but wholly our Torah which speaks through him. Z. H. Hajes, *Darche Moshe,* 1ᵇ, Zolkiew, 1840, reprinted in the volume on Maimonides, edited by Rabbi J. L. Fischman, Jerusalem, 1935.

51. *Guide,* Introduction.

52. Anent his exposition of Omniscience and Freedom of the Will, he once wrote to a correspondent: "Whoever disregards my explanations, built as they are on solid rock, and goes rummaging in the *Hagadah, Midrash,* or in the writings of the Geonim to ferret out a word here and there with which to challenge my arguments—arguments rooted in knowledge and un-derstanding—whoever does that is guilty of suicide." *Responsa,* I, 159, 34ᵃ; *cf.* also his *Epistle to the Jews of Marseilles* II, 25ᵃ&ᵇ, reprinted by Professor Alexander Marx in the *HUC Annual,* vol. III, 311-58, with emenda-tions, variants and a most valuable introduction and notes. Concerning his *Ma'amar ha-Ibbur* Maimonides writes: "No one but a man of faith and knowledge, diligence, and alertness in pursuit of the sciences will be able to understand it . . . provided he toils many years in metaphysics and achieves in it notable success. Otherwise my words will be (of no more value to him than) the price (with which to buy wisdom) in the hand of a fool." *Commentary on Mish. Rosh ha-Shanah,* 2, 6; *cf. Proverbs,* 17, 16.

53. *See,* for example, Saadia's *apologia* . . . "even though I confess that my intelligence is inadequate and my erudition limited, neither am I the wisest among my contemporaries." *Op. cit.,* 2, 39; *cf.* also Bahyah, *Hobot ha-Lebabot,* Introduction, 40.

54. Witness the extraordinary confidence of Einstein. Read the striking account in A. Moszkowski, *Einstein the Searcher,* 5, trans. Brose, New York, 1921. Moszkowski wanted to know Einstein's state of mind while his theories were being tested—the tension, uncertainty, etc. Einstein laconically replied: "Such questions did not lie in my path. That result could not be otherwise than right. I was only concerned in putting the result into a lucid form. I did not for one second doubt that it would agree with observation. There was no sense in getting excited about what was self-evident."

55. *Guide,* Introduction.

56. *Propositum nostrae intentionis in hoc opere est, ea quae ad Chris-tianam religionem pertinent, eo modo tradere, secundum quod congruit ad eruditionem incipientum . . . ea quae ad sacram doctrinam pertinent, bre-viter ac dilucide prosequi, secundum quod materia patietur. Opera Omnia,* etc., vol. IV, 5, Leonine ed. 1888. Maimonides writes in the Intro-duction to the *Guide*: "There is no need to notice them (the multitude of ordinary men) in this treatise."

57. *Hil. Yesode ha-Torah,* 2, 11.

CHAPTER VII

1. *Supra,* p. 55.

2. Albo, *op. cit.,* II, 5, 221.

3. *Quaedam vero sunt ad quae etiam ratio naturalis pertingere potest, sicut est Deum esse, Deum esse unum, et alia huiusmodi; quae etiam philosophi demonstrative de Deo probaverunt, ducti naturalis lumine rationis, Summa Contra Gentiles,* I, 3, 7ᵇ, *Opera* XIII.

4. *Qui autem probare nititur Trinitatem Personarum naturali ratione,*

fidei dupliciter derogat. Primo quidem, quantum ad dignitatem ipsius fidei, quae est ut sit de rebus invisibilibus, quae rationem humanum excedunt . . . Secundo cum enim aliquis ad probandam fidem inducit rationes quae non sunt cogentes, cedit in irrisionem infidelium, Summa Theologica, I, qu. 32, 1; 3, Opera, IV, 350. Cf. also Summa Contra Gentiles, loc. cit.

5. *b. Berachot,* 31^{b} and elsewhere.

6. *Guide,* I, 33; ibn Daud, *Emuna Ramah,* I, 1, 12, Berlin, 1919, writes: The fundamentals of metaphysics are not expounded in the prophetic books not to make them too difficult for the multitude.

7. *Nam, quandoquidem non possumus Lumine Naturali percipere, quod simplex obedientia via ad salutem sit, sed sola Revelatio doceat, id ex singulari Dei gratia, quam Ratione essequi non possumus, fieri; hinc sequitur, Scripturam magnum admodum solamen mortalibus attulisse. Quippe omnes absolute obedire possunt, et non nisi paucissimi sunt, si cum toto humano genere comparentur, qui virtutis habitum ex solo Rationis ductu acquirunt; adeoque, nisi hoc Scripturae testimonium haberemus, de omnium fere salute dubitaremus. Tractatus,* XV, end, *Opera,* II, 257-8.

8. *Supponit, Prophetas in omnibus inter se convenisse, summosque fuisse Philosophos et Theologos; idem,* VII, 188.

9. *Idem,* XIII, 238-9.

10. *Nam nihil aliud curaverunt, quam nugas Aristotelicas, et sua propria figmenta ex Scriptura extorquere; quo mihi quidem nihil magis ridiculum videtur; idem,* I, 97.

11. *Idem,* XIV, 245.

12. *Unicum verae vitae exemplar. Idem,* XIII, 242.

13. *Philosophiae enim scopus nihil est praeter veritatem; Fidei autem . . . nihil praeter obedientiam et pietatem. Idem,* XIV, 249.

14. *Idem,* XV, 250. The thesis had been vigorously advanced in the sixteenth century by the scholastic thinker Pomponatius. Not only the Prophets, he urged, but even the secular legislators were more concerned with making men virtuous than enlightened. Renan, *Averroès,* etc., 83.

15. *Idem,* XIII, 238.

16. *. . . hanc Maimonidae sententiam ut noxiam, inutilem, et absurdam explodimus. Idem,* VII, 189.

17. *Idem,* XII, 231. When Descartes heard of the condemnation by the church of Galileo because of his theory of the earth's movement, he wrote to the priest Mersenne: "*Et it* (the theory) *est tellement lié avec toutes les parties de mon Traité que je ne l'en saurois détacher, sans rendre le reste tout défectueux. Mais comme je ne voudrois pour rien du monde qui'l sortît de moi un discours ou il se trouvât le moindre mot qui fût desapprouvé de l'église,* etc. . . . from the letter of the end of November, 1633, *Oeuvres,* I, 171, Paris, 1897.

18. He might even have quoted in his support a contemporary Jewish authority. "Those among us," wrote the physician Joseph Solomon Delmedigo, "who love to philosophize and therefore believe that the Prophets were philosophers like themselves, whose words can only be explained philosophically, are mistaken. The Talmudists are the successors to the Prophets . . . and in their words will we find the true meaning of Scripture." *Mazreph le-Hochmah,* 77. An older and more distinguished authority had written: "Philosophy and the Torah cannot pursue one path. The wisdom of the Torah is based on the Sinaitic Mosaic tradition, whereas the 'wisdom' of Philosophy is natural." R. Asher b. Yehiel (Rosh) *Responsa,* 55, 9, 105^{a},

204   THE JEW AND THE UNIVERSE

Vilno, 1881; *cf.* I. H. Weiss, *Dor Dor ve-Dorshov*, V, 67. For a discussion of the double truth *cf.* Renan, *op. cit.*, 200-435; M. Maywald, *Die Lehre von der zweifachen Wahrheit*, etc., Berlin, 1871.

19. *Idem*, XV, 254. Spinoza, of course, did not have to go back to the Averroists. He could find this dichotomy energetically expressed in Hobbes' *De Cive* and *The Leviathan*.

20. . . . *An, quaeso, tenemur credere, quod miles Josua Astronomiam callebat? Idem*, II, 113-14.

21. *See* Karl Sass in the *Spinoza Festschrift*, 187, S. Hessing ed., Heidelberg, 1933.

22. *Joshua*, 10, 4.

23. *Numbers*, 27, 20.

24. *Deut.*, 39, 9.

25. *GR.*, 26, 8, 248 and note *a.l.* It is not, of course, our intention to refute Spinoza with citations from a tradition whose authority he did not recognize. Our aim is to show that persons credited with Divine Inspiration were assumed to know more than the laws of conduct. That assumption underlies the Bible as well as rabbinic literature.

26. Ginzberg, *Legends* V, 149, 53.

27. *PRE.*, 8, 13, Warsaw, 1885.

28. *GR.*, 67, 9; *ER.*, 1, 1; *b. Sotah*, 13ᵃ where the gift of prophecy is also ascribed to Miriam; *cf.* also *GR.*, 44, 14, 433 & note *a.l.*

29. *TG.*, 192 & 188.

30. Ginzberg, *loc. cit.*, 368, 391 & 379, 5.

31. *SD.*, 357, 149ᵃ&ᵇ; *TN.*, 162.

32. *Otiyot d'R. Akiba*, 16ᵃ & 6ᵈ Koretz, 5545; *cf. b. Rosh-ha-Shanah*, 21ᵇ & *b. Nedarim*, 38ᵃ, where we read: Fifty gates of understanding were created in the world and all of them but one were turned over to Moses.

33. *GR.*, 39, 16, 374; *YJ.*, 17. *Agadat Esther*, 9, 70.

34. *b. Hullin*, 24ᵃ. As preparation for the battle of Ai, Joshua spent the night in "the depths of the study of the Law." *b. Erubin*, 63ᵇ.

35. *j. Peah*, 1, 1, 15ᵇ.

36. Philo, *Biblical Antiquities*, 20, 133.

37. Ginzberg, *Legends*, VI, 464, 108.

38. *Idem*, VI, 180, 56.

39. *b. Temurah*, 16ᵃ.

40. *Antiquities*, V, 8, 4.

41. For literature *see* Ginzberg, *loc. cit.*, 282-3, notes 18, 24 & 25. For influence of Solomon on Aristotle add to Professor Ginzberg's sources, R. Moses Isserles' *Torat ha-Olah*, I, 11, 17ᵃ, Prague, 5330; *cf.* also I. B. Levenson, *Jehoshaphat*, 18, Warsaw, 1883. For earlier references to the influence of Jews on Aristotle, *see* Josephus, *Contra Apionem*, I, 22; Schuerer, *Geschichte des juedischen Volkes im ZAJ.*, ch. III, 10, 3rd ed., Leipzig, 1898. There was even a legend to the effect that Aristotle had embraced Judaism. Azariah di Rossi, *Me'or Einaim, Imrei Binah*, 22, 236, Vilno, 1863; *cf.* also Tatian, *Oratio ad Graecos*, chs. 40 & 41, Migne, *Patrologia*, vol. VI, 152-63; Tertullian, *Apologeticus*, 19, 1, writes . . . *respici potest tam iura vestra quam studia de lege deque divina doctrina concepisse. . . . Quod prius, hoc, sit semen necesse est* . . . it can be that your laws and your studies (Roman-Pagan) alike were fertilized from the law and teaching of God (Torah). The earlier must be the seed. *See* also F. A. Paley's Preface to *The Epics*

of Hesiod, xvi, xvii-xx, 2nd ed. Bibliotheca Classica, 1883, & Decharme's
La Critique des Traditions Religieuses chez les Grecs, 5-6, Paris, 1904, for
the possible influence of the Pentateuch on Hesiod. Delmedigo, *op. cit.*, 107,
also ascribes Greek philosophy to Jewish origin. *Cf.* Munk, *op. cit.*, I, 333,
n. 3; Malter, *JQR.*, I, 176, n. 29; L. G. Lévy, *op. cit.*, 42, n. 1.

42. *MPs.*, 5, 55; *cf.* also *b. Sanhedrin*, 102ᵃ.

43. *Psalms*, 25, 4 & 14.

44. *Prophetas non fuisse perfectiore mente praeditos, sed quidem potentia vividius imaginandi. Loc. cit.*, II, 107.

45. *Idem*, 108-9.

46. *Idem.*, 118; NR., 19, 3.

47. *Artem tantam tanque operosam et perinde fructuosam.* Cicero, *De Finibus*, I, 21, 72. One of the most noted of present-day scientist-philosophers does not hesitate to make the function of Reason the promotion of the art of life. Of course, Professor Whitehead's "art of life" is most comprehensive. *The Function of Reason*, 2, Princeton, 1929.

48. PR., 14, 121; NR., 19, 3; YKs., 178; Mish. Sanhedrin, 10, 3; b. idem, 110ᵇ; b. Nedarim, 20ᵇ; ExR., 23, 15; MEx., 44ᵇ; 72ᵇ. ARN. Appendix A, 148; YPs., 760.

49. *Loc. cit.*, III, 124-5.

50. *Loc. cit.*, 803-87, particularly chs. 1-5, 22, 29, 31.

51. *A pueritia opinionibus de Scriptura communibus imbutus fuerim. Loc. cit.*, IX, 207.

52. *Idem*, XIII, 2640. Spinoza's respect for Scripture goes even further. "Unless we would do violence to Scripture," he writes, "we must certainly admit that the Israelites heard a real voice, for Scripture expressly says, *Deut.*, 5, 4 'God spoke with you face to face,' i.e., as two men ordinarily interchange ideas through the instrumentality of their two bodies; and therefore it seems more consonant with Holy Writ that God really did create a voice of some kind with which the Decalogue was revealed." I, 96. Spinoza here uses several expressions found verbatim in Maimonides' letter to Hasdai Halevi Hasephardi, *ve-ilu lo shanah ha-katuv lomar, va-yishma et ha-kol medaber elav . . . hayiti modeh zeh* (namely, he would have accepted a more rational interpretation of the voice) . . . *ain lanu lomar ela kol nivra. Responsa*, II, 23ᵈ.

53. Shem Tov ibn Shem Tov, *Derashot, Balak*, 56ᵇ, Venice, 1547.

54. *Loc. cit.*, IV, end.

55. *See* how the *Emunah Ramah* assembles at the end of most chapters biblical verses under the heading, *Ketubim Romezim* or *Ketubim Me'idim*.

CHAPTER VIII

1. *Cf.* Professor Ginzberg's article in *JE.*, *verbum Allegorical Interpretations*. He regards already *Hosea*, 12, 5 as an interpreter of the early story of Jacob and the angel. Professor Ginzberg also finds instances of allegory in the *Book of Daniel. See* J. Z. Lauterbach, *The Ancient Jewish Allegorists in Talmud and Midrash, JQR.*, I, 290-333, 503-31. From the ninth century on the primary method of instruction in Europe was the *lectio*, i.e., commenting on a text. deWulf, *op. cit.*, I, 57.

2. Hatch, *op. cit.*, 52-6 and notes *a.l.* For allegoric interpretations of the Koran, *cf.* L. G. Lévy, *op. cit.*, 56, n.4.

3. *De Opificio Mundi*, 56, 157.

4. *Idem*, 59, 156; *Legum Allegoria*, III, 244; *De Mutatione Nominum*, 2, 12; 15, 96; *De Somniis*, I, 27; *cf.* Ginzberg, *op. cit.*, V, 304, 318. For the Patriarchs as the Chariot *see*, *GR.*, 82, 7.

5. *Legum Allegoria*, III, 59, 170.

6. *Exodus*, 33, 7.

7. *Legum Allegoria*, II, 15, 55.

8. *GR.*, 8, 7, 61; *MhaG.*, 52, 3.

9. *j. Peah*, 2, 6, 17[a]; *LR.*, 22, 1; *KR.*, 1, 29. See also L. G. Lévy, *op. cit.*, 55 & n.2.

10. Allegoric interpretation often went so far that it frightened and angered the more conservative proponents of literalness. *Zunz Jubelschrift*, 143.

11. *MEx.*, 53[a], W.

12. *SER.*, 13, 61-2; Ginzberg, *Legends*, V, 42, 142.

13. *GR.*, 64, 7.

14. Ginzberg, *loc. cit.*, V, 421, 128.

15. *Psalms*, 115, 16.

16. *MEx.*, 73[b]; *b. Sukkah*, 5[a]; *see supra.*

17. *b. B. B.*, 25[b]; *TN.*, 48.

18. Josephus, *Antiquities*, 4, 6, 3; *Midrash Agada Numbers*, 136.

19. Both Galileo and Giordano Bruno, unlike Spinoza and Hobbes, assumed that the Bible, intended for the people, spoke the language of the people. But, at the same time both of them were convinced that its authors knew more of natural science than a superficial reading of the scriptural text revealed. *Cf.* Lange, *op. cit.*, I, 233-4 and note *a.l.*

20. *Il Convito*, 3, 5, 189, Ferenze, 1879. Another distinguished Italian wrote: *Aristoteles imperator noster, omnium bonarum artium dictator perpetuus.* Scaliger, *Poetices*, VII, ii, 1, quoted in J. Spingarn, *Literary Criticism in the Renaissance*, 141. Cremonini, a colleague of Galileo at the University of Padua, refused to look through a telescope from the time the instrument, in utter disregard of Aristotle, revealed the satellites of Jupiter. Renan, *Averroès*, etc., 412, 476 to end; Lange, *op. cit.*, vol. I, 220.

21. *See* Preface to *Shem Tov's Commentary.*

22. Professor Friedlaender's first scientific work is entitled, *Der Sprachgebrauch des Maimonides*. It contains a vindication of Maimonides' Arabic style.

23. Past & Present, 205. *See*, however, Maimonides' letter to his son, *Responsa*, II, 39[a-d]. Such far-fetched interpretations are not unknown even in the *Guide*.

24. *Genesis*, 1, 21; *Guide*, I, 1.

25. Ch. Bigg, *The Christian Platonists of Alexandria*, 25-49, 2nd ed., Oxford, 1913.

26. *De Opificio Mundi*, 23, 69; *cf.* Saadia, *op. cit.*, II, 9, 96, in which he interprets *zelem, al derech ha-Gedulah veha-Hashivut*, exaltation and importance. Rabbi pseudo-Jacob Tam puts it most beautifully: Let us make man in our image . . . i.e., in the form most respected among us and most precious to the angels . . . for it is the form of knowledge and wisdom. *Sepher ha-Yashar*, 5, 31. *Cf.*, *GR.*, 8, 9; *PRE.*, 11 where all the angels come to bow before Adam and to call him holy.

CHAPTER IX

1. *b. Berachot*, 33ᵇ; *b. Hagigah*, 15ᵃ; *GR.*, I, 10, 4; *YEx.*, 285; *cf.* also *b. Yebamot*, 49ᵇ for the exculpation of Menasseh from the murder of the prophet Isaiah; Albo, *Sepher ha-Ikkarim*, III, 17, 154. *Cf. Mish. Sanhedrin*, 7, 10, for the legal formula, How shall we foresake our Heavenly Father and worship wood and stone.

2. *De Opificio Mundi*, 61, 171.

3. I, 50.

4. One would hardly need to add, were it not for the willful misunderstanding of Pharisaism, that this is equally characteristic of rabbinic literature. Weigh such utterances as: I shall not listen to you to shake off the yoke of the heavenly government even for one second. *Mish. Berachot*, 2, 5, With every breath that a man draws, he should offer praise to the Holy One Blessed Be He. *GR.*, 14, 9, 134; *DR.*, 2, 26.

5. *Isaiah*, 29, 13; *cf.* D. Neumark, *Toledot ha-Ikkarim be-Yisrael*, 75-7, Odessa, 1912.

6. I, 28.

7. I, 35.

8. *Idem.*

9. Italics mine.

10. *b. Hullin*, 13ᵇ.

11. I, 36.

12. As is evidenced by Maimonides' essay *Tehiyat ha-Metim, Responsa*, II, 8ᵃ; ben David's stricture to *Hil. Teshuvah*, 35, 5; *Nahmanides' Letter to the Rabbis of France* published in *Responsa*, III, 9ᵈ; Abraham Maimon's letter *Milhamot Adonai, idem*, III, 16ᵇ & 23-24. *See* also Yedayah ha-Penini ha-Bedarsi who claims that Maimonides was responsible for the complete eradication among Jews of the belief in corporeality. *Iggeret (Ketav) ha-Hitnazlut*, addressed to the famous R. Solomon b. Adret and published in his *Responsa*, 47ᵈ-48ᵃ, Libau, 5571; Munk, *op. cit.*, I, 34, n. 1.

13. *Guide*, I, 26.

14. Joad, *op. cit.*, 85.

15. *Philosophy*, 157, W. W. Norton & Co., 1927; published in Great Britain under the title *"An Outline of Philosophy."*

16. Dampier, *op. cit.*, 486.

17. Hoeffding, *op. cit.*, 46.

18. *Confessions*, VI, 3.

19. In his Letter to the Rabbis of France Nahmanides emphasizes that in the Bible and Talmud, in the writings of the *Geonim* and *Paytanim* incorporeality is the accepted belief. Already Abraham, he declared, no longer believed in a corporeal God. *Responsa*, III, 9ᵈ-10ᵃ.

20. The Torah, says Albo, expressly emphasizes the dogma of the Unity and Incorporeality and makes clear that God cannot be apprehended. *Op. cit.*, 3, 25, 223; *cf.* also Crescas, *Or Adonai*, 1, 3, 19ᵃ, *Ferrara*, 1555. None of the medieval Jewish, Arab or Christian philosophers ever experienced a shortage of biblical verses.

21. Maimonides notes that in the Bible the expressions burning anger, provocation or jealousy are applied to God, only in reference to idolatry

and that none but idolaters are called enemy, adversary, or hater of the Lord, *Guide*, I, 36.

22. *Exodus*, 20, 4; *Deut.*, 5, 8.

23. *Idem*, 4, 15.

24. *Idem*, 12.

25. *Isaiah*, 40, 18; *cf.* Maimonides, *Mish. Sanhedrin*, 10, Introduction, *Yesod*, 3. *See supra*, p. 48.

26. *Exodus*, 3, 13-14.

27. I *Samuel*, 19, 12. The still small voice has not yet lost its charm or effectiveness. *Cf.* Eddington, *Science and the Unseen World*, 26.

28. For Maimonides' deep appreciation of the efforts of Onkelos, *see Guide*, I, 26 and elsewhere.

29. The term is frequently employed in rabbinic literature. *MEx.*, 20ᵃ&ᵇ; *b. Erubin*, 22ᵃ; *Yoma*, 3ᵇ; *b. Hagigah*, 13ᵇ; *Sotah*, 35ᵃ; *b. B. K.*, 79ᵇ; *Mish. Sanhedrin*, 6, 5; *ER.*, 29, 7. Opinions differ as to the derivation of the term. Isaac Lamperonti, *Pahad Yizhak, verbum Kevayachol* regards it an abbreviation of *ki ba-adam ye-amer ken ve-lo be-loha*, Such a thing can be said of man but not of God.

30. S. D. Luzzatto, *Ohev Ger*, 1-25, Krakow, 1895; A. Geiger, *Urschrift und Uebersetzungen der Bibel*, 259, Breslau, 1857; H. Malter, *Saadia Gaon, His Life and Works*, 144 notes 310-11. Saadia as it is well known studiously eliminated all anthropomorphism from his Arabic translation of the Bible.

31. *GR.*, 19, 18, 178.

32. *ER.*, 28, end; Philo, *De Decalogo*, 9.

33. *Mish. Abot*, 5, 1; *b. Rosh-ha-Shanah*, 32ᵃ; *b. Megillah*, 22ᵇ.

34. Ginzberg, *op. cit.*, V, 111, 102.

35. *GR.*, 34, 10, 319.

36. *See supra*, p. 8.

37. There are, as is well known, verses which do ascribe a likeness to God. *Genesis*, 1, 26; 5, 1; *Numbers*, 12, 8; *Job*, 4, 16; *cf.* however, Neumark, *op. cit.*, 78.

38. *See* note 12 this chapter.

39. Note, for example, his explanation in *Mish. Sanhedrin loc. cit.* of the passage from *b. Hagigah*, 15ᵃ.

CHAPTER X

1. *Guide*, I, 18.

2. *Idem*, I, 26.

3. *Idem*, 23.

4. Aristotle, *Metaphysics*, IV, iv, 1007a, 34; *cf. Albo, op. cit.*, 2, 9, 1, 51.

5. *Guide*, I, 52.

6. Italics mine.

7. *Idem*, 50.

8. The origin of the doctrine of divine attributes, L. G. Lévy, *op. cit.*, 51, n. 3, finds in neo-Platonism, whereas Husik, *JQR.*, vol. IV, 506-7 discovers it in Christianity. *Cf.* Munk, *op. cit.*, I, 180, n. 1.

9. *Idem*, 52. In Kant's *Critique of Teleological Judgment* we read: "We can *think* the attributes of the Supreme Being only by analogy. How, indeed, could we investigate directly the nature of a Being to whom nothing

similar is given in experience? . . . the attributes by which we think the Supreme Being do not enable us to *know* Him as He is, nor can we theoretically predicate them of Him. To contemplate that Being as He is *in Himself* speculative reason must assume the form of the determinant judgment, and this is contrary to its very nature." *Selections*, 349.

10. Italics mine.

11. *Op. cit.,* I, 336.

12. *Guide, loc. cit.*

13. *Guide,* I, 56 & also 20; Hume employs almost the same language. "As all perfection is entirely relative, we ought never to imagine that we comprehend the attributes of this Divine Being, or to suppose that these perfections have any analogy or likeness to the perfections of a human creature. Wisdom, Thought, Design, Knowledge; these we justly ascribe to Him; because these words are honorable among men, and we have no other language or other conceptions, by which we can express our adoration of Him. But let us beware, lest we think, that our ideas any wise correspond to His perfections, or that His attributes have any resemblance to these qualities among men. *Op. cit.,* 29.

14. Italics mine.

15. *Cf.* Crescas, *op. cit.,* I, 1ᵃ.

16 *Guide,* I, 35.

17. *Idem,* 50.

18. *Deut.,* 4, 35.

19. *Isaiah,* 43, 10.

20. *Idem,* 44, 6; *cf.* also 45, 6 & 18; 48, 13; *cf.* Bahyah, *op. cit.,* 1, 6.

21. b. *Pesahim,* 50ᵇ; *YEx.,* 171; *Otiyot d'R. Akiba,* 1, 76; A. Marmorstein, *HUC. Annual,* I, 467-99.

22. *MEx.,* 45ᵃ; *TEx.,* 79; *PR.,* 21, 6.

23. *DR.,* 11, 5.

24. *Students, Scholars and Saints,* 29, The Jewish Publication Society of America, 1928.

25. *Otiyot d'R. Akiba,* 1, 7ᵇ; *YG.,* 1.

26. Moore, *Judaism,* I, 393.

27. *Guide,* I, 57.

28. *Idem,* 51.

29. *Idem,* 57.

30. *Idem,* 51.

31. The root of the question is already present in Plato's *Ideas.* The early Middle Ages found the problem in Porphyry's *Isagoge* or Introduction to Aristotle's Categories—through the medium of Boethius Latin translation. At the end of the eleventh century the controversy received added impetus through the work of Roscelin. de Wulf, in *Archiv fuer Geschichte der Philosophie,* 1896, 427; *idem, Le Probleme des Universaux dans son Evolution Historique des IVe au XIIIe siècle; cf.* Munk, *op. cit.,* I, 185, n. 2.

32. *Guide,* III, 18. Professor Finkelstein, in a letter to the author, argues on the basis of the present quotation that Maimonides was a conceptualist. We find it difficult to accept his interpretation. *Cf. Guide,* I, ch. 46.

33. *Idem,* I, 51.

34. *Idem,* 57.

35. *Metaphysics,* XII, v, 1070b, 36—1070b, 36—1071a, 1.

36. Saadia, *op. cit.,* 2, 1, 91-2; Bahyah, *op. cit.,* 1, 10, Kaufmann, *op. cit.,* 19-31, 141-54; Malter, *op. cit.,* 206.

37. The phrase belongs to Erasmus Darwin. *Cf. 19th Century*, vol. 90, 731.

38. *JAOS.*, vol. VI, 299 & *supra*, p. 5.

39. At the end of *Yodaim*, Maimonides notes that the tractate does not conclude with the verse from *Exodus*, "and Pharaoh said: 'Who is the Lord, that I should hearken unto His voice to let Israel go?'" (*Exodus*, 5, 2). His reason is characteristic. The verse is not a happy ending, since it contains Pharaoh's denial of God. Therefore, the redactor of the Mishnah added another verse. It is just such trifles that show how much more than a "Jew in letter" Maimonides was.

40. *b. Berachot*, 3ᵃ; *b. Megillah*, 29ᵃ; *b. Taanit*, 16ᵃ.

41. *Hil. Teshubah*, 10, 3; *cf.* also letter to ibn Gabbar, *Responsa*, II, 16ᵈ; *Guide*, III, 54. Lévy, *op. cit.*, 189-90.

42. Somewhere in his *Short Treatise*.

43. *Op. cit.*, IV, 2-3, 199-200.

44. Aristotle was even more ruthless. "The ultimate substrate," he writes, "is in itself neither a particular thing, nor a quantity, nor anything else. Nor indeed is it the negation of these; for the negations too will only apply to it accidentally." *Metaphysics* VII, 3, 1029a, 26.

45. *Guide*, I, 58.

46. *Idem*, I, 60.

47. *Idem*, 59.

48. *Idem*.

49. *Idem*, 60.

50. *Idem*, 34; *cf.* Albo, *op. cit.*, II, 1, end, 12 says: The Torah instead of beginning with an exposition of God's essence, begins with pointing to his work. "Science," says Professor Planck, "proves its validity by pointing to its achievement." *Op. cit.*, 135.

51. *Guide*, I, 54.

52. Maimonides was not the first to speak of negative attributes. The origin of the doctrine is to be found in Plato's theory of Ideas. Among Jews he was preceded by Philo, *Quod Deus Immutabilis Sit.*, V, 1, 275 & ibn Daud, *Emunah Ramah*, II, 3, 51-6; Kaufmann, *op. cit.*, 260-344. Philo's view was so extreme that he was charged with atheism. *Cf.* A. F. Daehne, *Geschichtliche Darstellung der juedisch-Alexandrinischen Religionsphilosophie*, I, 127-8, Halle, 1834. In a less extreme form the doctrine was taught by Bahya, ibn Gabirol, Halevi and ibn Zaddik. Al-Kindi introduced it to the Arabs. *See* Munk, *op. cit.*, I, 238, 1.
Scholasticism knew this method of defining Deity from pseudo-Dionysius the Areopagite. In his treatise on *Mythical Theology*, he spoke of God as non-being, and suggested that the highest knowledge we have of Him is a "mystic ignorance." God is beyond Good, Truth, Eternity, beyond the ten categories and all the perfections that man can attribute to Him. de Wulf, *op. cit.*, I, 101-2; Gilson, *op. cit.*, 16-17. Erigena was as insistent as Maimonides in his denial of positive attributes to God, even that of existence. He even refused to credit God with Knowledge of Himself. To the logician Scotus it seemed preposterous to allow the duality of the knower and the known in the Deity. *Deus itaque nescit se quid est, quia non est quid, incomprehensibilis quippe in aliquo est sibi et omne intellectui. De Divisione Naturae*, 1, 15, *Patrologia*, vol. 22, col. 463. *Idem*, 464, Scotus writes: *Nam qui dicit superessentialis est, non, quid est, dicit, sed, quid non est; dicit enim essentiam non esse, sed plusquam essentiam.* Gilson, *loc. cit.*, 18; de Wulf, I, 125-160; Bett, *op. cit.*, 23-4. The German mystic Suso defined God as "nameless nothingness."

53. *Exodus,* 33, end. Cf. *Guide,* I, 37 & 57; ibn Daud, *loc. cit.;* Crescas, *op. cit.,* I, 3, 17ᶜ. Earlier Crescas remarks that Moses never sought to comprehend the essence of God, 15ᶜ; Albo, *op. cit.,* II, 31, 15, 217 took his hint from the "silent still voice" of Elijah. Note also Abraham b. Maimon's comment on *Exodus,* 33, 20 "for man shall not see me and live." Nothing living can see God, not even the holy angels can conceive his greatness. *Milhamot Adonai, Responsa,* III, 16ᵃ; *Sifra,* 4ᵃ. Cf. *Guide,* I, 21, 53, 64.

54. *GR.,* 65, 5. Cf. also *b. Hagigah* & *b. Kidd.,* 40ᵃ. He who has no regard for the Glory of God, it were better he had not been born. Rabbi Abba interprets the dictum to refer to one who gazes into the rainbow. In *Hagigah, loc. cit.,* we also read: He who looks at three things, the rainbow, the Nasi, and the Priests (when they are on the priests' platform, pronouncing the benediction) his eyesight grows dim. On the other hand Moses as a reward for hiding his face was granted the shining face. *Exodus,* 3, 6; 36, 29 to end; *b. Berachot,* 7ᵃ; *Guide,* I, 5 & 59.

55. *MPs.,* 18, 2, 135.

56. *PK.,* 148ᵃ.

57. Kadushin, *op. cit.,* 35.

58. Aquinas, *Summa Theologica,* I, q. 3,a.2, p. 2.

59. *See* preceding page, note 52.

60. The "negativism" has been traced to Buddha himself. "Those whose minds are disgusted with a future existence, the wise who have destroyed the seeds of existence and whose desires do not increase, go out like this lamp." *Sacred Books of the East,* X, 2, 39, Hastings *Enc. Religion & Ethics verbum* Buddhism; cf., however, the interesting statement in Rhys Davids, *Gotama the Man,* 118-21, London, 1928. "Writers," Mrs. Davids puts in the mouth of Buddha, "test my teaching . . . saying that as philosophy I taught the 'not-self,' as religion I taught the 'not-Being' (or going out, Nirvana). In either case the judgment is very wrong. As philosophy my teaching should count as this: the worth of life lies in man's will in choosing the better; *not* in man being a no-thing. As religion my teaching should count as this: the life of man is a way through the worlds to the goal, and not a going out into not-life."

61. *Brihadāranyaka,* II, 4, 12 ff; M. Bloomfield, *The Religion of the Veda;* 269-78.

62. *See* note 52; cf. Hume, *op. cit.,* 27-8.

63. Lange, *op. cit.,* I, 74.

64. The problem of deducing the manifold from the One has not been solved by the old neo-Platonist or by the later mystics and absolute Idealists. On the other hand, Spinoza grants that we can only experience the modes, which are a plurality. Therefore to get back to a monism he takes unwarranted license.

65. In Judaism the attempts at rationalism resulted in many new and significant terms, but in the final analysis they explain nothing about Deity. Examine the terms *Logos, Ma'amar, Or, Kol, Razon,* etc.

66. "During the past fifty years two main conclusions have emerged from the criticism of the scientific method with which philosophers and scientific men alike have been busied. The first of these is that science is essentially analytical, mathematical and mechanical . . . . the second is that the scientific method possesses a remarkably strong subjective element, or in other words, that the world as seen by science is not the world as it really is." Joseph Needham, *Materialism and Religion* in his collection of essays, entitled *The Skeptical Biologist,* 245, London, 1929. Professor Jeans in his *The*

Mysterious Universe, 135, writes: "Many would hold that, from the broad philosophical standpoint, the outstanding achievement of twentieth-century physics is not the theory of relativity with its welding together of space and time, or the theory of quanta with its present apparent negation of the laws of causation, or the dissection of the atom with the resultant discovery that things are not what they seem; it is the general recognition that we are not yet in contact with ultimate reality."

67. Jeans, *loc. cit.*, 113-22.

68. Russell, *Skeptical Essays*, 68.

69. Crescas, *Or Adonai*, I, 2, 3, 15^d-18^c. Albo had never quite made up his mind about the attributes. He both agreed with Maimonides and differed from him. *Op. cit.*, II, 10, 5, 58, "the concept of unity which is predicated of God is negative and not positive." 21, 3, 124, "There is one class of attributes which we ascribe to Him because He is a necessary existent and the cause of all existing things, neither of which He can be conceived to be unless He has the attributes in question. Such attributes are, one, eternal, perpetual, wise, having will, possessing power, and others besides, which God must have in order to be the author of all existing things." 6, 126, "In this way we can ascribe to Him attributes of the second class also, which involve corporeal perceptions. Thus we attribute to Him the sense of smell, which is a sensuous perception, as we read, 'And the Lord smelled the sweet savor.' But we do not attribute it to God as being a corporeal perception, but with a view to the perfection which it involves, namely, that God accepts favorably the offering of a person who brings it with a worthy purpose; we do not think of God as deriving pleasure from the offering which would be a defect." 8, 128, . . . "the attributes are ascribed to God by reason of the perfection that is in them, and not by reason of the defect." *Cf.* also *idem*, chs. 22-26, 129-57. For an earlier attack on Maimonides' doctrine of attributes by Gersonides *see* his *Milhamot Adonai*, III, 3, 132-7, Berlin, 1933. For a discussion of Gersonides, Crescas and Albo *see* H. A. Wolfson *JQR*, vol. VII, 37-40, 198-213, 214-16. For Crescas *see* also M. Waxman, *idem*, vol. VIII, 460-72.

70. *Psalms*, 52, 2.

71. *Idem*, 4, 5.

72. *Guide*, I, 59.

73. *Idem*, 59; *b. Berachot*, 33^b; *cf.* Albo, *op. cit.*, II, 23, 10, 141.

74. *Guide*, Introduction, I, 31.

75. *Idem*, Introduction.

76. *Idem*, I, 21; *cf. supra*, p. 204, note 32.

77. *Idem*, 31. To Hasdai ha-Levi ha-Sephardi he writes: "To the knowledge of man there is a limit. As long as the soul remains in the body it cannot know the supernatural. . . . This I lay down, as a principle, no thinker or philosopher can offer definite proof of things beyond nature. . . ." II, 23^b & 24^b.

78. Schechter, *op. cit.*, 30.

79. *The Christian Faith*, 353, trans. Mackintosh & Stewart, Edinburgh, 1928.

80. *History of Medieval Jewish Philosophy*, 1st ed., 266, The Macmillan Co., 1930.

81. F. Ueberweg, *op. cit.*, 415.

82. *De Opificio Mundi*, 2, 8; *Guide*, I, 54. The knowledge obtained by Moses had not been possessed by any human being before him or after him.

83. *JQR.*, vol. IV, 638-9.

84. The quotations are from an article by one of the most brilliant students of Jewish philosophy we have had in many years. It is therefore the more painful. *Ve-has li.* . . .

85. *Op. cit.*, 3, 20. The fact that Zerahia ha-Yewani is the true author of the *Sepher ha-Yashar* or that he accepted much of the content of the *Hobot ha-Lebabot* does not make the work less important. Its language and spirit are unique and it was without hesitation attributed to the pious Rabbi Tam.

86. *Op. cit.*, 8, 51.

87. Yedayah ha-Penini ha-Bedarsi, *Behinat Olam*, 24; quoted in Albo, *op. cit.*, 2, 30, 9, 206.

88. *Idem*, 5, 31.

89. *Idem*, 2, 10.

90. *Idem*, 2, 17.

91. *Idem*, 3, 18.

92. Note the undisciplined language. The old fashioned word "heart" has replaced the active intellect.

93. *Idem*, 1, 10.

CHAPTER XI

1. *GR.*, 1, 12, 8 & note *a.l.*; *b. Hagigah*, 12ᵃ; *PRE.*, 3; Albo, *op. cit.*, I, 2, 50. *Cf.* Abraham bar Hiya, *Hegyon ha-Nephesh*, 1, 2ᵇ who completely equates the Greek *hyle* with *tohu*.

2. Catholic philosophers have not sufficiently acknowledged Aquinas' indebtedness to Maimonides on this point. They speak of the former's thoroughness, ingenuity, etc. with which he meets Aristotle, without in the least appreciating that the arguments in the *Summa* on the eternity of the universe follow the arguments of Maimonides hardly with any deviation or innovation. *Cf.* Guttmann, *op. cit.*, I, 188 ff.; Husik in *JQR.*, vol. II, 164; L. G. Lévy, *op. cit.*, 265-7 & notes *a.l.*

3. There were of course some philosophers who saw no conflict between creation & the eternity of matter. As usual Yehudah Halevi was not overwhelmed by the difficulty. "If," says he, "a believer in the Law finds himself compelled to admit an eternal matter and the existence of many worlds prior to this one, this would not impair his belief that *this* world was created at a certain epoch." I, 67, 54. *Cf.* L. G. Lévy, 79, n. 2.

4. In his attack on Astrology, Maimonides is decidedly unmedieval. "Fools," he writes, "have composed thousands of books vain and vacuous. . . . And this is a fatal mischief that whatever is found in books is instantly accepted as the truth, especially if the books are ancient. *Responsa*, II, 25ᵃ; *HUC. Annual, loc. cit.*, 350; *see* also his *Iggeret Teman*, II, 5ᵈ, "Regard not all that you see in books as convincing proof. The liar lies with his pen as readily as with his tongue." Also his *Kiddush ha-Shem*, II, 13ᵇ; *cf.* Lynn Thorndike. *A History of Magic and Experimental Science*, II, 211-12, The Macmillan Co., 1923.

5. *Guide*, II, 16.

6. *Idem*, I, 71.

7. *Idem*, II, 2.

8. *Idem*, I, 71.

9. *Idem*, II, 15; *cf.* also his letter to Hasdai ha-Levi ha-Sephardi, *Responsa*, II, 24ᵇ.

10. *Guide, loc. cit.*

11. *Idem,* 19.

12. *Idem,* I, 71.

13. *Metaphysics,* XI, vi, 1062b, 24-7.

14. *Guide,* II, 17.

15. *Idem.*

16. Jennings, *op. cit.,* 15-64. The theory has been best stated by C. L. Morgan in his *Emergent Evolution,* 1. "Evolution in the broad sense of the word," says Professor Morgan, "is the name we give to the comprehensive plan of sequence in all natural events. But the orderly sequence historically viewed, appears to present, from time to time, something genuinely new." On p. 8, Morgan writes: "The essential feature of a mechanical—or, if it be preferred, a mechanistic—interpretation is that it is in terms of resultant effects only, calculable by algebraical summation. It ignores the something more that must be accepted as emergent. It regards a chemical compound as only a more complex mechanical mixture, without any new kind of relatedness of its constituents. It regards life as a re-grouping of physico-chemical events with no new kind of relatedness expressed in an integration which seems, on the evidence, to mark a new departure in the passage of natural events. Against *such* a mechanical interpretation—*such* a mechanistic dogma—emergent evolution rises in protest." On p. 39, he writes: "Cognitive relatedness just emerges, as something genuinely new, at a critical stage of evolutionary advance." J. S. Mill to whom Morgan partly traces "emergence" speaks of it as "so radical, and of so much importance, as to require a chapter to itself. . . . The Laws of Life will never be deductible from the mere laws of the ingredients. . . . The different actions of a chemical compound will never, undoubtedly, be found to be the sums of the actions of its separate elements." *A System of Logic,* III, 6, 1 & 2. Whether the emergent evolutionists can still maintain that *ex nihilo nihil fit* will depend very largely on the conception of *nihil. See* Prof. J. B. Burke's highly technical and mathematical treatment of the many problems involved in the theory, in his *The Origin of Life,* particularly 244-52, 261-73, London, 1906.

17. *See* Prof. Z. Diezendruck's brilliant article in *Moznaim,* vol. III, 347 ff.; *cf.* particularly p. 50. For Diezendruck's other studies of Maimonides, see note at the beginning of his article.

18. *Guide,* II, 17.

19. *Idem,* 13.

20. *Idem,* 22.

21. *Idem,* 25; *cf.* also his letter to Hasdai ha-Levi ha-Sephardi, *Responsa,* II, 24ª.

22. *Idem,* 28.

23. *Idem,* 17.

24. *Idem,* 30. Italics mine.

25. *MPs.,* 1, 22.

26. *Metaphysics,* XII, ix, 1074b, 34-5.

27. *Guide,* II, 20.

28. *Idem,* 19. "The term 'Necessary result' is used by Aristotle in reference to the whole Universe, when he says that one portion is the result of the other, and continues the series up to the First Cause as he calls it, or first Intellect, if you prefer this term. For we all mean the same, only with this difference, that according to Aristotle everything besides that Being is the necessary result of the latter, as I have already mentioned; whilst, according

to our opinion, that Being created the whole Universe with design and will, so that the Universe which had not been in existence before, has by His will come into existence." *Idem,* 21; *cf.* also III, 13 & 14.

29. *Cf.* Diezendruck's penetrating analysis of purpose in Maimonides in his *ha-Tachlit veha-To'arim be-Torat ha-Rambam, Tarbiz,* vol. I, iv, 106-12, 124; vol. II, i, 30; H. Wolfson, *The Philosophy of Spinoza,* II, 426; *cf.* I Epstein in *MGWJ,* vol. 75, 335-47.

30. *De Opificio Mundi,* 2, 7-11. Philo, of course, also found the doctrine of purpose in the writings of the Stoic philosophers. Spinoza rejected purpose as a logical inconsistency. *Ethics,* I, *Props.* 33-6, demonstrations and particularly *Scholia* to 33, & Appendix at close of *Opera* I, 63-72. *Cf.* also Preface to bk. IV, 183, *"Ratio igitur, seu causa, cur Deus seu Natura agit, et cur existit, una eademque est. Ut ergo nullius finis causa existit, nullius etiam finis causa agit; sed ut existendi, sic et agendi principium, vel finem, habet nullum. Causa autem, quae finalis dicitur, nihil est praeter ipsum humanum appetitum, quatenus is alicujus rei veluti principium seu causa primaria consideratur."*

CHAPTER XII

1. *Responsa,* II, 15[d]; R. Abraham b. David's stricture to *Hil. Teshubah,* 8, 2.
2. Introduction to *Helek* toward end.
3. *Guide,* I, 71.
4. Introduction to *Zeraim.*
5. *Idem.*
6. Plato, *The Republic,* VII, 537B.
7. *Guide,* Introduction; *cf. Pirke ha-Hazlahah, Responsa,* II, 34[e].
8. The elasticity of reason is well seen by the various attitudes to the sense of touch among philosophers. Democritus had reduced all sensations to the one sensation of touch. Aristotle and his followers humbled this sense, which was accorded by Locke a position of the highest importance. *On The Human Understanding,* II, 2, 1, Dutton & Co.; Bishop Berkeley in his *New Theory of Vision* makes the sense of touch responsible for our awareness of time and space and rather redeems the sense "from the reproach of the centuries." *Cf.* also his *On The Principles of Human Knowledge,* I, 44, where he speaks of the ideas of sight as being the "marks and prognostics" of the ideas of touch. Professor Morgan, *op. cit.,* 47, finds the sense of vision of all senses "the most liable to illusion, conspicuously subject to error," unless it be co-related with other modes of sensory experience, especially "that of contact treatment founded on the more primitive data of touch supplemented by manipulation." *See* his detailed analysis of the senses, 210-42. *Cf.* also Husik's note in Albo, *op. cit.,* I, 192 & IV, 543 for Ginzberg's additional note.
9. *Guide,* III, 8. Italics mine.
10. Italics mine.
11. *Idem,* 9.
12. *Idem,* 33.
13. *Idem,* 51. Italics mine. At the end of *Mish. Kinim* Maimonides writes: "The older and weaker scholars grow and the more their bodies disintegrate,

the more they gain in wisdom, strengthen their intellect and approach perfection."

14. *Idem*, 7.

15. Introduction to *Zeraim*.

16. *DR.*, end. For twelve months the soul continues to visit the body in
the grave. It discontinues its visits only when the body perishes. *b. Sabb.,*
152[b]; *cf.* also *PRE.*, 34. The soul does not leave the body until it beholds
the *Shechina*. According to Professor Ginzberg, the *PRE* offers an incorrect
explanation of the word *be-Mitatan* employed in the older Tannaitic statement. *Cf. Sifra,* 4[a] & *SN.*, 103, 28[a].

17. *j. Kileaim,* 9, 4, 32[b]; *GR.*, 95, 1; *TG.*, 208-9; *KR.*, 5, 12; *YJb.*, 924.
It is true that one might cull scores of Talmudic dicta to the effect that the
reward of a *Mizvah* is not to be found in this world. *b. Kidd.*, 39[a]; *b. Hullin,*
142[a]; that the Rabbis time and again referred to the next world. We must
not forget, however, that the whole Biblical tradition was this-worldly as is
particularly evident from the Book of Job, that immortality was decidedly
corporeal and that the return to earth was so often stressed. One should
also remember that the whole purpose of existence was the observance of
the Law and that it was only upon earth that the Law could be observed.
Was not Elisha b. Abuyah representing the older and commonly accepted
tradition when he refused to see *Olam ha-Ba* in the *Deuteronomic* verse. Albo
notes that there are no promises of spiritual reward in the Torah. His
attempt to read into the Bible such reward is unsuccessful. *Cf., op. cit.,* II,
4, 39.

18. Christianity, too, at first emphasized bodily resurrection. *Resurgit igitur
caro et quidem omnis, et quidem ipsa, et quidem integra* was a creed pleasing and flattering to man. G. F. Moore, *op. cit.,* II, 394.

19. *Phaedo,* 66B-67B, Lewes, *op. cit.,* 1, 197. Of Plotinus it is reported
that he was ashamed that he had a body and would never mention his
parents.

20. Even the holiness of the Sabbath could be imposed upon for the
sake of making marriage arrangements. *b. Sabb.*, 150[a]. *Cf.* Maimonides on
Mish. Sabb., 23, 3. A childless man could not be a member of a court
sitting on capital cases. *Mish. Horoyot,* 1, 4. Maimonides, *a.l.* comments:
"Not knowing the love of children he will be hard-hearted and show no
mercy." An interesting contrast will be found between Nahmanides' *Iggeret
ha-Kedushah* & St. Jerome's *Letter to Eustochium, Epistolae* XXII. Nahmanides calls marriage holy. He contradicts Maimonides and Aristotle who
maintain that the sense of touch is a disgrace to man. The sex organs are
no disgrace. They were carefully wrought by God for their purpose. Were
the act of copulation impure and disgraceful, the Eternal would not have
commanded us to indulge in it. (Ch. 2, *see* particularly chs. 5 & 6 which
we need not quote here.) Jerome, on the other hand, hasn't a good word
for marriage. He lists its disadvantages: pregnancy, a crying baby, household
cares, etc. (2) "Why should you (nun), who are God's bride, hasten to
visit the wife of a mortal man? In this regard you must learn a holy pride;
know that you are better than they." (16) "I praise wedlock, I praise
marriage; but it is because they produce me virgins. I gather the rose from
the thorn, the gold from the earth, the pearl from the oyster. *Laudo nuptias,
laudo coniugium, sed quia mihi virgines generant: lego de spinis rosas, de
terra aurum, de concha margaritum.* (20)." *Cf.* also his *Letter to Laeta,
Ep.* CVII; *The Acts of Paul,* II, 3; *The Acts of Thomas,* XII, 144; Gibbon,
op. cit., V, 526-7; F. J. Foakes Jackson, *The Parting of the Roads,* 167.

21. *b. Sanhedrin,* 17ᵇ; Maimonides makes this a law. He adds to the list a water supply. *Hil. Deot.,* 4, 23. In *j. Kidd.,* end, R. Jose & in *b. Erubin,* 55ᵇ, R. Huna forbid living in a city that grows no vegetables.

22. B. *Nazir,* 19ᵃ; *cf. b. Taanit,* 11ᵇ, if a student fasts, let a dog eat his meal.

23. *j. Kidd.,* end.

24. *Tos. Sotah,* 15, 11-14, 322-3; *b.B.B.,* 65ᵇ.

25. *Memorabilia,* I, iii, 6-8.

26. *b. Pesahim,* 49ᵃ; *cf.* also *Mish. B.M.,* 7, 5; *ARN.,* 26, 82ᵃ.

27. *b. Yebamot,* 20ᵃ; *cf.* also Nahmanides *loc. cit.,* ch. 1.

28. *b. Yoma,* 39ᵃ; Nahmanides, commentary on *Leviticus,* 19, 2.

29. *j. Nedarim,* 9, 41ᵇ.

30. *b. Sanhedrin,* 72ᵃ.

31. A scholar, said the Rabbis, should not indulge in fasting for it interferes with his studies. *b. Taanit,* 11ᵇ.

32. *GR.,* 9, 9, 72.

33. *Midrash ha-Ne'elam* to *Toldot* on ch. 25, 21, in *Zohar G.,* 138ᵇ.

34. *Tos. Sabb.,* 16, end; *b. Yoma,* 85ᵇ; *b. Sanhedrin,* 74ᵃ.

35. A sentiment frequently given utterance in rabbinic literature, *b. Berachot,* 63ᵇ; *b. Sabb.,* 83ᵇ; *b. Sotah,* 21ᵇ; *b. Gittin,* 9ᵇ; *YJb.,* 915; *cf.* also *b. Erubin,* 54ᵃ; *b. Sanhedrin,* 111ᵃ; *b. Hagigah,* 15ᵃ; *j. idem,* 2, 1, 77ᵇ; *ARN.,* 28, 85ᵃ; *YJb.,* 916; *Aboda Zarah,* 5ᵇ; *LR.,* 19, 1 & 3.

36. *Mish. Kileaim,* 9, 4; *b. Niddah,* 61ᵇ; *YPs.,* 839 & 873.

37. *LR.,* 34, 3.

38. Italics mine.

39. *j. Nedarim, loc. cit.; cf. Tos. Yebamot,* 1, end, 242; *b. Erubin,* 6ᵇ; *YK.,* 968.

40. *Eight Chapters,* ch. 4.

41. *Hil. Deot,* 3, 1.

42. *Idem,* 4, 1-19. *Cf.* also his letter to his son, *Responsa,* II, 38ᵃ&ᵇ, know that the wholesomeness of the body precedes the perfection of the soul. It is the key that opens the palace.

43. *Hil. Yesode Torah,* 4 end.

44. *Mish. Abot,* 1, 13, *a.l.*

45. *Hil. Talmud Torah,* 3, 10.

46. *Idem,* 3, 11.

47. *Mish. Abot,* 4, 5, *a.l.;* the same opinion he expresses *Mish. Nedarim,* 4, 3. "It is in no wise permitted to accept tuition fees . . . I marvel at some of our great men whom greed has blinded. They falsify the truth and allow themselves to accept court expenses and tuition fees. . . ." It is hardly necessary to remind the reader that Maimonides was only expressing what the Rabbis both taught & practiced. *Cf. MEx.,* 95; *idem* R. Simon b. Yohai, 98; *Mish. Abot,* 2, 2; *Tos., B.K.,* 7, 10, 359; *b. idem,* 79ᵇ; *b.* Pesahim, 113ᵃ; *GR.,* 74, 12; *KR.,* 9, 4-5 & 7; *SER.,* 5, 26; *SEZ.,* 15, 197. Note particularly the painful remorse of R. Tarphon, who had once availed himself of the "crown" of the Torah, *b. Nedarim,* 62ᵃ.

CHAPTER XIII

1. No wonder Munk opens his *Préface* to the third book of the *Guide* with the following words: *La troisième et dernière partie de l'ouvrage de*

Maimonide est consacrée a des questions moins arides que les précédentes, et qui peuvent encore aujourd'hui intéresser, jusqu'a un certain point, le penseur et notamment le theologien juif.

2. "Although one ought to study the opinions of the philosophers (peoples), it is only for the purpose of refuting them. Beware lest any opinion of an infidel nestle in your heart." *Mish. Abot,* 2, 14, *a.l.*

3. ibn Ezra, *Commentary Hosea,* 1, 2; *idem, Numbers,* 22, 28.

4. For Maimonides' high opinion of ibn Ezra *see* the letter to his son, *Responsa,* II, 39ᵈ-40ᵃ, where he urges him to study diligently the works of ibn Ezra. Professor Ginzberg is not convinced that Maimonides was acquainted with the works of ibn Ezra. He regards the letter I cited a forgery. *Cf.* his article in *JE. verbum Allegorical Interpretations,* I, 406.

5. *Commentary Gen.,* 18, 21; *cf. Munk,* III, 131, n. 1.

6. *Commentary Deut.,* 4, 5.

7. *Emunot ve-Deot,* 3, 1 & 2, 105-9; *Yesod Mora,* 7, 26-36 (Hebrew), Frankfort a.M., 1840. On p. 32, ibn Ezra writes: "I found one verse which embraces all the *Mizvot* 'thou shalt fear the Lord, thy God and Him shalt thou serve. . . . 'The *Mizvot* will habituate man and lead him to cleave to the Blessed and Glorified Name, for it is to this end that man was created." Maimonides of course knew of many precedents much older than ibn Ezra. He went as far back as Solomon. Letter to Hasdai ha-Levi ha-Sephardi, *Responsa,* II, 23ᵈ; *Guide,* III, 26; *b. Sanhedrin,* 21ᵃ; *MK.,* 744. In rabbinic literature, it is true, no consistent effort was made to find a rationale for the *Mizvot,* but sporadic attempts were not wanting. They were sufficient to give Maimonides, with his propensity for logic, his lead. R. Johanan b. Zakkai suggested a reason for the boring of the ear of the slave who refused to be manumitted. *Ex.,* 21, 6; *Tos. B.K.,* 7, 5, 358; *j. Kidd.,* 1, 3, 59ᵈ; *b. idem,* 22ᵇ. He explained the prohibition against the use of iron in the construction of the altar. *Ex.,* 20, 25; *MEx.,* 81ᵇ (See Weiss' interesting note *a.l.*) ; *idem,* R. Simon b. Yohai, 116; *Sifra,* 92ᵇ; *Mish. Middot,* 3, 4; *Tos. B.K. loc. cit.; YJ.,* 18. R. Simon b. Yohai suggested a general principle for the *Mizvot. Tanhuma, va-Yigash,* 6, I, 196 Warsaw, 1902. Abba Arika had also offered a general explanation of the purpose of the *Mizvot. GR.,* 44, 1, 424-5 & note *a.l.* for further reference. Rabbi Meir found a reason for the *Zizit* wholly pleasing to Maimonides. *Numbers,* 15, 37-41; *j. Berachot,* 1, 5, 3ᵃ; *b. Sotah,* 17ᵃ; *b. Menahot,* 43ᵇ; *b. Hullin,* 89ᵃ; *MPs.,* 90, 394; *cf.* also *SN.,* 115, 34ᵇ. An explanation of the scapegoat on the Day of Atonement was attempted by later authorities, *b. Yoma,* 67ᵇ; *cf. DR.,* end. Even the ceremony of circumcision was accounted for. *TL.,* 35. *Cf. Guide,* III, 26-50; *Hil. Temurah & Hil. Me'ilah,* end; Bacher, *Agadat ha-Tannaim,* I, 1, 20-3; II, 1, 4 & 59-60. Z. H. Hajes, *op. cit.,* 8ᵈ-9ᶜ, says: In truth Maimonides followed Talmudic precedent (in his search of reasons for the commandments). C. Bardowicz, *Die Rationale Schriftauslegung des Maimonides,* 2-10, Berlin, 1893. Weiss, *op. cit.,* Introduction clxxvi; L. Finkelstein, *Proceedings, RAA.,* II, 98. Of the rituals of the Greek Religion Plato writes as follows: "These are subjects which we do not understand ourselves, and about which, in founding a state (referring to the ideal republic), we shall, if we are wise, listen to no other advice or exposition, except that of our ancient national expositor. For it is this God, I apprehend, expounding from His seat on the Omphalos, at the earth's center, who is the national expositor to all men on such subjects." *Republic,* IV, 427, B-C. The rationalism was evidently not altogether on the side of the Greeks.

8. *See supra,* 99 & note 52, *a.l.*

9. Guttmann, *op. cit.,* II, 234-5; Weiss, *loc. cit.,* clxxvi-vii.

10. Malter, *op. cit.,* 167, n. 309.

11. *Idem,* 212, n. 485; *cf.* also I. Heinemann, *Die Lehre von der Zweck-bestimmung des Menschen,* etc., 37-83, Breslau, 1926.

12. R. Zevi Ashkenazi (Hacham Zevi), *Responsa,* 18, trans. by L. Roth, in *Chronicon Spinozanum,* I, 278-82. Hague, 1921.

13. *Guide,* II, 29; letter to Hasdai ha-Levi ha-Sephardi, *Responsa,* II, 24ᶜ; for the Rabbis' attempts to rationalize miracles *see* Marmorstein, *op. cit.,* 175-6; ch. 8 of *Eight Chapters; GR.,* 5, 4-5, 34-5; *ER.,* 21, 10; Hajes, *op. cit.,* 9ᶜ-10ᵈ.

14. Whitehead, *op. cit.,* 514.

15. *Guide,* I, 72; Diogenes Laertius, VII, 1, 43.

16. For literature *see* Ginzberg, *Legends,* V, 64, 4; *MhaG.,* 454, reads: Everything found above or below was in the human body. *Cf.* Munk, *op. cit.,* I, 354, n. 1; Malter, *The Personification of Soul and Body in JQR.,* vol. II, 453-4.

17. Lynn Thorndike, *A History of Magic and Experimental Science,* II, 208, New York, 1923.

18. "Maimonides was not a Rabbi employing Greek logic and categories of thought in order to interpret Jewish religion; he was rather a true medieval Aristotelian using Jewish religion as an illustration of the Stagirite's meta-physical supremacy. . . . Maimonides is ruled by reason, nothing is true which is not rational, his interest is mainly logical." H. A. Wolfson, *JQR.,* II, 306.

19. Letter to Hasdai ha-Levi ha-Sephardi, *Responsa,* II, 23ᶜ. We are giving only a paraphrase.

20. *Hil. Melachim,* 8, 11. The condition at this place is original with Maimonides. Maimonides' source is *Mishnat R. Eliezer,* 121, Enelow. *Cf. Responsa,* 370, Freimann who has b. Jacob for b. Jose. I owe this reference to my teacher Professor Ginzberg. *Cf. Keseph Mishneh, a.l.* See also Mai-monides' comments on *Mish. Berachot,* 5, 3. The *Mizvah* of letting the mother bird go (*Deut.,* 22, 6-7) is to be observed not out of compassion, for "were it a matter of compassion, the slaughtering of beast and fowl would have been prohibited. The sending away of the mother is a tradition for which we know no reason." *See* also Maimonides' comment on *Mish. Hullin,* 7, end & *idem Makkot,* 105. *Cf.* also *Sifra,* 93ᵇ; *Tos. Sanhedrin,* 13, 2, 434; *b. idem,* 105ᵃ; *b. Abodah Zarah,* 64ᵃ. *Cf.,* however, *Guide,* III, 48.

21. *Cf. Yohasin ha-Shalem,* 219, Filipowski-Freimann, ed.; *Shalshelet ha-Kabalah,* Rambam; R. Aaron b. Meshullam, Responsa, III, 12ᶜ wrote: It is known that the Jewish community does not contain one to equal him in wisdom, piety, faith, or uprightness of heart. Hillel ha-Hasid, *loc. cit.,* 14ᵇ speaks of him as a second Moses. Ibn Duran writes, from the days of R. Ashi, there arose none like our teacher Moses, our great teacher, *op. cit.,* 30. Jedaiah ha-Penini ha-Bedarsi in his *Behinat Olam,* wrote: "The conclusion of the whole matter is, go either to the right, my heart, or go to the left, but believe all that R. Moses b. Maimon has believed, the last of the *geonim,* but the first in rank. Quoted in Schechter's *Studies in Judasim,* vol. I, 97. Professor Ginzberg called my attention to R. Joseph Yaabetz who despite his anti-rationalism repeats the famous dictum "from Moses unto Moses there arose none like Moses." *Or ha-Hayyim,* 9, Zalkow, 5608.

22. Azulai, *Shem ha-Gedolim,* 61ᵈ, *Wien,* 1864. Great praise of the *Yad*

ha-Hazakah is found in the letter of R. Aaron b. Meshullam to R. Meir Halevi, *Responsa*, III, 11[d], where it is spoken of as the greatest work since the Talmud. Ibn Duran, *loc. cit.*, 31, writes: "No one before and no one since has embraced everything in one work as he has done . . . this he erected into an impregnable fortress against those who deny the Torah. Nahmanides, *loc. cit.*, III, 8[e], speaks of it as a tower of strength. Even his opponents respected this *magnum opus. Cf.* Judah Alfakar, in his letter to R. David Kimhi, III, 2[d]. His severe critic ben David in a note most acrimonious nevertheless admits that in bringing together all there was in the Babylonian and Palestinian Talmud and in the Tosefta, Maimonides had achieved an extraordinary work. *Hil. Kil'aim*, 6, 2. *See,* however, the interpretation of this stricture by I. B. Levenson, *op. cit.*, 20, note *a.l.* For attacks on the *Yad ha-Hazakah, cf.* Z. H. Hajes, *Tif'eret le-Moshe, Petiha,* 4[a], Zolkiew, 1840; S. D. Luzzatto in *Kerem Hemed,* vol. III, 66-7, IV, 288-91.

23. *Guide,* II, 47.

24. *Hil. Abodat Kochabim,* 1, 3; *Iggeret Teman, Responsa,* II, 5[e]; letter to Marseilles, 25[e]; *Guide,* II, 42, III, 29.

25. *Guide,* III, 17.

26. *Eight Chapters,* end of fourth reads: "The maid servant at the Red Sea saw more than Isaiah, Ezekiel, and all the Prophets, *MEx.,* 44[a] & 72[a]; *DR.,* 7, 9, *Guide,* I, 5; *cf. Mish. Sanhedrin,* 10, 1; *b. idem,* 110[b], for R. Akiba's opinion of the *Dor Midbar. See supra,* p. 748, note 48, *a.l.* Maimonides' conception of prophecy evidently remains, after it is divested of all its rationalism, only traditional. Moral worth and intellectual fitness are no guaranty for obtaining the gift. In the last analysis the inspiration of the Prophets remains miraculous. *Guide,* II, 32, 36; Introduction to *Zeraim*; see particularly his Letter to Hasdai ha-Levi ha-Sephardi, *Responsa,* II, 23[e] as well as the Letter to Samuel ibn Tibbon, 228. Professor Diezendruck evidently finds, after a brilliant discussion, the problem of prophecy in Maimonides insoluble. It is an *"Abkehr von jedem Intellektualismus und ein Einfueren des nichtintellektualen-aber auch nicht sinnlichen Vermoegens in den Bereich der Erkenntniss und einer Erkenntniss von besonderem und hoeherem Grade." Jewish Studies in Memory of Israel Abrahams,* 74-134.

27. *Guide,* I, 66; *cf.* also *Mish. Yadaim,* 4, 5, for Maimonides' comments.

28. *Mish. Abot,* 5, 6; *Guide,* I, 66.

29. *Hil. Torah,* 8; *cf.* also *Iggeret Teman, Responsa,* II, 3[d], there has not been the least change in the Torah even from a *kamatz ha-taph* to a *sheruk. See* also his *Beur Shemot Kodesh va-Hol* published by Gaster. *Devir,* I, 191-222 and reprinted later separately, Berlin, 1923.

30. Introduction to *Helek; b. Sanhedrin,* 100[b]. Professor Ginzberg is of the opinion that Maimonides did not know the genuine b. Sira and that he was referring only to the "Alphabet of b. Sira."

31. *Hil. Sotah,* 3, 16-22; *Commentary Mish. Peah.,* I, 1; *Guide,* III, 47; *b. Hagigah,* 7[a]; Crescas, *op. cit.*, I, 2, 3, 26[d].

32. *Guide,* II, 43; *Iggeret Teman, Responsa,* II, 3[a] & 5[b]; Letter to Hasdai ha-Levi ha-Sephardi, *loc. cit.*, 23[e]; Josheph ibn Aknin, 30[b]; *Pirke ha-Hazlahah,* 32[a]; Letter to his son, 39[e]. In rabbinic literature Moses was occasionally put beneath the Patriarchs. The Messiah is sometimes placed above him, Samuel and Isaiah on a par with him. *SN.,* 101, 27[b]; *b. Hullin,* 89[b]; *TG.,* 139; *MPs.,* 25, 212 & n. 24; *PR.,* 4, 46; *MT.,* 186.

33. Introduction to *Zeraim.*

34. *Hil. Tum'at Zoraat,* 16, 10; *cf.* also *Guide,* III, 47; Munk, *op. cit.,* III, 393, n. 4 & 394, n. 2.

35. *Iggeret ha-Shemad* or *Kiddush ha-Shem, Responsa,* II, 12ᵈ; *cf. PR.,* 11, 2, 96; *YI.,* 406.
36. Comm. *Mish. Taanit,* end.
37. *Hil. Berachot,* 109.
38. Introduction to *Zeraim; Iggeret Teman, Responsa,* II, 3ᵃ; letter to ibn Gabbar, II, 16ᵃ.
39. Comm. *Mish. Kelim,* 17, 12.
40. *Responsa,* I, 76, 17ᵃ; *cf. b. Berachot,* 57ᵇ.
41. Introduction to *Zeraim; Hil. Yesode Torah,* 9, 2, reads: "The prophet does not come to institute laws but to command and warn the people not to transgress the words of the Torah." *Cf. Hil. Melachim,* 11, 12. See *b. Sabb.,* 104ᵃ, *b. Yoma,* 80ᵃ; *b. Yebamot,* 90ᵇ; *b. Temurah,* 16ᵃ; *j. Taanit,* 2, 1, 65ᵃ; *j. Megillah,* 1, 5, 70ᵈ, reads: "The *Prophets* and the *Hagiographa* will be abolished but never the *Five Books of Moses.*
42. Introduction to *Zeraim; Hil. Yesode Torah,* 10, 1.
43. *Hil. Berachot,* 2, 4; *cf.* Introduction to *Helek* toward end: Whoever opposes this family denies the Blessed Name and the words of the Prophets. In *Iggeret Teman, Responsa,* II, 6ᵃ, he writes: "It is inconceivable that there will not arise a descendant of Solomon to gather together our dispersions. This, brethren, is one of the vital principles of our faith." The persecutions of his day Maimonides regarded as the "pains preceding the coming of the Messiah," *loc. cit.,* 1ᶜ. With all his objections to the "calculators of the end," he nevertheless earnestly believed in a family tradition which he was certain originated with the year 70, to the effect that prophecy in Israel would be restored in the year 4976. *Idem,* 6ᵇ.
44. Comm. *Mish. Adayot,* end; *cf.* also *Pirke ha-Hazlahah, Responsa,* II, 34ᶜ.
45. *Hil. Tephillah,* 12, 12; Comm. *Mish. Megillah,* end.
46. *Hil. Tephillin,* 3, 1.
47. *Hil. Lulab,* 7, 15.
48. *Hil. Hanukah,* 3, 2. Rashi, *b. Sabb.,* 22ᵇ, explains that the miracle of *Hanukah* was in the "flask," because that was unnatural. See *Ma'amar Tehiyat ha-Metim,* II, 11ᶜ&ᵈ; Hajes, *op. cit.,* 10ᶜ-11ᵃ.
49. *Guide,* II, 43; Ginzberg, *Legends,* VI, 119, n. 687.
50. *Hil. Melachim,* 11, 1-2; *cf.* Comm. *Mish. Menahot,* end, where Maimonides stresses the importance of studying the laws of sacrifices.
51. *Hil. Issure Bi'ah,* 13, 14-15.
52. *Hil. Kle ha-Mikdash,* 10, 11.
53. Introduction to *Helek; Guide,* II, 30. For the beauty and fertility of Paradise, *cf.* Ginzberg, *Legends,* V, 31, 90.
54. *Hil. Bet ha-Behira,* 2, 2-5.
55. *Guide,* III, 45.
56. Comm. *Mish. Abot,* 5, 5.
57. *Hil. Me'ilah,* end.
58. *Guide,* II, 30.
59. *Idem,* 34. Italics mine.
60. *Idem,* III, 22.
61. *Ps.,* 104, 2.
62. *Job,* 37, 6.
63. *Guide,* II, 26. In his letter to Hasdai ha-Levi ha-Sephardi he again exonerates R. Eliezer. *Responsa,* II, 24ᵈ.

CHAPTER XIV

1. In his *Code* where Maimonides gives in detail the rules of the "Golden Mean," one of his commentators casually and laconically remarks: "These regulations are based on the sayings of the teachers of ethics, who in turn took them from the Rabbis, whose logia fill the Talmud to overflowing." *Migdal Oz* of R. Shem Tov b. Abraham to *Hil. Deot*, 1, 1; *cf.* Cassel, *Kuzari*, II, 50, 4th ed. 150, n.2. All Jewish philosophers equally quoted Biblical and Talmudic sources for the Golden Mean. Saadia Gaon, *op. cit.*, X; Bahya, III, 3; IX, 1, 3; Halevi, *loc. cit.*, II, 50; ibn Daud, 98. Why they are all passed off as Aristotelian is hard to tell. Malter who notes that the *media via* was known to the Arabs before they learned of Aristotle, nevertheless makes the same claim, *JQR.*, I, 160-1, n. 25.

2. *Deut.*, 30, 15.
3. *Idem*, 19.
4. *j. Hagigah*, 2, 1, 77ᵃ; *Tos., idem.*, 2, 6, 234; *ARN.*, 28, 86ᵃ & n. 22, *a.l.*
5. *Tos. B. K.*, 2, 12, 349.
6. Ginzberg, *Legends*, VI, 90, 486. "The statutes of the Law," says Maimonides, "do not impose burdens or excesses as are implied in the service of a hermit or pilgrim, and the like; but, on the other hand, they are not so deficient as to lead to gluttony or lewdness, or to prevent, as the religious laws of the heathen nations do, the development of man's moral and intellectual faculties." Guide, III, 39.
7. C. H. Moore, *Religious Thought of the Greeks*, 127; M. Hutton, *The Greek Point of View*, 26-32.
8. Lucretius, II, 1095-8.
9. *Isaiah*, 40, 12.
10. G. F. Moore, *op. cit.*, I, 493.
11. *Sifra*, 110ᶜ; *j. Sabb.*, 1, 1, 3ᵇ.
12. *GR.*, 8, 4, 59.
13. *b. Baizah*, 32ᵇ; *cf.* also *b. Sabb.*, 151ᵇ; *b. Yebamot*, 79ᵃ.
14. *Tos. B. K.*, 9, 29-30, 306; *j. idem*, 8, 8, 6ᶜ; *GR.*, 33, 3, 304.
15. *b. Sabb.*, 12ᵇ; *b. Nedarim*, 40ᵃ; *YPs.*, 741.
16. *b. Sukkah*, 49ᵇ. *Cf. Guide*, I, 53, III, 28, 38. E. von Lasauex, *Untergang des Hellensimus*, 68, Muenchen, 1854, points out that the Christian care of the poor was something new in the ancient world. Even Julian, the Apostate, with all his contempt for Christianity, could not help but praise the Christian care of the poor. *"Denn schimpflich ist es, wenn von den Juden keiner bettelt, die goetterfeindlichen Galilaer aber nicht nur die ihrigen ernaehren, sondern auch die unsrigen, die wir hilflos lassen."* That which historians so frequently designate as Christian is of course the Jewish element in the religion of Jesus.
17. *Isaiah*, 52, 13-53, end.
18. Ezekiel, 4; *cf. Albo,* III, 25, 23, 239.
19. *b. Sanhedrin*, 39ᵃ. The reading in the text is *Zeduki.* We do not mean to imply that the Greeks had no social outlook. We remember Aristotle's famous dictum that, man is by nature a social being. *Nicomachean Ethics,* I, vii, 7. Or, "to secure the good of one person only is better than nothing; but to secure the good of a nation or a state is a nobler and more divine achievement." *Idem*, I, iii, 8. Despite such utterances our strictures are not

unfair. Ethics remained among the Greeks a branch of philosophy. It was never impassioned, aglow with the warmth of pity and channeled into social conduct. The Greeks, I believe Goethe somewhere remarks, were friends of freedom, yes, but each one only of his own freedom; and so in every Greek there was a tyrant.

20. *Tos. Kidd.,* I, 13, 336-7; *b. idem,* 40^b.

21. The expression is to be found in Maimonides' commentary on *Nezikin,* the exact reference escapes me; *cf.* also *Iggeret Teman, Responsa,* II, 2^d, "we shall never cease to be a pious people . . . this pure clean seed." In this letter (3^b) too he lovingly applies to Israel verse, 7, ch. 4 of the *Song of Songs:*

> "Thou art all fair, my love;
> And there is no spot in thee."

22. *Responsa,* 370, 1, 339, ed. A. Freimann.

23. *Deut.,* 33, 4. *Cf.* Maimonides, *Sepher ha-Mizvot,* 3, ed. Heller, 6^a, Pietrokov, 1914.

24. IV *Esdras,* 3, end; *cf.* A. Kaminka in *Mozndim,* vol. IV, 51.

25. *MEx.,* 51^b; *Saadia, op. cit.,* III, 115.

26. *Ut id sua sponte facerent, quod cogerentur facere legibus. De RePublica,* I, 2, 3.

27. *Mish. Abot,* 1, 3.

28. *Cf. Crescas,* II, 6, 1, 38-41.

29. *Deut.,* 4, 6.

30. I *Kings,* 3, 9.

31. *Hosea,* 4, 6.

32. *Isaiah,* 2, 4.

33. *Idem,* 11, 9.

34. *Jeremiah,* 9, 23.

35. *b. Yoma,* 28^b.

36. *GR.,* 63, 7.

37. *b. Abodah Zarah,* 3^b; *cf.* also *TN.,* 117, when Moses ascended to Heaven he heard the voice of God, entoning the discussion about the red heifer.

38. *GR.,* 1, 2, 1; *cf.* note *a.l.*; *MPr.,* 9, 61, 1, 49; *YPr.,* 944.

39. *MEx.,* 29^a. Elsewhere the Rabbis say that God keeps the scholars poor in order that they do not waste their time with idle affairs, and neglect study. *MPs.,* 5, 51; *YPr.,* 934.

40. *b. Sabb.,* 88^b & 89^a; *PRE.,* 46.

41. *b. Berachot,* 33^a; *b. Sanhedrin,* 92^a; *MS.,* 5, 9, 19; *YS.,* 84; the Rabbis refer to the expression *El Deot Adonai,* I *Sam.,* 2, 3.

42. *b. Sabb.,* 30^a, bottom; *b. Makkot,* 10^a, bottom, *cf.* also *b. Erubin,* 63^b; *b. Megillah,* 3^b; *b. Sanhedrin,* 44^b; *b. Menahot,* 110^a; *YL.,* 509.

43. *b. Megillah,* 16^b; *AE.,* 9, 82.

44. *YREx.,* 105, Warsaw, 5582.

45. *SER.,* 9, 50.

46. At the conclusion of a list of ethical acts, the redactor of the *Mishnah* placed Study as excelling all things. *Mish. Peah,* 1, 1; *cf.* also *YPr.,* 934, all the *mizvot* of the Torah are not equal to one thing of the Torah, viz., its study.

47. *ARN.,* 48, 131^b.

48. *b. Sotah,* 21^a; *cf.* also *SN.,* 119, 39^b.

49. *b. Sotah, loc. cit.;* *cf.* also *b. Hagigah,* 15^b, where we read: Suffering which does not interfere with study is to be considered "chastisement of

love." *Cf.* also *YD.,* 850. Since the body was born to weariness, one might as well toil for Torah. *b. Sanhedrin,* 99ᵇ. Why is a scholar compared to a nut? To suggest that even like the nut, although soiled with mud and filth, the inside is not repulsive, even so with the Torah of a scholar who has sinned. *See* also *idem* for the punishment of R. Judah the Prince because he refused assistance to the daughter of Elisha b. Abuyah.

50. *ARN.,* 3, 14.

51. *b. Berachot,* 5ᵃ; *YD.,* 942.

52. *b. B. M.,* 86ᵃ; *cf.* also *LR.,* 11, 8; *SER.,* 1, 4.

53. Although there were thirteen synagogues in Tiberias, Rabbis Ami and Asi would offer their prayers between the columns where they studied; *b. Berachot,* 30ᵇ. *Cf. Hil. Talmud Torah,* 4 end; *Hil. Tephillah,* 8, 3; *cf. Keseph Mish., a.l.; cf.* also *b. Berachot,* 64ᵃ, he who leaves the Synagogue and enters the Beth ha-Midrash and engages in the study of the Torah, receives the Divine Presence.

54. *SER.,* 15, 69.

55. 4th Benediction of *Amidah. b. Megillah,* 17ᵇ; *b. Berachot,* 33ᵃ; *cf.* S. Baer, *Abodat Yisrael,* 90, Roedelheim, 1868.

56. *LR.,* 2, 1; *MPs.,* 116, 476; *MS.,* 8, 7, 30; *YS.,* 97.

57. *b. Hagigah,* 12ᵃ; *YPr.,* 935.

58. *MPs.,* 34, 245; *cf.* the interesting comment in *YS.,* 131, wisdom is more pleasing than anything except folly.

59. *b. Kidd.,* 40ᵇ; *b. Sanhedrin,* 7ᵃ; *YPr.,* 956; *cf.* also *b. Sabb.,* 31ᵃ bottom & *Tos., Sanhedrin, loc. cit.*

60. 8, 22.

61. *LR.,* 19, 1; *GR.,* 1, 1, 2 & 6; *YPs.,* 942. The Torah preceded creation by 2000 years; *cf.* also *Zohar Ex.,* 321; Ginzberg's brilliant analysis of *Mahashavah* in his epoch-making lecture delivered at the Hebrew University, Jerusalem, and published under the title "*Mekomah shel ha-Halachah be-Hochemat Yisrael,*" 32 to end, Jerusalem, also A. Kaminka in *Moznaim,* vol. IV, 48.

62. *b. Pesahim,* 68ᵃ *cf.* also *Otiyot d'R. Akiba,* 2. Without understanding the world cannot subsist. If a man engages in the study of Torah and wisdom, the Eternal regards it as though he had set up the entire world. *MPr.,* 9, 61 & *YPr.,* 944.

63. *Prov.,* 12, 1; *b. Berachot,* 17ᵃ *YPs.,* 870; *MPr.,* 1, 42. The last two sources read: If man has wisdom, the Torah is entrusted to him; if he has no wisdom, the Torah is not entrusted to him.

64. *Cf.* further *MPr.* 1, 43.

65. *Cf.* Prof. L. Roth's article in *Moznaim,* vol. III, 373.

66. *Students, Scholars and Saints,* 164.

67. *Mish. Abot,* 2, 8.

68. *b. Pesahim,* 26ᵃ; *b. Sukkah,* 28ᵃ.

69. *Mish. Hagigah,* 2, 1; *see b. Sabb.,* 80ᵇ for the story of a certain Galilean; *b. Megillah,* 24ᵇ: Many looked forward to the study of the Chariot, etc. Note Rav's vigorous opposition to such study in *j. Hagigah,* 2, 1, 77ᶜ & *b. idem,* 13ᵃ for its pursuit by his contemporaries; *Guide,* I, 33; note also the remarkable statement in *Sepher ha-Bahir,* he who frees himself from worldly affairs and engages in the study of the Chariot, the Holy One Blessed Be He accounts it to him as though he were engaged in prayer the whole day. Quoted in Delmedigo, *op. cit.,* 57.

70. *Tos. idem,* 2, 1, 234; *b. idem,* 14ᵇ-15ᵇ; *j. idem,* 77ᵃ&ᵇ; *b. Yoma,* 54ᵇ; *GR.,* 12, 11, 109.

71. *Tos. Hagigah,* 2, 1, 234; *j. idem,* 2, 1, 77ᵃ; *b. idem,* 14ᵇ.

72. *GR.,* 98, 3.

73. *Sepher ha-Yashar,* 1, 4; 2, 17 reads: The intellect is the basis of reverence and love . . . the quality of the reverence, love and their perfection will depend on the quality of the intellect . . . without intellectuality the worship of God will not be worthy. Lublin, 1873. *Cf. supra,* ch. X, end.

74. *See* Maimonides' reference in the *Guide,* II, 34 to R. Eliezer & R. Joshua of whom he speaks as the scholars of Israel in the "absolute meaning of the word."

75. *Guide,* I, 32. Maimonides undoubtedly had in mind the story of the *Pardes* as well as the rabbinic statement to the effect that there were things revealed to R. Akiba which were held back from Moses. *NR.,* 19, 4; *TN.,* 117; *PR.,* 14, 125; *PK.,* 4, 39ᵇ; *cf.* also the statements in *MPs.,* 19, 165, concerning Mar Samuel & R. Hoshia.

76. *Prov.,* 3, 6.

77. *b. Berachot,* 63ᵃ.

78. *Guide,* I, 32; *cf.* also closing chapter of *Guide* for an analysis of Wisdom.

79. Abravanel divides the forty days into four periods of ten each, because of the mystic value of the number 10. *Ateret Zekenim,* 39ᵇ-40ᵃ, Amsterdam, 1839; *cf.* also *Shalshelet ha-Kabalah, verbum* Moses.

80. *Nicomachean Ethics,* I, viii, 1099b, 16.

81. *Iliad,* IX, 514; *Symposium,* 214, B.

CHAPTER XV

1. *b. Megillah,* 27ᵃ; *b. Kidd.,* 40ᵇ; *b. B. K.,* 17ᵃ.

2. *b. Berachot,* 17ᵃ.

3. For a long time the Middle Ages knew of Aristotle only through his *Organon,* and his reputation was first made as a logician.

4. *Op. cit.,* VI, 30. The Chronicler Abraham b. Yehiya in his *Shalshelet ha-Kabalah* comes near making a similar distinction between Plato & Aristotle. *Cf.* also Husik in *JQR.,* II, 1, 61. Professor Ginzberg maintains that the matter is not quite so simple. *Vide,* the influence of Plato on Alexandrian Judaism and early Christianity. He is of the opinion that the vogue of Aristotle in Medieval philosophy may be due to the accident of translation. The medievalists were not under the influence of Aristotle simply because they knew more of him. It may, however, also be that Alexandrian Judaism and early Christianity were more tolerant of Plato's Athenian imagery.

5. Of course for a long time only Plato's *Timaeus* was known to the Middle Ages, and of that only a fragment. The obscurity of this dialogue certainly did not tend to add to Plato's popularity.

6. Diogenes Laertius, III, 80. *Cf.* Plato, *Timaeus,* 426. The discussion on the origin of the universe in this dialogue concludes as follows: "It (universe) is, therefore, an image of its maker, a god manifest to sense, the greatest and best, the most beautiful and perfect of all creatures, *even the one and only begotten universe."* Italics mine. *Timaeus,* end. Elsewhere in the same Dialogue we read: To know or tell the origin of the other divinities is beyond us, and we must accept the traditions of the men of old time who affirm themselves to be the offspring of the gods—that is what they say and they must surely have known their ancestors. How can we doubt the word

of children of the gods? . . . Oceanus and Tethys were the children of
Earth and Heaven, and from these sprang Phorcys and Cronas and Rhea, and
all that generation; and from Cronas and Rhea sprang Zeus & Hera. . . ."
40d, 1-41a, 1.

7. Caird, *op. cit.*, I, 93; *cf.* Zeller, *op. cit.* II, 355 & 361.

8. *Metaphysics*, Bks. XIII & XIV; *cf.* W. Windelband, *A History of
Philosophy*, I, 3, 11-13, 116-54. Eng. trans. J. H. Tufts, New York, 1914.

9. Professor Wolfson argues that Maimonides' loyalty to Judaism had "its
basis in his heredity and practical interests; it is not a logical implication of
his philosophy. Judaism designated the established social order of life in
which Maimonides lived and moved and had his being, and it was logically
as remote from his intellectual interests as he was historically remote from
Aristotle." *JQR.*, II, 3, 14-15. Professor Wolfson evidently believes that
between a man's intellectual interests and his life and being there is a wall.
In his social order Maimonides, for the major part of his life, was a kind of
Robot mechanically complying with the requirements of his environment. He
lived automatically all his life, wrote the extensive commentary on *Seder
Tohorot*, codified every minutia of the laws of purity & impurity, sacrifices,
leprosy, *Tephillin, Zizit, Mezuzah, Kashrut*, etc., carried on an extensive
correspondence about a *hazan, mikvah*, the style of a *Talit*, etc., all this, we
repeat, he did in Robot fashion to the spite and perversion of his own philosophy. Is it not too harsh a penalty to inflict on a man just because he
borrowed a few terms in logic from the Greeks?

10. The well-known commentator on Aristotle, Alexander of Aphrodisias
in Caria, c. 200 C.E., called *Exēgētēs, Responsa*, II, 28[d]; Munk, *Le Guide,*
etc., I, 107, n.1 & II, 51, n.2; L. G. Lévy, *loc. cit.*, 45, n.1.

11. *Guide*, II,•3; italics mine.

12. Whitehead, *op. cit.*, 25. "A great number of scholastics," writes Professor deWulf, . . ." openly reveal their own personal sentiments. Even when
he is developing his own doctrines, John Scotus delights to speak of himself
and the part he plays. Abelard and John of Salisbury are romantics, influenced by the spirit of chivalry; St. Anselm and St. Bernard reveal to us
what is passing in their souls; Alan of Lille and others have recourse to
allegory, letting us perceive their personality behind their didactic methods."
Of course deWulf for his own temperamental reasons makes of *the 13th century* scholastics pure rationalists free from all previous conditioning. *Op. cit.*,
I, 267.

13. Of Franz Rosenzweig, Albert Lewkowitz writes: *"Es ist in der Tat der
Irrtum des spekulativen Idealismus zu meinen, Glauben in Wissen verwandeln
zu koennen. Auch Rosenzweigs glaeubiges Denken ist nicht anderes also eine
Erlebnisstheologie, die als Aussage des religioesen Bewustseins tief und
wahr, wenn sie aber als wissenschaftliche Erkenntnis gelten will, dogmatische
Behauptung ist."* MGWJ. vol. 79, 6.

14. *Loc. cit.*, 512.

15. "Science is an art. . . . He regards the distinctions we now make
among these activities (religion, art & science) as entirely unreal. . . ."
In an Interview with J. W. N. Sullivan, *The Observer*, April 13, 1935,
p. 19. Professor Schroedinger, *op. cit.*, 98-9, writes: "Those fortunate individuals who can devote their lives to the profession of scientific research
are not merely botanists or physicists or chemists, as the case may be. They
are men and they are children of their age. The scientist cannot shuffle off his
mundane coil when he enters his laboratory or ascends the rostrum in his
lecture hall."

16. Cornford, *op. cit.*, 138.

17. *Guide*, I, 50.

18. I, qq. 27-43, *Opera* IV, 305-454. Note some of the chapter headings: *de Processione divinarum Personarum, de relationibus divinis, de Personis divinis, de pluralitate Personarum in divinis, etc.*

19. Scholastics had argued that there is nothing contrary to nature in the miracle of the Holy Eucharist since the essence of nature consisted in always obeying the will of God,

ut a quo est semper eius obtemperat iussis.

20. Italics mine.

21. *b. B. B.,* 116[a]; *b. Menahot,* 65[b]; *cf.* Philo, *de Aeternitate Mundi,* 23-27.

22. Aristotle was, of course, not quoting Sabian stories. Maimonides is following Islamic writers who applied the name Sabian to star worshipers & idolaters in general. The name is mentioned in the Koran three times along with Jews and Christians. The Sabians seem to have been a semi-Christian sect which was confused with the Elkesaites, Harranians & Maandeans. D. Chwolson, *Die Ssabier u. der Ssabismus,* vol. I, 2-471, 689-96, St. Petersburg, 1856. Munk, *Le Guide,* etc., I,280, n. 2; III, *Préface,* vii & 217, n. 1; Mulvi Muhammad, *The Holy Qur-án,* 2, 66, n.103, Surrey, 1917. *Cf.* also *Guide,* III, 39.

23. *Metaphysics,* XII, ciii, 1074b, 1-14.

24. *Consuetudo suetem, et praecipue quae est a puero, vim naturae obtinet: ex quo contingit ut ea quibus a pueritia animus imbuitur, ita firmiter teneat ac si essent naturaliter et per se nota. Contra Gentiles,* I, 11, vol. XIII, 24[a]. Aquinas, of course, uses the thought in a different connection—to deny that the knowledge of God's existence is intuitive.

25. Lange, *op. cit.,* I, 83.

26. Professor Nilsson writes: "In the trace of cosmogony which is to be found in Homer it seems to be water, *Okeanos,* that is the first principles." In Hesiod, *Theogony,* 105-8 we read: "The deathless gods . . . were both of Earth and Water. Heaven and gloomy Night and briny Sea." For other gods sprung from Oceanus and Tethys, *see idem,* 300. In Aristotle's *Metaphysics* we read: . . . they (the ancients) represented Oceanus and Tethys to be the parents of creation, and the oath of the gods to be by water—Styx, as they call it. Now, what is most ancient is most revered and what is most revered is what we swear by. I, iii, 983b, 30-984a, 1.

27. I, 12.

28. *Five Stages of the Greek Religion,* 67, Columbia University Press, 1925.

29. "All things," said Democritus, "happen by virtue of necessity, the vortex being the cause of the creation of all things. Diogenes Laertius, IX, 7.

30. P. Decharme, *op. cit.,* 9-22.

31. *Protagoras,* 345[d], quoted by Plato from Pittacus of Mitylene, one of the Seven Wise Men; also by Diogenes Laertius, I, 77.

32. "He declared the sun to be a mass of red-hot metal. . . . He was indicted by Cleon on a charge of impiety, because he declared the sun to be a mass of red-hot metal." Diogenes Laertius, II, 3, 8 & 12. The same author offers an epigram on Anaxagoras:

The Sun is a molten mass
Quoth Anaxagoras;
This is his crime, his life must pay the price . . .

idem, 15. Even Socrates, Plato and Xenophon were shocked by such heresies.

In the *Apologia*, Plato takes great pains to point out that Socrates does not accept the "absurdities" of Anaxagoras that "the sun is a stone and the moon earth." 26 D-E. Xenophon reports Socrates to have said "that he who meddles with these matters (the phenomena of the heavens—the secrets of the gods) runs the risk of losing his sanity as completely as Anaxagoras, who took an insane pride in his explanation of the divine machinery." *Memorabilia*, IV, 7, 6. P. Decharme, *op. cit.*, 157-9.

33. Cicero, *De Natura Deorum*, I, 13, 34; Decharme, *op. cit.*, 220-21. *Cf. Responsa*, II, 23^d & 25^d.

34. For the identification of the stars with angels in rabbinic literature, see *b. Moed Katon*, 16^a; for the *Hayyot* of *Ezekiel* identified with Michael, Gabriel, Uriel and Raphael, see *PRE.*, 4; *cf.* also *ARN.*, 43, 120^b-21^a for the dependence of angels on the *Shechinah*, *PK.*, 6, 57^a; *ER.*, 32, 4; for angels as the symbols of God's activity with regard to the universe, *GR.*, 97, 3; *ER.*, 2, 8 & 9; Husik, *op. cit.*, 268; for apocryphal, pseudo-epigraphic and rabbinic literature on subject, Ginzberg, *Legends*, V, 34, 100; 40, 112; 162-4, 61.

35. *Op. cit.*, 74.

36. Diogenes Laertius, VII, 1, 135.

37. "The Great Architect of the universe," writes Professor Jeans, "now begins to appear as a pure mathematician." If the illustrious Englishman is deeply convinced that the universe cannot owe its origin to chance, it would be well to remember that he was raised on the Bible. *The Mysterious Universe*, 144, The Macmillan Co., 1931.

38. *Guide*, II, 15; *cf.* Munk, *op. cit.*, II, 126, & note 4.

39. *The Quest for Certainty: A Study of the Relation of Knoweldge and Action*, 14, Gifford Lectures, 1929.

CHAPTER XVI

1. G. Wallas, *The Great Society*, 101, The Macmillan Co., 1920.

2. *Cf. Metaphysics*, VI, i, 1026a, 22-3.

3. *Idem*, XI, vii, 1064b, 3-4.

4. *Idem*, XII, ix, 1074b, 35; *cf.* also vii, 1062b, 27-30. "What peculiar privilege," asked Hume, "has this little agitation of the brain which we call *thought*, that we must thus make it the model of the whole universe? Our partiality in our own favor does indeed present it on all occasions; but sound philosophy ought carefully to guard against so natural an illusion." *Dialogues*, 40. He believes that the world resembles more animals and vegetables and could be better explained on the principle of vegetation or generation than on the basis of pure reason, 93-4. Cassendi, too, was of the opinion that the world may just as well be inferred from any other action as from thinking. *Lange*, op. cit., I, 261.

5. *Metaphysics*, VI, i, 1026a, 28-33.

6. *Idem*, 10-12. In the *De Anima*, I, i, 403b, 16 we read: "Insofar as they (affections of the body) are separable they are the sphere of the Metaphysician (the first philosopher)."

7. *Metaphysics*, loc. cit., 31-2.

8. Réné Guénon, *op. cit.*, 54. "Philosophy," writes Professor Bergson, "ought . . . to follow science, in order to superimpose on scientific truth a

knowledge of another kind, which may be called metaphysical." *Creative Evolution*, 199, trans. Mitchell, Henry Holt & Co., 1911.

9. *The Advancement of Learning*, II, vii, 3, The World's Classics, 1906.

10. *Metaphysics*, XI, i, 1059a, 1.

11. *Op. cit.*, I, 78.

12. *Idem*, 192.

13. *Idem*, 91. Professor Lange is of course only echoing Bacon as did Bertrand Russell, but recently: "Aristotle," he writes, "has been one of the great misfortunates of the human race." *The Scientific Outlook*, 42, Norton & Co., 1931.

14. *Ou gàr linai tòn hpeónton epistēmēn. Idem*, XIII, iv, 1078b, 18.

15. *Idem*, I, iv, 987b, 6, 7.

16. *Idem*, XI, ii, 1060a, 27, 28.

17. *Idem*, IV, v, 1010a, 29-32.

18. *Idem*, XI, vi, 1063a, 16-18.

19. *Idem*, XII, viii, 1073a, 27-28.

20. *Cf. Guide*, I, 69: The series of successive purposes terminates in the will or wisdom of God.

21. *Op. cit.*, 70.

22. *Critique of Pure Reason*, II, 3, 5; F. Paulsen, *Immanuel Kant*, 224-8, Chas. Scribner's Sons, 1916.

23. Jennings, *op. cit.*, 64; *cf.* Lange, *op. cit.*, I, 21-2.

24. *Op. cit.*, 12; Professor Planck was only fulfilling a wish long ago expressed by Ernst Mach. "I hope," said he, as early as 1893, "that the science of the future will discard the idea of cause and effect, as being formally obscure . . . (containing) a strong tincture of fetishism." *Popular Scientific Lectures*, 254, trans. T. J. McCormack, The Open Court, 1898.

25. *Ésti gár ti hó aei tà kinoúmena. Kaì tò próton kinôun akineton auto. Metaphysics*, IV, end.

26. *Idem*, XII, vii, 1072a, 21-6; *cf. Guide*, II, 1.

27. The Rabbis certainly display a finer poetic sense when they suggest that all created things long for infinity: When the Holy One Blessed Be He created the world it continued to expand, when He created the sea it did likewise. *b. Hagigah*, 12ᵃ, *b. B. B.*, 74ᵇ; *ExR.*, 15, 22; *YJb.*, 913; *MhaG.*, 29. *Cf. Guide*, I, 69: "It is the aim of everything to become, according to its faculties, similar to God."

28. *Dialogues concerning Two New Sciences*, trans. Crew-Salvio, 153-60; J. J. Fahie, *Galileo, his Life and Work*, 355-62, 367-9, London, 1903; Whitehead in *Science and Civilization*, ed. by E. S. Marvin, 170, Oxford, 1923.

29. *Op. cit.*, 105.

30. *Summa Theologica*, I, q.; XLVI, art. 2, 8, *Opera*, IV, 481; *cf.* also *mundum incopisse, sola fide tenetur*.

31. Ch. 3, 11.

32. *GR.*, 9, 1, 68 & note *a.l.*; *cf. Guide*, II, 31 & III, 25. It is interesting to find Hume employing a similar idea although for a different purpose. "Many worlds might have been botched and bungled, throughout an eternity, ere this system was struck off. . . ." *Op. cit.*, 76.

33. Real existence, Aristotle argues, cannot submit to . . . bad rule. Had not Homer said that many kings were bad and that only one should rule? *Iliad*, 11, 204; *Metaphysics*, XII, end. To which we might add, let's not have even one. These kings are earthly, human, tyrannical, vindictive, jealous cutthroats. To allow several of them to rule is to invite catastrophe. But how about the unmoved movents? Are they, too, not to be trusted? Evidently

Aristotle had for the moment overlooked an important statement from Euclid. Of an argument from analogy, he had said that "it must be taken either from similars or dissimilars. If it were drawn from similars, it is with these and not with their analogies that their arguments should deal; if from dissimilars, it is gratuitous to set them side by side." Diogenes Laertius, II, 10, 107.

34. *Timaeus*, 29e-30a, 6.

35. *Reden ueber Religion*, 1st published, 1799, trans. J. Oman, London, 1893, Introduction & 26-146, particularly, 36-42, 56-62.

36. Kant's chief work on religion is his "*Religion innerhalb der Grenzen der blossen Vernunft.*" Morality is discussed in his "*Kritik der praktischen Vernunft.*" The reader not overambitious will find extracts from the latter work in Professor John Watson's Selections from Kant (*The Philosophy of Kant*), 261-303, Jackson, Wylie & Co., 1927. On page 299, we read: "Practical reason brings us to the conception of a Supreme Being. This conception speculative reason was able to think, but it could not show it to be more than a transcendental *ideal*. Practical reason, on the other hand, gives meaning to this idea, by showing that a Supreme Being is the supreme principle of the highest good in an intelligible world, and is endowed with the sovereign power of prescribing moral laws in that world." The less ambitious reader may welcome a few citations from *Kant's Lectures on Ethics*, trans. by Professor J. MacMurray, The Century Co., 1930. "Religion must be not only theological but also moral. But what kind of theology is necessary as a basis for religion? Ought it, for instance, to concern itself with the question whether God is a Spirit and whether He is omnipresent and pervades all space? No. Such questions as these belong to the sphere of speculative theology and are extraneous to that theology which is requisite to natural religion. . . . But to enable us to do our duty it does not matter what notions we have of God provided only they are a sufficient ground for pure morality. The theology which is to form the basis of natural religion must contain one thing, the condition of moral perfection. We must conceive a Supreme Being whose laws are holy, whose government is benevolent and whose rewards and punishments are just. In short, the theology of natural religion need only postulate a holy lawgiver, a benevolent ruler and a just judge, and assuming all these functions to be supplied by one being, we have the conception of God required by the theology which is to be the basis of natural religion. Here we have the moral attributes of God. His natural attributes are necessary only in so far as they increase the effectiveness of the moral attributes. The omniscience, omnipotence, omnipresence and unity of the Supreme Being are the conditions requisite to His moral attributes, and relate only to them. The being who is the most holy and the most benevolent must be omniscient if He is to give heed to that inner morality which depends upon our dispositions. For that reason, too, He must be omnipresent. But the principle of morality is inconceivable except on the assumption of a supremely wise will which must be one and so must be the will of a single being. This constitutes the essence of the theology of natural religion. Its sources are to be found not in speculation, but in sound reason. Speculation is necessary to satisfy our craving for knowledge: for purposes of religion, for the purpose of knowing what we ought to do and what to leave undone, no more is necessary than that which sound reason can grasp and recognize. . . . The outstanding characteristic of natural religion is its simplicity. Its theology is such that the least intelligent among us can grasp it as completely as the most thoughtful and speculative. Apart from its simple rudiments

there are other things in theology, but these are no concern of natural religion and serve only to satisfy our thirst for knowledge. Religion and
morality must go hand in hand. The philosophers of old did not appreciate
this. Religion is the application of the moral laws to the knowledge of God,
and not the origin of morals. . . . The basis of religion must, therefore, be
morality. Morality as such is ideal, but religion imbues it with vigor, beauty
and reality. It would indeed be splendid if all men were righteous and
moral, and the thought might induce us to be moral. But ethics tells us that
we ought to be moral in and for ourselves, no matter whether others are
moral or not; it tells us in effect to pursue the Idea of morality apart from
any hope of being happy. But this is impossible; and as without a Being to
give actuality to the Idea, morality would be merely ideal. It follows that
there must exist a Being to give vigor and reality to the moral laws, and
this Being must be holy, benevolent and righteous. Without such a representation ethics is merely an Idea. It is religion which gives weight to morality:
it ought to be its motive . . . *Religion stands in no need of any speculative
study of God.*"

37. *Op. cit.,* 121-2.

38. *Strife of Systems and Productive Duality,* 25-6. Professor Sheldon
quotes from H. G. Wells, *Marriage,* 408-9. "Each," says Wells of two philosophers, "contradicted the other fundamentally upon matters of universal
concern." To which Professor Sheldon adds, "the remark is of general application."

39. *Op. cit.,* 65.

CHAPTER XVII

1. *Op. cit.*
2. *Idem,* 101.
3. *Idem,* 103.
4. *Idem,* 106.
5. *Idem,* 150.
6. *Idem,* 161.
7. *Idem,* 164.
8. *Idem,* 201.
9. *Idem,* 202.
10. *Idem,* 211. Except that it is really unfair to blame this "objectionable
nonsense" on England's great literature and Professor Eddington's elegant
style. The "nonsense" comes from Germany. Professor Schroedinger writes,
"The Universe is itself indeterminate. The ultimate happenings in the physical universe are not predestined. We can say what will happen to a large
aggregate of elements such as atoms or electrons but not what will happen to
individual members . . . something like free will is placed at the basis of
natural phenomena." *The Observer,* April 13, 1930. Professor Schroedinger
it will be recalled is himself a Nobel Prize winner and holds the Chair which
the great Planck has graced for so many years.

11. *Philosophy,* 223.

12. *See supra,* pp. 43-4.

13. *See* the Lectures on *Conditioned Reflexes,* particularly 275-281, 296-
304, 329-38. Eng. trans. by W. H. Gant, New York, 1928. *Cf.* his note on
281. Professor Pavlov resents the intrusion of psychology. He can barely

recognize it as a science. For him physiology suffices—since "the complicated nervous (psychical) activity is, like the lower, made up of reflex acts", 282.

14. *Science and Religion*, 126.

15. *Cf.* his *Science and the Human Temperament*, 39-80. On p. 43 Professor Schroedinger writes: "We have the paradox that from the point of view of the physicist, chance lies at the root of causality." And again on p. 50: . . . "undetermined chance is primary and is no further explicable. Law arises only statistically in mass phenomena owing to the cooperation of myriads of chances at play in these phenomena."

16. *Hil. Teshubah*, 5, 2-4.

17. *Guide*, III, 20. At the end of his commentary on *Mish. Berachot* Maimonides writes: "Scripture bears witness to the principle that God rewards the good and punishes the wicked in keeping with justice. But the nature of this justice is beyond the comprehension of man, just as his intellect cannot embrace the knowledge of God. From Scripture we know 'For as the heavens are higher than the earth, so are My ways higher than your ways, and My thoughts than your thoughts.' (*Isaiah*, 55, 9)." *Cf.* also letter to Marseilles, *Responsa*, II, 26ª & ᵇ and to Hasdai ha-Levi ha-Sephardi, II, 23ᶜ, 24ᵈ.

18. *Hil. Teshubah*, 5, end. However, at the conclusion of the statement quoted in the preceding note, Maimonides advises against becoming absorbed in the problem. For all those who labored on it, both Jews and non-Jews have toiled in vain. They dived into deep waters and brought back a potsherd.

19. *See* Abraham b. David's stricture, *a.l.* "Concerning the intellect," writes R. pseudo-Tam, "the philosophers have been most loquacious and have meticulously distinguished between the intellect, the intelligent and the intelligible. Some say that all three are one and others claim that they are disparate. Such discussion is neither beneficial nor harmful . . ." *Op. cit.*, 5, 24.

20. *Guide*, I, 34.

21. *Idem*, II, 40.

22. *Hil. Deot*, 6, 1; *cf.* also *Kiddush ha-Shem*, II, 15ª.

23. *Nec.* . . . *nanctos, sed natura insitos esse sapientiam.* Minucius Felix, *Octavius*, XVI, 5.

24. *Neminem posse ex mandato sapientum esse, non magis quam vivere et esse.* Spinoza, *Tractatus Theolo.-Polit.* XIII, Opera, II, 240.

25. *Daniel*, 2, 20; *b. Berachot*, 55ª.

26. *Guide*, I, 34.

27. *Idem*, III, 8.

28. Aristotle, *Nicomachean Ethics*, III, iii, 19.

CHAPTER XVIII

1. Holt, Marvin, etc. *The New Realism*, 22, The Macmillan Co., 1925.

2. . . . the substance or essence as contrasted with its attributes is no more than a name, a gesture, or some one of its attributes, arbitrarily singled out for the purpose of identification. *Present Philosophic Tendencies*, 67, Longmans, Green & Co., 1912; *cf.* also his *General Theory of Value*, 402-406, Longmans, Green & Co., 1926. In that year Professor Perry was still afraid of "misguided anthropomorphism." However, that "matter" was nothing but a mere name was already the view of Hobbes. There is evidently nothing new under the philosophic sun, not even in New Realism.

3. Planck, *op. cit.*, 82; Lange, *op. cit.*, III, 111.

4. Quoted *supra*, p. 69.

5. H. Wolfson, *The Philosophy of Spinoza*, vol. II, 4-5, Harvard University Press, 1934.

6. *Utopia*, Bk. I.

7. The original German reads: *"Deutschland ist das einzige Land der Erde, in welchem der Apothekar kein Recept auffertigen kann, ohne sich des Zusammenhangs seiner Taetigkeit mit dem Bestand des Universums bewusst zu sein."* Hermann Cohen, ed., Leipzig, 1908; Lange, II, 88, 263; on p. 133, Eng. ed., vol. II, Professor Lange writes: "The bad habit of setting definitions out of which nothing essential results was deeply rooted in the nation. It envelops still, like rank weeds, the whole system of Kant, and only now is the fresher spirit brought by the development of our poetry, of the positive sciences, and of our practical efforts, gradually freeing us by a process not yet completed from the nets of the metaphysical."

8. J. Dewey, *Character and Events*, I, 33-48, ed. by J. Ratner, Henry Holt & Co., 1929; *Idem, German Philosophy and Politics*, passim, particularly the last chapter, Henry Holt & Co., 1915.

9. Hegel's *Naturphilosophie erschien, den Naturforschern wenigstens, absolut sinnlos. Von den ausgezeichneten Naturforschern jener Zeit fand sich nicht ein Einziger, der sich mit den Hegl'schen Ideen haette befreunden koennen. Da andererseits fuer Hegel es von besonderer Wichtigkeit war gerade in diesem Felde sich Anerkennung zu erfechten, die er anderwaerts so reichlich gefunden hatte, so folgte eine ungewoehnlich leidenschaftliche und erbitterte Polemik von seiner Seite, die momentlich gegen J. Newton, also den ersten und groessten Rapraesentanten der wissenschaftlichen Naturforschung, gerichtet war.* H. Helmholtz, *Populaere Wissenschaftliche Vortraege*, I, 8, Braunschweig, 1865. *Cf.* also Lange, *op. cit.*, I, 313 and 248, note 69 for Descartes' "perverse and disparaging judgment" of Galileo's doctrine of motion; also I, 223 for the indissoluble bond between Averroistic rationalism and belief in astrology. According to Professor Whitehead it was Kant who "drove the wedge between Science and Reason." *The Function of Reason*, 49, Princeton University Press, 1929. We shall not debate the question. Both Hegel and Kant were noted High Priests of Reason.

10. Professor Lenard won the Noble Prize for physics in 1905 and is now the head of the Philipp Lenard Institute of Physics at Heidelberg. Professor Stark was the winner in 1919 and is today the President of the German Physics Institute and the German Research Association. Both of these Prize winners have engaged in furious attacks in the *Voelkische Beobachter* on Einstein, Planck, Schroedinger and Heisenberg. The last three are, of course, not Jewish but only the victims of "Jewish propaganda."

11. Lange, *op cit.*, III, 343-4. *Cf.* also the absolutely ridiculous quotation from Professor Meier's *Metaphysik*, in Lange, *loc. cit.*, 16.

12. Holbach, *op. cit.* Préface.

13. Witness the testimony of even the prejudiced Tacitus.

Evenerant prodigia, que neque hostiis neque votis piare fas habet gens superstitione obnoxia, religioniobus adversa, Hist. V, 13.

14. Ch. 10, v. 2.

15. *The Jewish Wars*, VI, 5, 3.

16. *Matthew*, 2, 9.

17. Leopold Loew, *Gesammelte Schriften*, II, 117-21, Szegedin, 1819; *JE., verbum Astrology;* W. M. Feldman, *Rabbinical Mathematics and Astronomy*, 217-8, London, 1931.

234   THE JEW AND THE UNIVERSE

18. A. Marx in *HUC Annual, loc. cit.,* 312-14; Loew, *loc. cit.,* 122-6. Among other illustrious Jews of the Middle Ages who did not escape the influence of astrology may be mentioned: Eliezer ha-Kalir, Shabbetai Donolo, Solomon ibn Gabirol, Abraham bar Hiyah, Yehudah Halevi, Abraham ibn Daud, Abraham b. David, the critic of Maimonides, Solomon b. Adret, Joseph Albo, Isaac Arama, Isaac Abravanel, Azariah di Rossi. Nahmanides despite his great respect for Maimonides cannot rid himself of the superstition. Here he altogether abandons Maimonides and in his commentary on *Deut.* 18, 9 he writes: Many jeer at omens saying there is no truth in them . . . we, however, cannot deny things for which there is the testimony of eyewitnesses.

19. *Cf.* Marx, *loc. cit.,* 322 & 356.

20. *Idem,* 350-6; *Responsa* II, 25-26[b].

21. *Numb.,* 23, 23.

22. *Deut.,* 18, 14.

23. *Hil. Abodat Kochabim,* 11 end. The translation is free.

24. *Guide,* III, 26; *Sepher ha-Mizvot, Negative Commandments,* 365, Heller, 136; *Hil. Me'ilah,* 8, 8; *Hil. Temurah,* end.

25. *Guide,* III, 31 & 37.

26. *Idem,* III, 29.

27. *Idem,* III, 37; Bardowicz, *op. cit.,* 54.

28. *Prov.,* 15, 15; *Guide,* I, 62.

29. *See* his *Introduction to Tohorot.* S. L. Rappoport in his epistolar Introduction to Abraham b. Hiya, *op. cit.,* 1st ch. writes: "Maimonides was most careful to bring in his book (*The Code*) every legal statement in the Talmud relative to practice."

30. *MEx.,* 20, 104[a].

31. *Iggeret Teman, Responsa,* II, 2[a]. *Cf.* also *Guide,* III, 27.

32. *b. Sanhedrin,* 92[b]; *cf.* also *b. Sotah,* 46[b] bottom; *YK.,* 226.

33. There is nothing in the wide world concerning which the Holy One Blessed Be He did not give Israel some command. If a Jew goes out to plow . . . sow . . . reap . . . etc., *NR.,* 17, 7.

34. *See* his letter quoted *supra,* p. 200 to the simple ibn Gabbar. Some of Maimonides' contemporaries resented that he had written to so ordinary a person so fine and respectful a letter. *Responsa,* IV. He answered a correspondent when his son Abraham was critically ill and of whose recovery he well-nigh despaired. End of letter to Hasdai ha-Levi ha-Sephardi, II, 24[d]. Despite his many labors and his only chance for rest on the Sabbath he spent a good part of it in planning the communal affairs for the week. Letter to ibn Tibbon, II, 28[e]. To the community of Lunel he writes that he can find no time to translate his books or to revise his manuscripts for publication, neither during the day or night can he find a moment's leisure to write as much as a paragraph. "Nevertheless," he adds, "because of my respect for your community I troubled and wearied myself to write this letter completely with my own hand," II, 44[a]&[b]. In the same letter he pleads with the leaders of Lunel to labor for their people for he himself is no longer able to. "Whatever of perfection God has bestowed upon a man," he writes, "he should make every effort to share it with mankind." *Pirke ha-Hazlahah,* II, 232[d]. Those who did not observe punctiliously the social laws that make for the preservation of society, Maimonides excluded altogether from the category "man." *Comm. Mish. B.K.,* 4, 3.

35. *Hil. Megillah,* 2, 17.

36. *See* the interesting letter from Maimonides to Samuel ibn Tibbon,

the translator of the *Guide* from the Arabic into the Hebrew, *Responsa*, II, 28°; quoted in Yellin and Abrahams, *op. cit.*, 202-3.

37. To the Yemenites he writes: "It is your duty to be most attentive to what I present before you. Teach that to your children and wives to remove their doubts and strengthen their faith. . . . Brethren, be strong and of good courage, rely on these true verses (which Maimonides has quoted in the letter) and let not the persecutions frighten you." *Idem*, II, 1°&ᵈ & 2ᵈ.

38. *Responsa*, I, 7, 17, 81, 85, 87, 88, 104, 112, 113, 114, 145, 153.

39. *Idem*, I, 158, 34ª&ᵇ.

40. *Ps.*, 92, 6-7.

41. *b. Kidd.*, 33ª.

42. *MEx.*, 50ᵇ.

43. *Mish. Abot*, 2, 5; *Tos. Berachot*, 7, 18, 16. Maimonides defines the boor (rude man) as both empty of knowledge and good conduct. *See* his *comm.* on *Mish. Abot, loc. cit.* & *Mish. Mikwaot*, 9, 6.

44. *b. Sabb.*, 63ª; *SEZ.*, 16, 4.

45. *b. Pesahim*, 49ᵇ.

46. *Mish. Abot*, 3, 17.

47. *Idem*, 3, 14.

48. *Tos. Yebamot*, 8, end; *GR.*, 34, 20, 326.

49. *Leviticus*, 19, 18; *Sifra, a.l.*, 89ᵇ; *j. Nedarim*, 9, 5, 41°; *GR.*, 24, end, 237 & extensive note *a.l.*; *ARN.*, 26, 53ᵇ.

50. *b. Pesahim*, 49ᵇ; *ARN.*, 33, 71ᵇ.

51. *Idem*, 21, 74ª.

52. *j. Kidd.*, end, 61ᵈ; *cf.* controversy of R. Johanan & R. Simon b. Lakish in *b. Sanhedrin*, 111ª. Maimonides, in his Comm. on *Mish. Makkot* end, adopts view of R. Akiba; *cf.* also Albo, *op. cit.*, III, 29, 1, 269.

53. *ARN.*, 36, 109.

54. *Idem*, 12, 56ª.

55. *b. Sanhedrin*, 92ª.

56. *b. Niddah*, 31ª.

57. *CR.*, 2, 16.

58. From the eulogy of R. Ilai at the death of R. Simon b. Zavid: There are four things indispensable to civilization, if any of them is lost it can be replaced,

> For there is a mine for silver,
> And a place for gold which they refine.
> Iron is taken out of the dust,
> And brass is molten out of the stone (*Job*, 28, 1 & 2),

But when a scholar dies who will provide us a substitute?

> Whence then cometh wisdom?
> And where is the place of understanding?
> Seeing it is hid from the eyes of all living (*Job*, 28, 20-21),

j. Berachot, 2, 8, 5°; *GR.*, 91, 11; *YJb.*, 915; *cf.* also *b. Horoyot*, 13ª; *NR.*, 6, 1.

59. *b.Yoma*, 1, 38ᵇ.

60. *b. Moed Katon*, 25ᵇ.

61. *GR.*, 68, 7; *RR.*, 2, 12; *cf. SD.*, 38, 77ᵇ.

62. *b. Nedarim*, 20ᵇ. In *b. Gittin*, 62ª, the scholars are compared to kings. *Cf.* also *j. Shekalim* beginning.

63. *b. Yoma*, 38ᵇ.

64. *GR.*, 39, 18, 377.

65. *b. Sabb.*, 119ᵇ; *YCh.* end.

66. *MS.*, 7, 27.

67. *b. Sabb.*, 114ᵃ; *b. Berachot*, end; *Mish. Mikwaot*, 9, 6; Maimonides, *a.l.*, following *b. Sabb.*, *loc. cit.*, explains that the scholars are called *bannaim* (builders) because they are engaged in the building of the world. In our *Mishnah* the word is used as antonym for boor and probably means a cultured, refined person; *cf. MGWJ.*, vol. 71, 8-13.

68. *b. Sabb.*, *loc. cit.*, where several similar dicta will be found. Maimonides in *Mish. Mikwaot*, *loc. cit.*, states: "It is incumbent on the scholar in our midst to be refined and most neat in his attire." *Cf.* also *b. Berachot*, 43ᵇ.

69. *b. Sabb.*, 119ᵇ.

70. *b. Ketubot*, 103ᵇ; Albo, *op. cit.*, 29, 9, 276.

71. *b. Taanit*, 7ᵃ.

72. *b. Sabb.*, 152ᵃ.

73. *b. Megillah*, 15ᵇ; *b. Sanhedrin*, 111ᵇ; *AE.*, 5, 46; *cf.* also *b. Sabb.*, 152ᵃ; *b. Taanit*, 9ᵇ.

74. *b. Nedarim*, 81ᵃ; *b. Berachot*, 30ᵃ.

75. *b. Berachot*, 63ᵃ.

76. *b. Yebamot*, 64ᵃ top; *YN.*, 731; *Seder Olam R.*, 15.

77. *Tos. Sukkah*, 1, 9, 133; *b. idem*, 27ᵇ; *cf.* also *NR.*, 14, 25, all the tribes are equal and beloved before God.

78. *Mish. Abot*, 2, 4; *b. Berachot*, 30ᵃ, 40ᵇ; *j. idem*, 7, 3, 11ᶜ; *cf.* also *b. B.B.*, 91ᵇ & *RR.*, 1, 5, where the punishment of Elimelech and Mahlon is attributed to the shirking of public responsibility.

79. *b. B.B.*, 16ᵇ; *b. Taanit*, 23ᵇ.

80. *b. Taanit*, 11ᵃ; *SEZ.*, beginning; *cf.* also *LR.*, 28, 6; *PK.*, 8, 71ᵇ.

81. *Sifra*, end; *b. Berachot*, 32ᵃ; *ExR.*, 42, 1; *YEx.*, 391. See *TD.*, 12 & *YD.*, 821 for the extraordinary statement put in the mouth of Moses: "Perish Moses and a thousand like him but not one Jew." *Cf.* also *DR.*, 2, 2; *cf.* Albo *op. cit.*, III, 12, 2, 107.

82. A workingman was not permitted to rise before scholars while on his job, *b. Kidd.*, 33ᵃ. That, says Maimonides, is an important principle with us. Nevertheless do we obligate the workingmen to rise and welcome the pilgrims when they are entering Jerusalem because they come in large numbers. The respect due a crowd is a different matter. *Comm. on Mish. Bikkurim*, 3, 3.

83. *Sifra*, 112ᵇ; *b. Shabuot*, 39ᵃ, bottom; *b. Sanhedrin*, 27ᵇ, bottom; *YL.*, 675.

84. *CR.*, 2, 9.

85. *LR.*, 1, 14; *NR.*, 15 end; *Joel*, 3, 1, 2; *Numb.*, 11, 29.

86. *b. Gittin*, 57ᵇ; *b. Sanhedrin*, 96ᵇ; *cf.* also *b. Megillah*, 14ᵇ; *NR.*, 8 end; *RR.*, 2, 1; *MS.*, 9, 6, 33; *AE.*, 5, 49; for the priests and prophets who were descendants of Rahab, among them are mentioned Jeremiah, Huldah, Baruch and Ezekiel.

87. *b. Hullin*, 92ᵃ. Was it, by the way, difficult for Maimonides to find here his thesis of the subservience of the many to the one? Rashi certainly no metaphysician and as yet not charged with exaggerated intellectuality comments on ben Lakish's statement as follows: The leaves of the vine are exposed and protect the clusters against the heat, sun and winds. Even so the peasants plow, sow and reap what the scholar eats. For the philosophy of R. Simon b. Lakish *see Jahrbuch der juedisch-literarischen Geselschaft*, vol. XIV, 126-48.

88. *ARN.*, 12, 64[a].

89. *See* the penetrating dictum of the Rabbis: I created, says the Holy One Blessed Be He, the evil tempter, I also created the Torah as an antidote. *b. Kidd.*, 30[b]; *b. B.B.*, 16[a]; *SD.*, 76[b].

90. *j. Bikkurim*, 3, 3, 66[c]; *b. Berachot*, 6[a]; *LR.*, 35, 3; *cf.* Schechter, *Aspects*, 203.

91. Better known as *Ari ha-Kadosh*, founder of practical or miraculous *Kabbalah. JE.*, *verbum Luria*; Schechter, *Studies in Judaism*, 2nd series, 251-66; D. Kahana, *ha-Mekubbalim, ha-Shabeta'im veha-Hasidim*, I, 22-48, Tel Aviv, 1926. Note that he was warned by R. David b. Zimra not to violate either the letter or spirit of rabbinic Judaism. *The Shulhan Aruch* published by the disciples of the *Ari* in his name does not invalidate any of the laws of traditional Judaism.

92. Famous Kabbalist, contemporary, townsman, disciple and colleague of Ari., *JE.*, *verbum Vital;* Schechter, *loc. cit.*, 267-83; Kahana, *loc. cit.*, 18-48.

93. Israel Baal Shem Tov, founder of *Hasidism.* Schechter, *op. cit.*, 1st series, 1-38; Kahana, *op. cit.*, III, 65-8; S. A. Horodetski, *ha-Hasidut veha-Hasidim*, I, 1-73, Berlin, 1922; S. Dubnov, *Toledot ha-Hasidut*, I, 41-74, Tel Aviv, 1930; J. S. Minkin, *The Romance of Hasidism*, 58-105, The Macmillan Co., 1935.

94. Grandson of the Besht, of the most distinguished of the Hasidic Rabbis. Horodetski, *loc. cit.*, III, 18-81; Dubnov, *loc. cit.*, II, 290-309; Minkin, *op. cit.*, 231-72.

95. Greatest Talmudic authority of Russian Jewry, opponent of Hasidism, Schechter, *loc. cit.*, 73-98; Ginzberg, *Students, Scholars and Saints*, 125-44; Kahana, III, 59-117; Dubnov, I, 106-10, 114-17, 138-50, II, 242-57.

96. *Iggeret Teman, Responsa*, I, 3[c]; *cf. b. Sabb.*, 104[a]; *b. Yoma*, 80[a]; *b. Megillah*, 2[b], bottom; *b. Temurah*, 16[a]; *Sifra*, end; *YL.*, 682; also *b. B.M.*, 59[b].

97. *Idem*, II, 4[c].

98. *Cf. Responsa, L.*, I., 140, 26[a].

99. *See Introduction to Tohorot.* The evidence is writ large on every page of his *Code.*

100. *Es giebt in dem dreibaendigen Werke keinen Theil, aus dem nicht fundamenttalle, den Stempel der Originalitaet und Vollendung tragende Lehren ihren Weg in Leben und Litteratur hineit genommen haette.* D. Kaufmann, *Der "Fuehrer" Maimunis in der Weltlitteratur. Archiv fuer Geschichte der Philosophie XI*, 339, reprint.

101. *Crescas' Critique of Aristotle*, 1, Cambridge, 1929.

102. *Philosophy of Spinoza*, I, 14. Speaking of Maimonides' solution to the philosophic problems Munk writes: *"Elles offrent du moins un puissant intérêt historique, en nous permettant d'embrasser d'un coup d'œl les problèmes qui pendant plusieurs siècles occupèrent les esprits supérieurs des trois communions, et les efforts qui furent faits pour concilier ensemble deux autorités en apparence ennemies, celles des livres saints et celle d'Aristote."* *Op cit.*, II, *Préface*, v.

103. J. Pagel in Guttmann, *op. cit.*, 247; Isak Muenz, *Die juedischen Aerzte im Mittelalter*, 8-10, 57, Berlin, 1887.

INDEX

Aaron, 138, 185-186
Aaron b. Meshullam, 199, 219-220
Abaye, 24, 125, 140
Abba, 211
Abba Arika, 135, 218, 224
Abd al-Mu'min, 59
Abel, 131
Abélard, 226
Abodat Yisrael, 224
Abraham, 3-8, 14, 16, 28, 85, 105, 112-113, 129, 131, 135, 137, 140, 146, 156, 185-186, 207
Abraham bar Hiya, 171, 185, 234
Abraham b. Yehiya, 200, 225
Abrahams, I., 200
Abravanel, 141, 225, 234
Absalom, 138
Absolute idealism, 149, 168, 211
Abstract, 2, 9, 11, 16, 45, 49, 101, 170
Abuhah, 155
Abulafia, 199
Accidents, 33, 57, 88-89, 93, 165
Achad Ha'am, 199
Acquired intellect, 120
Active intelligence, 108
Acts of Paul, The, 216
Acts of Thomas, The, 216
Actual, the, 33
Adam, 4, 76, 131, 135, 185, 206
Adlerblum, N. H., 199
Adolph Schwartz Festschrift, 185
Advancement of Learning, 229
Agadat ha-Tannaim, 189, 218
Ahijah the Shilonite, 73
Akiba, 18, 20, 22-24, 28-29, 76, 120, 122, 140, 160, 176, 180, 185, 191, 193, 201, 220, 225, 235
Alan of Lille, 226
Albalia, 58

Albo, 102, 189-190, 212, 216, 234
Alcibiades, 134
Alexander of Aphrodisias, 143, 226
Alexander, S., 33, 35, 52, 54, 89, 196, 198
Alfakar, 220
Al-Fārābi, 62
Al-Kindi, 62, 210
Allegory, 76-78, 206
Almohades, 60
Altar, the, 131
Ambrosius, 83
Am ha-Arez, 176-177
Ami, 224
Amor Dei, 49
Amos, 20, 22, 186
Analogy, 43, 45, 52, 230
Analysis of Mind, The, 195-197
Anaxagoras, 148, 227-228
Anaximander, 5
Anaximenes, 5
Angels, 228
Anselm, 201, 226
Antediluvians, 129
Anthropomorphism, 6, 7, 84-85, 208
Antiquities of the Jews, 204, 206
Antisthenes, 31
Antologia shel ha-Pilosophiah ha-Ivrit, 198
Apocrypha, 1, 54
Apologia, 228
Apologeticus, 204
Apotheosis vel Consecratio Homeri, 76
Apple, the, 49
Aquinas, 15, 55, 62, 65-67, 145, 147, 158, 188, 213
Arabic Thought and Its Place in History, 200
Arabs, 222

239

Religion innerhalb der Grenzen der blossen Vernunft, 230
Religion in the Making, 186
Religion of the Veda, The, 211
Religious Thought of the Greeks, 192, 194, 222
Republic, The, 32, 194, 218
Responsa, 54
Responsa (Maimonides), 175, 187, 199, 200, 202, 205-207, 210, 213-215, 218, 220-221, 223, 226, 228, 232, 234-235
Responsa (Rosh), 203
Responsa (Zevi), 219
Resurrection, 116, 120
Revelation, 58, 68, 75, 77, 92, 110, 128, 156
Reymond, Du Bois, 193
Robin, L., 187
Romance of Hasidism, The, 237
Roscellin, 63, 209
Rosenzweig, F., 226
Roth, L., 199, 219, 224
Rousselot, P., 188
Royce, 199
Ruskin, 10, 35, 38-39, 46, 188
Russel, B., 33, 39, 40, 83, 162, 195, 197, 229

Saadia Gaon, 55, 64, 96, 127, 188, 199, 202, 208
Saadia Gaon, His Life and Work, 208-209, 219
Sabbatai Zevites, 179
Sabbath, the, 216
Sabean stories, 146, 227
Sacred Books of the East, 211
Sacrifices, 131, 221
Sages, *see* Rabbis
Samson, 72, 131
Samuel, 185, 187, 220
Samuel, Mar, 225
Samuel, Maurice, 187
Saragossa, 58
Sass, K., 204
Sat, 5
Satan, 23-24, 187
Scaliger, 206

Scapegoat, 218
Scepticism, 32
Sceptics, 16
Schechter, S., 6, 16, 142, 187, 219
Schiller, F., 117
Schleiermacher, 104, 156
Scholar, 137, 177-178, 223-224, 235-236
Scholasticism, 143, 149, 210
Scholastics, 95, 157, 226-227
Schroedinger, 40, 163, 167, 196, 198, 226, 231-233
Science, 16, 19, 44-46, 50, 56, 144, 154, 157-158, 160, 196-197, 210-211, 226
Science and Civilisation, 229
Science and Religion, 194, 232
Science and the Human Temperament, 195, 198, 232
Science and the Unseen World, 186, 196-197, 208
Scientific Outlook, The, 194, 229
Scientist, 41
Scotus, *see* Erigena
Scotus, D., 158
Sectarianism, 179
Seder Olam Rabbah, 236
Selection of Israel, 74
Selections from Kant, 195, 209
Sennacherib, 178
Senses, the, 47, 49, 87, 143, 152, 197, 215
Sepher ha-Bahir, 224
Sepher ha-Ikkarim, 189-190, 194, 202, 207-208, 210-213, 215, 222, 236-246
Sepher ha-Mizvot, 223-224
Sepher ha-Pardes, 190
Sepher ha-Yashar, 105, 140, 183, 185-186, 206, 213, 225
Septuagint, 85, 99
Seth, 72
Seville, 58
Shaddai, 17
Shakespeare, 45, 47
Shalshelet ha-Kabalah, 200, 219, 225
Shammaites, 31, 193
Shape, 46

THE JEWISH PEOPLE

HISTORY • RELIGION • LITERATURE

AN ARNO PRESS COLLECTION

Heine, Heinrich. **The Prose Writings of Heinrich Heine.**
Edited, with an Introduction, by Havelock Ellis. 1887

Hirsch, Emil G[ustav]. **My Religion.** Compilation and
Biographical Introduction by Gerson B. Levi. **Including
The Crucifixion Viewed from a Jewish Standpoint:** A Lecture
Delivered by Invitation Before the "Chicago Institute for
Morals, Religion and Letters." 1925/1908

Hirsch, W. **Rabbinic Psychology:** Beliefs about the Soul
in Rabbinic Literature of the Talmudic Period. 1947

Historical Views of Judaism: Four Selections. 1973

Ibn Gabirol, Solomon. **Selected Religious Poems of Solomon Ibn
Gabirol.** Translated into English Verse by Israel Zangwill
from a Critical Text Edited by Israel Davidson. 1923

Jacobs, Joseph. **Jesus as Others Saw Him:** A Retrospect
A. D. 54. Preface by Israel Abrahams; Introductory Essay by
Harry A. Wolfson. 1925

Judaism and Christianity: Selected Accounts, 1892-1962.
1973. New Preface and Introduction by Jacob B. Agus

Kohler, Kaufmann. **The Origins of the Synagogue and
The Church.** Edited, with a Biographical Essay by H. G. Enelow.
1929

Maimonides Octocentennial Series, Numbers I-IV. 1935

Mann, Jacob. **The Responsa of the Babylonian Geonim as a
Source of Jewish History.** 1917-1921

Maritain, Jacques. **A Christian Looks at the Jewish Question.** 1939

Marx, Alexander. **Essays in Jewish Biography.** 1947

Mendelssohn, Moses. **Phaedon; or, The Death of Socrates.**
Translated from the German [by Charles Cullen]. 1789

Modern Jewish Thought: Selected Issues, 1889-1966. 1973.
New Introduction by Louis Jacobs

Montefiore, C[laude] G. **Judaism and St. Paul:** Two Essays. 1914

Montefiore, C[laude] G. **Some Elements of the Religious
Teaching of Jesus According to the Synoptic Gospels.** Being
the Jowett Lectures for 1910. 1910

Radin, Max. **The Jews Amongs the Greeks and Romans.** 1915

Ruppin, Arthur. **The Jews in the Modern World.** With an
Introduction by L. B. Namier. 1934

Smith, Henry Preserved. **The Bible and Islam;** or, The Influence
of the Old and New Testaments on the Religion of Mohammed.
Being the Ely Lectures for 1897. 1897

Stern, Nathan. **The Jewish Historico-Critical School of the
Nineteenth Century.** 1901

Walker, Thomas [T.] **Jewish Views of Jesus:** An Introduction
and an Appreciation. 1931. New Introduction by Seymour Siegel

Walter, H. **Moses Mendelssohn:** Critic and Philosopher. 1930

Wiener, Leo. **The History of Yiddish Literature in the
Nineteenth Century.** 1899

Wise, Isaac M. **Reminiscences.** Translated from the German and
Edited, with an Introduction by David Philipson. 1901